All About Asthma
and Allergy

<u>All About</u>
<u>Asthma And Allergy</u>

Dr. H. Morrow Brown
MD FRCP

The Crowood Press

First published in 1985 by
Harper & Row Ltd as *The Allergy and Asthma
Reference Book*.

This revised edition published in 1990 by
The Crowood Press
Ramsbury
Marlborough
Wiltshire SN8 2HE

British Library Cataloguing in Publication Data
Brown, Harry Morrow
  All about asthma and allergy.
  [Allergy and asthma reference book] All about asthma and
  allergy.
  1. Man. Allergies
  I. [Allergy and asthma reference book] II. Title
  616.97

ISBN 1 85223 324 9

Typeset by Acorn Bookwork, Salisbury, Wiltshire
Printed in Great Britain by Biddles Ltd, of Guildford and King's Lynn

Contents

Acknowledgements

To all of the following who helped in the preparation of this book, I offer my sincere thanks – especially to my daughter Caroline for the long and painstaking hours spent on preliminary structure and planning, and to Dominic Newbould, of the editorial department of the Open University for his business acumen and editorial expertise. I am indebted to Mrs Felicity Jackson for her excellent preparation and arrangement of the art work, and to Dr Morag Stern and Mrs Anne Harries for reading and re-reading the manuscript, which was typed by Mrs Sheila Marsh who interpreted my jumbled text with skill, patience and unfailing good humour. Above all this book is dedicated to my wife Freda, without whose encouragement and help this book would never have been finished.

Introduction

Why is this book necessary and what is its purpose?

Allergy victims often encounter great difficulties in obtaining sound advice and treatment. A book describing all the afflictions which can be caused by allergy should, therefore, fulfil a real need for the millions who suffer from allergic complaints.

I have attempted to describe all the illnesses which may be caused by allergy from the trivial to the terrifying. How symptoms are produced anywhere in the body is explained, and the many causes of allergy are described and classified. How the causes may be tracked down, identified and avoided, or immunized against, is also dealt with. The effective use of modern drugs has been described in much greater detail than is usual in a book intended for the general public. This is because the side-effects of drugs are so often mentioned in medical programmes on radio and television today that patients often become very worried about their treatment, and a sense of perspective is needed.

Allergic problems are usually complex, are individual to each sufferer, and require time and expertise to sort out, so as to organize effective management. Some years ago, many family doctors were single-handed, and knew every detail about their flock of patients, whom they looked after from the cradle to the grave. Today, when patients may not see the same family or hospital doctor twice, and notes may be missing, inadequate or illegible, the continuity of care which is so essential for the effective management of the allergic patient may not be available. Allergic problems can be a life sentence for some, and the family doctor should be their helpful partner in making day-to-day living more tolerable, supported by consultant advice as necessary. I hope that this book will help the sufferer to understand his or her problems, and make them easier to control and to endure.

How should one approach reading this book?

This book has been designed as a reference book for the non-medical reader, but the answers should not be consulted as one would a dictionary because this would be to obtain information out of context, and to risk gross misunderstandings. The reader is, therefore, advised to read the book from the beginning, as otherwise the later chapters will prove difficult to understand. To understand how allergic symptoms are produced, and what can trigger them off, could be the first step in coping with your problems more effectively. It may also be helpful to know the reasons for the capricious and unpredictable behaviour of allergic symptoms.

It is hoped that this book will help to dispel much of the confusion, anxiety and fear which exists today amongst allergy sufferers. It is important to emphasize that this is not a do-it-yourself allergy manual, and that symptoms of serious organic disease can be identical with those produced by allergy problems. If you are considering a dietary approach you must consult with your family doctor and undergo any specialist examinations or tests advised *before* coming to the conclusion that allergy may be the cause of your symptoms. Obviously the author disclaims all responsibility for any independent action taken by readers of this book, with or without medical advice.

What is allergy?

The word 'allergy' is used so loosely today that it is essential to define at the outset the meaning of the word as used in this book. A narrow scientific definition would be too restrictive. It would exclude a wide range of reactions to substances in the environment where the only available evidence of their allergic nature is the repeatable demonstration of a clear relationship between exposure and symptoms which can mimic organic disease, can affect any part of the body, and may be mental as well as physical. Thus a practical working definition should be deliberately broad, so as to encompass the full range of 'allergic' reactions. The following is an attempt at such a definition.

An individual who reacts adversely and repeatedly every time a specific substance is inhaled, eaten, touched or injected should be regarded as being 'allergic' to that substance if it can be tolerated without adverse reaction by the majority of normal persons.

This is to talk of allergy in terms of a specific sensitivity to a specific substance. The most essential characteristic of an allergic reaction as defined here is the reproduction of the same effects at each and every encounter, often after a similar delay period, in the same system of the body.

What is immunology and what is an immunologist?

The main task of the scientific services in a hospital, such as bacteriology, pathology, and immunology is to produce reports on specimens from patients. These are interpreted by the physicians or surgeons in charge of the case along with all other information on the problems of the patient.

The fastest growing speciality since the War, with effects throughout medicine and surgery, has been the science of immunology. The effects on the study of allergic disease have been far-reaching, providing the explanation of some types of allergic reaction, and the invention of many tests. Progress in the laboratory has been spectacular, but the effects on the actual clinical management of allergic disease have been disappointingly small. At one time it seemed possible that allergy problems could be solved by producing accurate answers from a blood sample, but this has not yet happened nor seems likely to do so.

Immunologists, who are non-medical, cannot treat patients, but those who are medically qualified may do so, and are called clinical immunologists. Immunology, however, is only one of the scientific disciplines necessary to deal effectively with the allergic patient.

Why is it so difficult to find a family doctor interested in allergy?

The family doctor is usually the first to be consulted, but very few are well-informed and the view that allergy is 'all in the mind' is common. Hence the suggestion that your problems or those of your children might be due to 'allergy' may not be greeted with interest, enthusiasm, or sympathy. Rejection is a particularly common response if food allergy is mentioned. It is only fair to state that medical students very rarely get any instruction regarding allergic problems, and that many doctors are acutely aware of these gaps in their knowledge and want to help their allergic patients more effectively. Unfortunately there are practically no facilities for them to study allergy if they should wish to do so. The unpredictable behaviour of asthma can also create an antagonistic response in many otherwise excellent doctors, who may become irritated or even frightened by this capricious disease.

It is probable that many doctors regard the clinical practice of allergy with grave suspicion, a sceptical attitude which may be enhanced by the fact that the symptoms of allergy are often the same whatever the cause, a presentation which is the complete opposite of most medical problems. Yet the family doctor, presumably knowing the whole family history and environment, is in the ideal position to assess the allergic patient. However, because the knowledge and expertise is often lacking, treatment tends to rely excessively on drugs, with little emphasis on finding the cause of the problem. But remember that asthma, and eczema also, are very frustrating to treat, especially when emotions trigger an attack in an already primed situation. The belief that asthma is primarily a psychosomatic illness is not confined to doctors, but often shared by the patients themselves, and their relatives. Yet to suffer from such a protracted and unpredictable illness must be stressful and disturbing, so that asthmatics must be quite stable people to tolerate their problems as well as they do.

Why was clinical allergy not recognised as a medical specialty until 1987?

Allergies are probably commoner than any other medical problem, especially in developed western nations, yet the study of allergy failed to be recognized as a separate medical specialty in Britain until 1987. Allergic disease has failed to share in the rapid development of many branches of medicine since the war, and it is relevant to try to account for this.

In 1930 a few British pioneers formed the 'Allergy Research

Club', but they were not taken seriously, had a cranky reputation, and achieved little recognition before the Second War. Since then rapid scientific advances have made the curriculum of the British medical student more and more overcrowded. As a result special subjects not already established as specialties have little or no chance of being included, and medical students very seldom receive any instruction regarding allergic diseases, as part of their medical training.

In consequence, when patients are referred to hospital the potential importance of allergic factors in the causation of the problem is frequently misunderstood or not taken seriously. For example, skin testing in hospitals is often delegated to nurses and junior doctors, who may not know the correct methods or how to interpret the results, and who have had no instruction as students. In acute contrast to attitudes throughout Europe, particularly in Scandinavia, and in America, the treatment of allergic patients in Britain is often unsatisfactory, especially in children's departments. It is not surprising that many British allergy sufferers tend to be dissatisfied with the service, even when referred for a consultant opinion. For example, out-patients with allergic disease of the skin, the nose and the chest often attend three different departments, and the family doctor may receive contradictory advice. Ideally the patient would attend an Allergy Department which could deal with all these problems at once.

In Britain much unnecessary suffering is caused by the lack of availability of specialist advice about allergic problems, which drives some patients into the hands of unorthodox practitioners using untried or doubtful methods of diagnosis and treatment.

In 1987 the Royal College of Physicians belatedly recognized allergic disease as a specialty, but up to now the requirements for training potential allergists and who should train them, are still undecided. Also the numbers and location of consultant posts must be agreed by the Ministry of Health. Obviously, it will be many years before an Allergy Service can be established.

How effective is the management of chronic asthma in Britain?

In Britain at least two million adults and half a million children suffer from asthma, and 2,000 adults die from asthma each year.

The management of *acute* asthma in hospital has become very efficient during the last 25 years, but the management of *chronic* asthma has lagged behind and has improved little. It has been written that chronic asthma is frequently misunderstood, mismanaged, misjudged, and mistreated and this is true. Several investigations to find out why so many people still die from asthma have repeatedly confirmed the view that most patients died as a result of inadequate treatment. In a recent survey 77 out of 90 deaths were considered preventable. Many more thousands of asthmatics gasp out a limited existence, yet it is true that effective treatment already available could often improve the quality of life, if not to cure. Asthma is not only an occasional killer, but also destroys the health and prosperity of the victims. It is deplorable that today the treatment of asthma at all ages should be so inadequate when effective drugs are more freely available than ever before.

It is hoped that this book, which includes a large section devoted to the management of asthma, will make a significant contribution towards improving the control of asthma and other allergic problems. This objective can be achieved most effectively by fruitful collaboration, not confrontation, between patients and their medical advisers.

PART 1

The Scientific Background of Allergy

1   Basic biology

Most of us live for at least 70 years, often without serious illness. We often take health for granted, as the body stands up to all sorts of adversity and abuse without maintenance. Even a hundred years ago, when there were few effective medicines and doctors could do little except give comfort, relief and advice, the majority were healthy and survived. Today, new medicines have conquered most infectious diseases, so that early death from infection is rare in the developed western nations, but even in the plagues of black death or smallpox of the past, some people always survived. The reason for survival was, and still is, successful adaptation to the external environment, and a healthy immune system to protect from disease.

A simplified explanation of the workings of the immune system, and of the ways by which the body adjusts itself to ever changing circumstances, is fundamental to the understanding of allergic diseases, because these diseases are usually the result of an excessive immune reaction which does more harm than good – 'immunity gone wrong'.

The simplest forms of life are uni-cellular organisms, such as the amoeba, and bacteria, which have all the equipment required for continued life and reproduction built into one single cell. A microscope is necessary to see an amoeba, although it is much bigger than most cells. When we look at this simple organism we see that it has a cell wall to separate it from the environment in which it lives, usually dirty pond water, and from which it absorbs essential chemicals and captures food by engulfing and digesting it. The denser portion in the centre is called the nucleus, and the rest of the cell is filled with jelly-like material called cytoplasm. The amoeba can move from place to place by means of a flowing movement of the cytoplasm which can be easily seen under the microscope.

All the very complicated systems essential for continued life are contained in the one cell, each part of which has a specialized function, all working as a team in order to survive in the

environment in which it lives. Reproduction is by simple split-
ting, so that when it gets too big the cell just divides into two.
The light microscope reveals only the main parts of the amoeba,
and fuller understanding of how even such a simple organism
functions has had to wait for the development of the electron
microscope and molecular biology.

How are the higher forms of life organized?

Unlike the amoeba and other uni-cellular organisms, such as
bacteria, the more highly developed animals consist of large
groups of identical cells, each group having specialized functions, and governed by centralized control systems.

A group of identical cells will form recognizable organs, such
as the heart, liver, lungs and kidneys. Different parts of each cell
have special tasks, so that the cells also function as a team within
a team. Each organ has a unique part to play towards the efficient
functioning of the whole animal, and each vital organ depends
on every other so that if one fails all fail. This is why we have
two of most of the important organs, such as the kidneys, and
also why very large reserve capacity is found in all vital organs.

There are also very important specialized cells which are
scattered throughout the body instead of forming a recognizable
organ. The immunological system, which is responsible for
defence against disease, is made up of such cells. Allergic diseases are usually due to excessive reactions by the immunological system, so that it actually damages the tissues instead of
protecting them.

How is the blood circulated?

The basic constituent of blood is a fluid in which the red blood
cells, which carry oxygen, and many other important blood cells,
are suspended. This fluid is called plasma and contains large
amounts of proteins, which in turn, have very large molecules.
The task of the circulatory system is to ensure that the blood is
ceaselessly pumped around the body so as to nourish every cell
in it.

The blood is pumped by the right side of the heart through the
lungs to absorb oxygen and get rid of carbon dioxide, then drains

back into the left side of the heart to be pumped out at high pressure into the large arteries. These divide into smaller and smaller arteries and finally to tiny arterioles, which still have a thick muscular wall which controls blood pressure. The blood vessels then become even smaller, finally forming tiny capillaries with walls which are composed of only one layer of flattened cells. This arrangement enables the watery part of the plasma to pass out easily into the tissues to nourish the cells, but the proteins in the plasma, being big molecules, cannot get through and are retained in the circulation, along with the red cells. This watery fluid is called the *extra*-cellular fluid, because it lies in the spaces between the actual cells, which contain the *intra*-cellular fluid.

In the tissues outside the capillaries there are also other tiny capillary vessels with open ends. These are the lymphatic capillaries, which have the task of draining away any surplus extra-cellular fluid to the lymphatic glands, and eventually back into the huge veins inside the chest to join the circulation again.

After the blood passes through the capillary blood vessels, they join together again to form bigger and bigger venules, then bigger and bigger veins, and the blood finally passes at low pressure into the right side of the heart to be pumped round again. It has taken much longer to read this brief account of the circulation of the blood than for it to happen, because the time for the complete circuit is only 15 seconds!

How do the lungs work?

To continue living we must have air, because without oxygen our cells will die. Even an office worker needs to breathe 15–20 cubic metres of air a day, and someone doing hard physical work needs much more. When we take a breath the air is warmed and filtered in the nose, or passes direct into the windpipe, which passes down into the chest and divides into the two main bronchi which supply each lung with air.

The bronchi are tubes, but tubes very specially constructed to do an important job. The walls are fairly strong so that they cannot collapse, and there are muscles which are partly controlled by the involuntary nervous system. The inside is lined with living cells, which have tiny hair-like structures on the side nearest the air passages. These cilia, as they are called, continually wave about in such a manner as to pass the mucus constantly upwards towards the throat where it is swallowed or spat out. There are special glands which produce mucus to keep the lining moist, but if the mucus is too thick or excessive the cilia cannot do their job and it accumulates in the tubes. The lining of the bronchus is also richly endowed with cells of all kinds for the purpose of defence against infection, engulfing and removing dirt and bacteria, and has many of the mast cells which are so important in causing allergic reactions.

If there is infection or an allergic reaction taking place, the lining of the bronchial tubes may swell or produce too much mucus. The muscles surrounding the tubes may also contract and squeeze the bronchi so that they become narrower. In this way the amount of air which can pass into the lungs can be obstructed or restricted by swelling, sputum or spasm. Spasm may be a protective reflex to prevent inhalation of irritating fumes, and the cough reflex helps to keep the tubes clear. On inspiration the tubes open up, and on expiration they contract. Hence, the asthmatic finds it easier to breathe in than out.

Within the lung the bronchi divide again and again, becoming smaller and smaller, finally becoming a tiny bronchiole which opens into several tiny air sacs, the alveoli. In the walls of these alveoli are the tiny capillaries of the lungs, separated from the air by a single layer of cells only, so that oxygen can be transferred to the blood, and carbon dioxide removed.

Thus, the bronchial 'tree' has very dynamic properties which serve the vital function of supplying oxygen to the blood. Visualize the system as a tree upside down, and the leaves as the alveoli. In the lung, however, there is also the blood supply to and from the heart, and the blood vessels, also arranged like a tree, accompany each branch of the bronchi. Actually the blood vessels resemble two trees intertwined but with the leaves finally shared by both trees.

The severity of obstruction of the bronchi in asthma is influenced by swelling of the lining of the tubes, clogging with secretions, and by factors influencing nervous control of the bronchial muscles. The degree of obstruction often varies from hour to hour, so that for adequate monitoring of the situation it is best if the patient has some means of measurement which can be used at home.

This is provided by the 'peak flow meter', a portable instrument which is indispensable for the good management of asthma of any severity (*see* Chapter 9).

What is the internal environment?

It is a surprising fact that our bodies contain more water than anything else. For example, a person weighing 70 kilograms (about 11 stone) will contain 45 litres of water weighing 45 kilograms. Only 3 or 4 litres is in the blood, being pumped round and round to distribute oxygen and nutrients to every part of the body.

The fluid which filters out of the capillaries, the extra-cellular fluid, continuously bathes the cells, and amounts to about 12 litres. Its task is to supply oxygen and other essential nutrients through the cell wall to nourish the structures inside, and to remove waste products. To do this it is essential to maintain a constant concentration of sodium chloride (salt) and many other substances in this extra-cellular fluid.

The concentrations of salts and nutrients in the extra-cellular fluid are maintained constant by many regulatory mechanisms, particularly by the kidneys and the sensation of thirst. The kidney will get rid of excess salt and water when necessary, but will also conserve salt and water if required, so as to maintain the extra-cellular fluid constant. This is only one of the many mechanisms which work together to maintain constancy in the extra-cellular fluids, ensuring that each cell of the body lives in an ideal constant environment. This is the 'internal environment' for the cells of the body, as opposed to the 'external environment' to which the whole person must adapt.

Some staggering statistics will illustrate how this is accomplished. The kidney is composed of millions of tiny kidney units, which filter 2,000 litres of blood every day. There are 200 litres (45 gallons) of urine filtered out of the blood but about 198 litres are reabsorbed back into the blood, leaving only 2 litres passed as urine. Reabsorption is selective, being regulated according to whether the levels of salts and sugars in the blood need to be increased or decreased. The blood is filtered and reabsorbed about thirteen times a day so that each individual cell in the body remains healthy and efficient.

All these complicated arrangements are directed at the maintenance of the cells of the body in as healthy a state as possible, in spite of all adverse factors. The cells selectively absorb what they need from the extra-cellular fluid, and contain potassium instead of sodium chloride. The cells contain another 30 litres of fluid, the remainder of the 45 litres. Thus, any cell in the body can be contacted by any substance which gains access to the circulation. This fact is very important to the understanding of allergic reactions, as illustrated in Figure 3.1 (page 24).

How does man relate to the external environment?

It is essential for warm-blooded animals, such as man, to maintain the body temperature within fairly narrow limits. Failure of the temperature-regulating mechanism in winter causes hypothermia, to which infants and the aged are most vulnerable, while tropical heat may cause an excessive rise in body temperature resulting in heat-stroke, or heat exhaustion due to loss of salt.

Temperature regulation is only one of the many interlocking control systems of the body, which automatically adjust the function of all vital organs, while consciousness of hunger and thirst control the input of food and water. The objective of all these complex and wonderful arrangements, of which we are almost totally unaware, is to survive in a state of continuous adaptation to the constantly varying conditions in our external environment.

2 Basic immunology

What are the non-specific defences of the body?

Elaborate defence systems are essential in order to deal with a hostile external environment full of potentially deadly bacteria, viruses, parasites, and many other threats to health. This is in addition to maintaining the internal environment constant so that each cell of the body can live and function efficiently in spite of all environmental stress.

The first response to infection is non-specific or generalized. The blood contains not only the red cells, but also the white cells or leucocytes, some of which have the function of attacking and killing any invading bacteria or other organisms by engulfing and digesting them. There are also substances which coat the invaders to help the leucocytes engulf them, ready-made antibiotic substances such as lysozyme in the tears and saliva, and interferon which is made by the cells in response to virus infection.

In addition, when any part of the body is injured or attacked by an infecting organism various chemical substances are liberated as a result of damage to the tissues. These chemicals pass into the circulation and act as messengers to summon the right sort of white cells to the scene of the battle to engulf the invaders, help in repair, and even remove the dead cells and tissues. The capillaries are slightly damaged, and become leaky, so that the special cells required to cope with the emergency can squeeze out between the cells which form the wall of the capillary and enter the tissues. This also allows the large protein molecules of antibodies in the plasma to escape into the tissue fluid to fight infection. We can observe this happening in our own bodies: when we have a pimple on the nose we can see and feel the pain, redness and heat in the affected area.

Thus the primary response to infection is wide-ranging, non-specific and relatively primitive. The mechanisms of specific immunity are much more complex and correspondingly difficult to explain.

Why do we need an immune system?

To continue living, it is vital that the immune system, the invisible security and surveillance system of the body, can distinguish friend from foe. This system must build up a memory bank to enable enemy cells or foreign substances to be recognized, neutralized or destroyed, usually without any disturbance to the stable functioning of the body.

Conversely, all the tissues and proteins of the body itself must be tolerated by the immune system, i.e. it must not react against them. Perhaps the simplest way to express this idea is to regard everything which belongs to the body as 'self', and everything else as 'non-self'. In attempting to clarify this relationship further, it is best to start at the beginning of life.

In pregnancy the foetus, in spite of the father's genetic contribution, is tolerated by the immune system of the mother. From conception to birth the memory of the developing immune system is being patterned, so that all the tissues of the foetus are recognized as 'self'. At birth the baby enters a hostile environment full of danger and infection, so the developing immune system now has to recognize all 'non-self' material, and produce antibodies as quickly as possible. The donation of ready-made antibodies from the mother, representing her acquired immunity to the diseases to which she has been exposed, helps to tide the baby over until it can make its own antibodies. If the baby cannot make antibodies because of a defect of the immune system, death may soon occur, unless nursed in the germ-free atmosphere of a plastic bubble. It is important for the baby to be breastfed, even if only for the first few days, because the first milk (or colostrum) contains ready-made IgG antibodies, and also immunoglobulin A (IgA). This coats the lining of the gut of the child, acts protectively against bacteria, and prevents entry of food proteins into the blood.

Where is the immune system?

The immune system is not a recognizable organ, but, like the secret police, it is everywhere, looking for foreign cells or substances. The antibodies made in the immune system are distributed in the blood plasma, and their job is to destroy or neutralize foreign antigens anywhere in the body.

What are the different types of immunity?

There are two main systems, the 'humoral' system of antibodies, which may be available for instant use, and 'cell-mediated immunity'. Both systems depend on lymphocytes, special cells which are found in the bone marrow, lymph glands, spleen, and also in every type of tissue. Lymphocytes all look very much alike, so it was many years before it was discovered that there are two main types of lymphocyte, and several minor ones, all with different jobs. The main types are 'T' lymphocytes, which originate in the thymus gland, and 'B' lymphocytes from the bone marrow.

B lymphocytes, when stimulated by so-called 'helper' T cells, transform into another very special type of cell called a 'plasma cell', which makes antibodies which are released into the blood plasma and so are instantly available to neutralize any foreign antigen which is 'non-self'.

T lymphocytes also control the activities of the B lymphocytes in producing antibodies by suppressing or stimulating them. Other varieties are killer T cells, which may be a surveillance system for cancer cells, and cytotoxic T cells, which can dissolve cells infected by viruses, or indeed the cells of organ grafts from another person.

The main role of the T cell is to become sensitized to a foreign substance, so that on future contact, the cell will liberate chemical messengers (lymphokines) which summon more lymphocytes and other cells to the site to help to destroy or reject the foreign material.

What is an antigen?

Any foreign substance which stimulates the plasma cells to produce an antibody is called an antigen. Bacteria contain many antigens and after an infection has been overcome the plasma cells which produced the antibody remain dormant. When the same infection is encountered years later the antigen will jog the memory of the group or 'clone' of plasma cells which produced the antibody the first time, and the correct antibody will be produced very rapidly. Thus, contact with the many antigens in the environment speedily builds up an immunity bank with a memory, but the newborn immune system has to work overtime to become self-supporting.

How do antigens become allergens?

This question is posed to clarify this distinction. For example, the environment is full of antigens, to which a normal immune system adapts perfectly. Most of us are quite unaware of this unseen protective process, but the minority who are predisposed to become allergic react quite differently, and may develop an allergic disease. They have become hypersensitive to the antigen, which can now be referred to as an allergen because it is causing allergy.

Any antigen can act as an allergen, making the possible causes infinite, but fortunately there are relatively few *common* allergens. Many are sexual material such as pollen and spores, or insect venom or animal dandruff. Why it is commoner for some substances to act as allergens than others is a complete mystery, but it is a great help in narrowing down the possibilities.

The intensity of the reaction depends on the amount of allergen, and the degree of sensitivity of the patient. Thus a minute amount of allergen can produce a frightening effect on a very highly sensitized person, while it may take a much larger amount of the same allergen to produce even a moderate reaction in a patient who is only slightly sensitized.

Can chemicals act as allergens?

Small molecules of simple chemical compounds do not act as allergens, and the normal body proteins count as 'self', so neither can trigger an immune reaction. On the other hand, if a small chemical molecule becomes united with a large molecule of a body protein, the resulting combination, called a 'hapten', may be recognized as foreign ('non-self') by the immune system. Reactions against this new molecule may take the form of a T lymphocyte reaction, local contact sensitization to the chemical, or production of circulating antibodies. Self-damaging reactions may thus be brought about by simple chemicals.

Today we are all exposed to myriads of new chemicals which the human body has never encountered before. Recent research has already proved clearly that certain chemicals can act in this way. Perhaps some of us are indeed reacting to twentieth-century chemicals in the environment, but the full extent of illness caused by chemicals cannot be assessed until accurate and reliable laboratory tests for sensitization to haptens have been developed.

Where and how are antibodies produced?

The plasma cells could be described as an antibody factory producing large protein molecules called immunoglobulins, which are the antibodies. Several different types of immunoglobulin are made in the plasma cell, and have been labelled immunoglobulins G, A, M, D and E. Much of the information about these proteins has been gained from the experiments of nature, as when some unfortunate patient has a cancer of the plasma cells which makes them produce huge amounts of one type of immunoglobulin. Conversely, the effects of congenital absence of the immunoglobulins have been closely studied.

The detailed functions of the immunoglobulins are not relevant here, but they are all large molecules, and there is more immunoglobulin G (IgG) than any other (80 per cent). It contains the readily available antibodies to the various diseases to which the body has previously been exposed, and IgG can cross the placenta to donate passive or ready-made immunity to the foetus so that these antibodies are available at birth.

IgA is not so abundant in the blood (16 per cent) but it is found in abundance in the colostrum, tears, nasal and bronchial secretions, saliva, and in the gut secretions. The function of IgA seems to be both protective and preventive, by acting as a sort of inter-cellular cement in the gut to control the entry of antigens. Infants who develop food allergies have been found to have a temporary deficiency of IgA which coincides with their feeding problems. Last to be discovered, but the most important for allergic reactions, is IgE, found in such small amounts in normal persons that until quite recently, it was completely overlooked.

What is special about immunoglobulin E and how was it discovered?

It was in 1919 that a Dr Ramirez of New York reported that a patient who had recently had a blood transfusion developed severe asthma for the first time in his life while driving in a horse carriage in Central Park. The doctor found out that the donor had severe horse asthma, and suggested that his blood had contained some substance which had sensitized his patient to horses.

Two years later two German scientists, Prausnitz and Kustner, demonstrated the presence of this tranferable factor in the serum (the clear fluid left after blood has clotted). Kustner was known to react violently to fish, so a little of his serum was injected into the skin of Prausnitz. When tested on the same place the next day with a fish extract the skin test was positive for the first time in his life. The rest of his skin remained negative because only the cells near the site of the injection had been sensitized, but if he had had a blood transfusion from Kustner every cell in the body would have been sensitized and he would have reacted violently to eating fish. When Prausnitz ate fish he reacted only where he had been given Kustner's serum, because some fish allergen absorbed from the gut reached this site via the bloodstream.

The next significant observation was that some patients who had received diphtheria anti-toxin made by immunizing horses against diphtheria began to react to horses, and some became so sensitive that another injection of horse serum could cause a fatal reaction, and the tiniest amount injected into the skin would produce a large skin reaction.

When the immunoglobulins were discovered nearly 50 years later none of them could be shown to contain this skin-sensitizing factor. In 1968 American and Swedish investigators finally found that it was a new human immunoglobulin, which they called immunoglobulin E.

They found that allergic patients had a great deal of IgE, but normal people had so little it was difficult to measure, suggesting that the intensity of an allergy depended on the amont of IgE. It was then discovered that allergic subjects possessed IgE *specifically* directed against the allergens to which they were sensitive. Methods for the measurement of total and of specific IgE were soon developed, so that it became possible to detect what the patients were allergic to from a blood sample, and to measure it. Because of the way the test is done it was called the radio-allergo-sorbent test (RAST). The clinical significance of this test, which has now been used worldwide for over 10 years, is discussed later in this book.

Why do only some people get allergies?

Most of us can be exposed to the common causes of allergy such as grass pollen, dust mites, and animals all our lives without becoming sensitized and producing IgE against these allergens. A minority are unlucky and easily sensitized because they react in an abnormal way to allergens by producing an excess of IgE. Being easily sensitized runs in families, but it is not known why some are afflicted and not others, or why people suddenly become allergic.

In many parts of the world infestation with worms and other parasites is very common, and the plasma cells make lots of IgE as a defensive response. In developed western countries worms are uncommon, so IgE in excess is usually associated with allergic illnesses and simply causes problems. The IgE, instead of being protective, is a useless antibody which causes excessive and self-destructive reactions to specific allergens.

How can IgE, the apparently unnecessary antibody, produce so much trouble?

To explain this it is necessary to introduce the reader to two very special types of cell which are to be found in every part of the body – the *mast cell*, in the tissues, and the *basophil*, in the circulating blood, both being similar and reacting in the same way. Mast cells are found everywhere, including the skin, and abound near the capillary blood vessels, bronchial tubes, the lining of the nose, and the gut and lymphatic glands.

In the individual predisposed to allergy the plasma cells produce an excess of IgE when contact is made with an allergen. This specific IgE then attaches itself to the mast cells and the basophils. A molecule of IgE is shaped like a Y, and the foot of the Y sticks to the wall of the mast cell. One single mast cell has the capacity for 100,000 sensitized spots on its surface, so the possibilities for attachment of different sorts of IgE, each specific for one allergen, is very large.

When molecules of specific allergen enter the circulation and extra-cellular fluids of a sensitized individual the allergen will contact the sensitized cells, and stick to the free arms of the molecules of specific IgE. The result is bridging of the IgE thus

$$\frac{\text{Y} \quad \text{allergen} \quad \text{Y}}{\text{mast cell}}$$

and the effect is to trigger off the discharge of mediator chemicals, such as histamine, from the mast cells or basophils. These mediators are already stored in very tiny coils like watch springs inside the cell, ready to be pushed out through the cell wall when triggered by the allergen.

The mediator chemicals which are set free into the fluids surrounding the cell are the cause of the allergic symptoms, and the magnitude of the effects depends on how many cells discharge their load of mediators at one time. For example, if all the mast cells are discharged simultaneously there may be enough released into the circulation to cause anaphylactic shock, but this is very unusual.

Why are allergic reactions so specific?

It may be helpful to introduce a lock-and-key analogy, in which the patient may be regarded as the lock, and the allergen the key which will turn on the allergic reaction. Allergens are different, just as keys are, but all patients sensitive to the same allergen, such as grass pollen, have the same lock, so all can be 'turned on' by the same key. Patients who are sensitized to several allergens have a lock for each – so they have several 'key' allergens which turn on their symptoms whenever these allergens appear in the environment. The same part of the body may be affected by all the allergens, or different parts may be turned on by different allergens.

This leads to the very important principle that if no allergen is present no reaction can occur. Therefore, if the allergen can be avoided the problem is completely solved, thus effecting a cure without drugs. To complete the analogy, if the key is thrown away the allergic reaction cannot be turned on, but the lock is still present.

It follows that if a skilled allergist can identify the causative allergen or allergens, great benefit may ensue, without dependence on drugs, which suppress but never cure. The principle is also illustrated by seasonal allergies, such as summer hay fever, occurring only when grass pollen is in the air. Deliberate exposure to grass pollen in the winter will turn on the symptoms at once, demonstrating the hidden 'lock'. Obviously, if the patient arranges to be in another country, or on a cruise liner, in the pollen season, the hay fever can be avoided. Allergens present in the environment all year round, such as the house dust mite, cannot be so easily avoided.

How do lymphocytes become sensitized?

The cellular defence system is another realm in which 'self-damaging' (i.e. allergic) reactions can take place. When a 'non-self' foreign antigen makes contact with T lymphocytes, this encounter is imprinted in a large number of identical cells, called a 'clone'. For the rest of life that clone of cells will rally round to deal with that specific antigen whenever it appears in the body. This memory function is so strong that if a few lymphocytes taken from the blood of an animal which has been sensitized to a specific antigen are injected into a second animal known not to react to that antigen, the sensitivity is transferred permanently to the second animal.

The memory reaction of T lymphocytes to a known antigen is not immediate, like an antigen–antibody reaction in the blood, but takes 6–48 hours at least. What happens is that when the antigen sticks to the sensitized T lymphocytes they liberate chemical messengers, the lymphokines, to summon other cells called macrophages, which attack the infecting bacteria or viruses and liberate enzymes which help dissolve them. All this activity is partly due to non-specific defences, and inflammation, and partly because the T cells are hypersensitive to the antigen. The cellular immune system is so sensitive that it may overreact, and often causes considerable damage in the process of localizing and exterminating an invasion by bacteria or viruses.

Perhaps it is worthwhile explaining a common example of such a phenomenon – the effect of a skin test for tuberculosis on a school child. This is something which may have worried thousands of parents because the explanation given is seldom clear, and sometimes no explanation is given at all.

A negative 'Heaf' test means that the child has never been infected with tuberculosis. This is not good news, because it also means vulnerability to tuberculosis infection. It is safer to make the child hypersensitive to tubercle bacilli by giving a deliberate infection with a harmless strain of tubercle bacilli called BCG vaccine, rather than risking a future infection with a wild and virulent strain. A tiny dose of BCG is injected under the skin, and spreads though the body to contact all the lymphocytes, but without causing illness. After 6 weeks the Heaf test will become positive, indicating that the whole body is now sensitized, and that if the child should encounter tuberculosis in future the bacilli will immediately be localized and dealt with.

A positive Heaf test means that the child is already sensitive because of a previous infection with tuberculosis, without obvious illness, but caused by a wild strain of tuberculosis. Forty years ago nearly everybody was positive, but today a positive test suggests that somebody with active disease was in contact with the child. Very rarely an intense reaction to the Heaf test will indicate that there is active infection now.

This simplified account of how cellular immunity works is relevant to our allergy theme, because an exaggerated hypersensitivity response coming on slowly is also an allergic reaction because it is a self-damaging immune response. Cellular immunity plays a major part in defence against bacteria, viruses and cancer and also causes rejection of transplants from other than identical twins. The immunological memory can last a lifetime.

What are auto-immune diseases?

A whole group of unusual diseases has been identified in recent years where the immune system makes a mistake, and reacts against and may even destroy an organ, such as the thyroid gland, or some specific type of tissue which is widespread in the body. These self-destructive reactions, which could be referred to as immunological suicide, are called the auto-immune diseases. This is well illustrated by the analogy that if you were to buy a gun to defend yourself it would be essential to be able to distinguish friends from foes before pulling the trigger, and to take care not to shoot yourself – unless suicide is intended. An allergic reaction resembles inability to recognize a foreign substance as harmless, and reacting unnecessarily against it. When the immune system becomes unable to distinguish 'self' from 'non-self' this is analogous with suicide or shooting yourself accidentally.

What are the diseases of adaptation?

Successful and continuing adaptation to our environment is an expression of continuing life itself, failing only at death. Partial failure of adaptation may take many forms and have many causes. For example, the excessive defensive reactions found in allergic disease justify classifying these disorders as diseases of adaptation. In relation to the immediate type of allergic reaction characterized by circulating specific IgE antibody and specifically sensitized mast cells and basophils, the great mystery is how and why some specific allergen becomes selected for the role of sensitizing agent, or why only certain specific organs may be affected. For example, an individual may develop only an allergy towards one specific substance in the environment, and all that is necessary is to avoid that allergen in future, if known. Some individuals are easier to sensitize than others, and while some people are very selective about their allergens, other unfortunate individuals are easily sensitized to large numbers of allergens, and develop allergic diseases of all kinds.

'Adaptation' to the environment can be perfect, an automatic adjustment which depends on many complex bodily mechanisms. If there are any inbuilt defects, the adaptive response will be inadequate or insufficient, or exaggerated and excessive to the extent of being self-damaging – i.e. an 'allergic' reaction. For the mast cells to be sensitized by excessive amounts of otherwise useless IgE is clearly a defect of adaptation to specific foreign proteins. Self-damaging reactions by the cellular defence system are clearly in the same category, just as the 'auto-immune' diseases are caused by the immune system mistaking self for non-self.

3 A holistic approach to the allergy problem

Allergy can afflict one or more organs or systems of the body, and the cause can be one or several allergens. Only by close observation of numerous allergic patients over many years is it possible to build up the complex picture of allergic disease as a whole-body problem, and to recognize all its subtle variants. Although a major complaint such as asthma or eczema may be obvious, problems in other systems may also co-exist. The key to the understanding of allergic disease is the diagram (Figure 3.1) which illustrates how the allergens are distributed by the blood and tissue fluid to every cell, no matter by what route they enter the body. No sensitized area can escape the allergens, hence allergic disease is not limited by boundaries between medical specialties. This is why referral to specialized departments such as skin, or ear, nose and throat for advice may not be helpful unless all the specialists work closely together for the benefit of the allergic patient as a whole.

Today some doctors, and many patients, have become disillusioned with conventional medical specialization, and prefer what has become known as the 'holistic' approach. This should imply treating the patient as a whole person once more, but the public can confuse holistic with alternative or even fringe medicine.

Allergy victims desperately need the true 'holistic' approach because although the study of allergic disease is specialized in one sense, it must be generalized in another. Thus, the true clinical allergist should treat allergic disease anywhere in the body, but ideally should also possess sufficient scientific background to be familiar with a laboratory as well as with a clinic.

How may allergic problems change during a lifetime?

Allergic symptoms arising from one organ of the body may clear up spontaneously as time goes by, only to break out in another organ to produce another set of symptoms, perhaps caused by a different allergen.

Studies of large groups of cases over long periods of time have shown that quite often problems begin with infant feeding, when there is vomiting, diarrhoea, colic or eczema, which may perhaps be succeeded by head banging and hyperactivity. After parents have been driven almost frantic, these problems usually clear up (although the eczema may not), only to be often followed by asthma and hay fever in later childhood. These problems may fade out in adolescence but 'growing out of it' is seldom as common as it is made out to be. Unfortunately a period of freedom when the sufferer is in his/her twenties and thirties may be followed by the late-onset type of asthma in the forties and fifties. In fact, even old age is not exempt, as an increasing number of people are developing allergic asthma for the first time in their seventies and eighties. Problems such as nasal polyps, loss of smell and taste, and perhaps ear problems as well, may also return in later life after having last been a problem in childhood.

What is the difference between allergic and non-allergic individuals?

It is almost impossible to answer this question, as there are too many unknown aspects. For example, identical twins from very allergic families do not always both develop allergic disease. Being born in the season for grass pollen, birch pollen, or ragweed pollen predisposes to seasonal allergies, presumably because one is sensitized in the cradle. However, many individuals have positive skin tests *and* antibodies in the blood, yet have no symptoms.

In general terms, a great many individuals are primed ready to become allergics. Gross overexposure to allergens such as pollen, mites and animals may be more than these primed individuals can take. The result is that the allergies are turned on, and then it is very difficult or impossible to turn them off again. Very little good evidence exists regarding what turns allergics on or off. For example, slow recovery takes place over the years in many cases of hay fever, but we do not even know why they get better.

Are there any unusual ways in which allergy may cause problems?

Many physical and some mental problems are caused by allergy, but the presentation of the symptoms can be so bizarre that the possibility of allergy may not be considered. It is accepted that allergic reactions are responsible for asthma, hay fever and eczema, and sometimes migraine, but the extent to which allergies play a significant part in disease affecting the gut, joints, vascular system, nervous system, kidneys, and so on, is much more controversial. My experience suggests that, although it is uncommon, allergy can be very important in a few of these cases, so that the possibility should not be discarded, but considered seriously. Fever, with temperatures up to 40°C (104°F), has sometimes been noted in cases of undiagnosed allergy, especially to foods. The physician may not be aware of the possibility that allergy can cause fever, and it may be very difficult to establish the diagnosis, after more serious causes have been eliminated by many investigations.

Because similar symptoms can be caused by other organic diseases, it is unwise and unsafe to jump to the conclusion that the cause of a problem is always an allergy of some kind. All other possible causes should be excluded by conventional modern tests before considering allergy as a possibility in an unusual case, so that nothing equally or more serious is missed. The conclusion that a physical or emotional problem is due to an allergic reaction, usually to a food, is normally based on observations of repeated cause/effect relationships, because there are no reliable laboratory tests. Confirmation by modern methods of scientific laboratory investigation in order to convince the sceptics may not be possible at the present time.

Do different allergens tend to cause manifestations of allergic disease which suggest the cause?

It would seem logical if this were so, and to a limited extent it is true. For example, inhaled allergens usually cause respiratory allergy, contactants skin trouble, and foods intestinal problems. But this is an oversimplification, because this rule is so often broken that what might seem at first to be a relatively simple problem may turn out to be complex, only to be disclosed bit by bit, like peeling the layers of an onion. The ways in which allergic reactions cause symptoms are quite limited, but the number of allergens is legion. For example, many allergens can cause asthma, but the asthma caused by one allergen is identical with that caused by another.

In the gut the presentations of allergic symptoms are much more varied, because of the many ways in which the gut lining and the digestive processes can be interfered with. A further complication is the fact that many other causes of bowel disease can cause identical symptoms.

How can allergies affect any tissue in the body?

Whatever the route of entry of the allergen to the body may be, some of it must enter the general circulation of the blood, and thence the tissue fluids which are in contact with every cell in the body. This foreign material has no effect on a normal person, but in the allergic individual the effects depend entirely on exactly which tissues have become sensitized, and how intense the degree of sensitization happens to be.

An example is the case of a woman who reacted intensely with asthma to certain mould spores found in the air in large numbers in August and in September. This was proved by producing a mild attack of asthma in February by inhaling a little aerosol of the correct mould-spore extract. She complained not so much of the wheezing, which she could understand, but of an intolerably itchy back and ears from which she had always suffered in August and September. Obviously the tissues in these areas were sensitive to minute amounts of the allergen in the circulation,

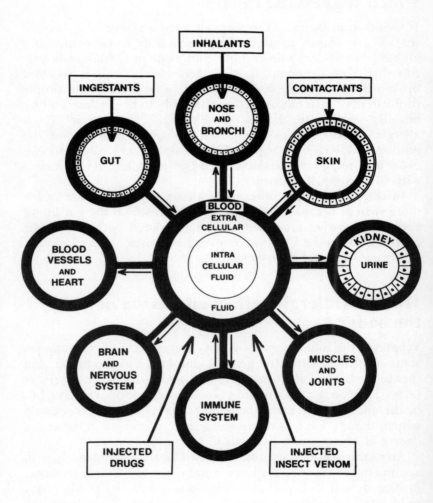

Figure 3.1 A holistic concept of allergic disease.

thus explaining her seasonal itch. Housewives, on being deliberately provoked with aerosols of dust mites, sometimes complain of severe itch on the chin, which they had previously noted as occurring when they were exposed to dust in the course of their household chores.

So there is good evidence that allergens gain entry to the circulation and eventually present themselves to each and every cell in the body, thus giving the opportunity for the cell to react if sensitive. I have deliberately quoted clinical examples which showed that the allergen can reach specifically sensitized areas of skin, because this example connects the eczema, urticaria or nettle rash with exposure to allergens from *within* the body as well as from *without*, and demonstrates how these afflictions may be caused by allergic sensitization of the skin. Just as the circulating allergens can reach the skin, so they can contact the brain and nervous system, joints, kidney, small and large intestine or gut, and all the blood vessels of the circulatory system which is distributing the allergen throughout the body, as shown in Figure 3.1.

Why some doctors find allergy difficult to understand

Doctors are trained to recognize the patterns of disease by the history of the complaint, the findings on physical examination, and the results of laboratory tests, x-rays, and so on. The results may give a definite diagnosis, or suggest several possible diagnoses, which may be narrowed down by further investigation.

Allergic syndromes differ in fundamental ways from more conventional diseases. The symptoms of the illness depend on the part of the body affected, not on the causative allergen to which that part has become sensitive, and the symptoms give no clue to the cause, which may be any allergen. There may be several causative allergens, mixed up with physical and emotional factors, and different allergens may, or may not, affect different parts of the body.

Furthermore, other diseases may be simulated so that allergy is not recognized as the basic problem. Recognition of the allergic nature of the problem is vital, as it may lead not only to the correct treatment, but even to the identification and removal of the cause, resulting in 'cure'.

PART 2

The Causes of Allergic Disease – the Allergens

4 The nature and distribution of the perennial allergens

What is an allergen?

Recognition that a substance is acting as an allergen will be shown by the fact that inhalation, ingestion or contact will repeatedly trigger off the same excessive reaction in a sensitized individual but produce no effect on other people.

This definition is a deliberately broad one because if we regard 'allergic' reactions as due to faulty adaptation to the environment – a sort of revolt against a specific substance – all types of reaction will be included. The reaction may occur at the first point of contact, or the allergen may provoke a reaction in a distant sensitized organ, but the presence of the allergen is essential for a reaction to occur.

Thus, perennial symptoms are caused by allergens which are always present, seasonal by those which are only present in their season, and intermittent symptoms when the allergen is only sometimes present. Allergic people are often sensitive to more than one allergen, and the effects of multiple allergy can be cumulative. Symptoms caused by a perennial allergen may be considerably worsened by a superimposed summer allergen.

What are the major perennial allergens?

These allergens can be constantly in the environment and therefore cause problems all year round, unlike seasonal allergens, which present only in the summer and autumn. The most frequent perennial allergens in order of importance are house-dust mites, house dust, animals, moulds, foods and chemicals. Awareness of the possible causes of allergic symptoms, where the

Table 4.1 The perennial allergens

Allergen	Usual sources	Most frequent problems caused
Dusts House dust: house-dust mite, feather particles, human skin scales	bedding and carpets, soft furnishings	rhinitis and asthma, sometimes eczema
Textiles Wool, feathers, cotton, synthetics, kapok	bedding and dust; sometimes occupational; clothing factories, etc.	rhinitis and asthma
Organic dusts Sawdust, grain dust, flour dust, cattle feed, hay, straw	occupational exposure or hobbies	asthma, rhinitis, contact dermatitis, alveolitis
Storage mites	stored foodstuffs or grain	
Animals Dogs, cats, birds, horses, cows, rabbits, guinea pigs, rats, mice, etc.	pets and occupations associated with close contact with animals	rhinitis, asthma and eczema
Moulds Aspergillus, *Penicillium*, dry rot, *Cladosporium*, *Botrytis*	damp houses or workplaces, cellars, farms, breweries, indoor plants, conservatories	rhinitis and asthma
Micropolyspora faeni	mouldy hay on farms	farmer's lung
Yeasts	breweries; beer, wine and sherry; breads and other foods; vineyards, vinegar, airborne wild yeast	rhinitis, asthma, sometimes eczema

Table 4.1   The perennial allergens

Allergen	Usual sources	Most frequent problems caused
Chemicals Metals: nickel, mercury chromium	home or work; dental fillings, jewellery, money, cement	contact dermatitis – localized, sometimes generalized symptoms
platinum, salts	refineries	asthma
Cosmetics and toiletries Eye shadow, hair dyes, powders, perfumes, hairspray, bleaching agents, aftershave, deodorants, toothpaste, shampoo, soap, camomile	home or work as beauticians or hairdressers	contact dermatitis, rarely asthma and unusual syndromes
Fumes and pollutants Oils, paints, inks, fumes from plastic foam manufacture, cavity wall insulation, natural-gas fumes, air-fresheners, aerosols, insecticides	home and work	asthma and unusual syndromes; cavity wall insulation is controversial; difficulties in proof frequently encountered
pine resin (colophony)	pine trees, solder flux, violinists' resin, glossy paper, etc.	asthma, rhinitis, unusual syndromes
Plastics and rubber Rubbers, leather, oils, paints, polishes	protective clothing, rubber gloves, wellingtons, etc; plastics found everywhere – clothes, seating, shoes, etc.	contact dermatitis; paint and plastic fumes cause asthma in some people
Food additives Dyes, preservatives, antioxidants	additives in foods, medical tablets and syrups, coloured sweets, soft drinks, etc.	sometimes behaviour problems in children, eczema, asthma; unusual syndromes

Table 4.1 The perennial allergens

Allergen	Usual sources	Most frequent problems caused
Medicines (drugs) Antibiotics, aspirin, anti-rheumatic drugs, adhesive plaster, injected drugs, and anti-sera animal extracts	can be occupational in factories or in a pharmacy; added dyes or fillers in tablets or syrups	skin rashes, anaphylaxis, gut reactions, asthma etc.
Cleaning agents Detergents – washing powder, washing-up liquid, scouring powders, etc., enzyme-based washing powders	home or work – the list is endless	contact dermatitis and unusual syndromes
Insects Bees, wasps, locusts, etc.	anywhere	anaphylaxis, skin reactions
Semen	men	rash, anaphylaxis, unusual syndromes
Foods For details *see* Chapter 22 – main foods are milk, cereals, yeast, fish, eggs, nuts, etc.	all foods and drinks	asthma, rhinitis and eczema, gut problems
Plants Primula, chrysanthemum; poison ivy and oak (USA only)		contact dermatitis, rarely asthma

allergens may be found, and how they can be identified is information which could be useful to the reader in search of a cause for his or her problems. Table 4.1 summarizes perennial allergens, their origins and the symptoms they cause, while Figure 4.1 summarizes the causes of allergic disease.

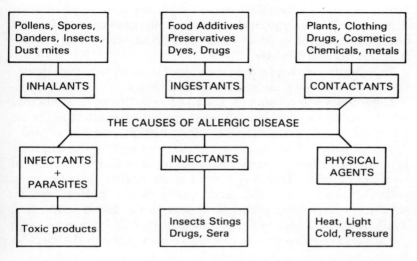

Figure 4.1   This diagram summarises the causes of allergic disease.

How do allergens enter the body?

Inhalants are allergens which enter the nose or bronchi with the inhaled air and will vary according to whether the patient is at home being exposed to allergens derived from the home environment, at work inhaling dust, spores or chemicals, or out in the open air where seasonal and perennial spores and pollens may be important.

When inhaled the particles land on the warm and moist lining of the nose and bronchi (the respiratory system). The allergens are dissolved out of the inhaled particles on the lining of the nose or bronchi. What happens next is a reaction by the nose or the bronchi, or both. It is also important to realize that the soluble allergens are also being absorbed into the bloodstream, whether or not a local reaction is being produced, and distributed to the whole body.

Contactants are allergens affecting the skin, mouth and eyes through direct contact. This class of allergen involves cosmetics, creams, ointments, detergents, metals and all manner of substances which can cause local sensitization, therefore contact dermatitis. Certain plants such as primulas, chrysanthemums, begonias (and in the USA poison ivy) can also cause contact dermatitis. Pollens and other air-borne allergens can act directly on sensitized eyes or skin; foods and drinks can affect mouth, tongue or throat directly.

Injectants are substances introduced directly into the circulation by bee or wasp stings, or injected drugs.

Ingestants are substances such as foods, drinks or medicines which can cause local symptoms directly in the intestine, or be absorbed into the circulation to affect distant sensitive organs.

It was believed for many years that the wall of the intestine presented an effective barrier to the entry of large molecules or of particles of food. This has proved quite untrue, because even pollen grains, yeast cells, and spores of the puffball fed to volunteers have been found to appear in the blood soon after. Thus, not only large molecules of food proteins but even large particles like pollen grains can easily gain entry to the circulation.

How much allergen is required to cause a reaction?

Allergens vary a great deal in their capacity to sensitize people, just as people are infinitely variable in their capacity to become sensitized. Massive exposure for many years may not sensitize those with little or no tendency to allergic disease, but at the other extreme very slight exposure to the same allergen can sensitize those who are very susceptible. For example, a fish-meal factory sensitized a few people living a mile away, but others could work all their lives in the factory without trouble. Some patients react to traces of allergen in the air which cannot be detected by the most sensitive scientific methods available. This enormous variation in sensitivity and in potential to sensitize may cause rejection of a patient's problems as 'all in the mind' if this is not understood. For example, a little boy who had acute asthma attacks whenever he saw his grandmother was eventually found not to be reacting to her but to traces of peanut on her clothes, as her job was packing peanuts.

What is the main cause of allergy to house dust?

There can be no doubt that the mites in household dust are the commonest cause of perennial asthma and rhinitis (perennial hay fever) in the world, and are particularly prevalent in developed western countries. Factory dust, building dust and garden dust have no relationship to household dust.

The role of mites as allergens is by no means fully investigated. In 1968 I found that many patients were allergic not only to the ordinary dust mite, but to several other species commonly found in the environment, especially on farms. Subsequent research has shown that mites are a major cause of allergy in farmers because they infest the cereals used for feeding the animals. Mites contaminate and destroy stored food, such as flour, and are found in huge numbers in stored grain. Isolation, identification and testing of patients for mites is difficult and tedious. Allergy can be limited to one type of mite, or extended to several.

What do mites look like, how big are they and what do they live on?

They are about 0.25 mm in size, white, and just visible to the naked eye when moving against a black background. They are surprisingly difficult to find, partly because they move away from the light. Dust mites live on human skin scales, and also on mould spores and yeasts.

Which part of the dust mite contains the allergen?

A recent British discovery is that the excreta of the mite contains most of the allergen. On the way down the gut of the mite the excreta forms into tiny lumps, which become covered in a layer of material derived from the mite. The result is a tiny rounded pellet about 20 microns in diameter, about the same size as a pollen grain, which can become airborne.

We are blissfully unaware that when we fling off the bedclothes and spring out of bed in the morning we create a shower of flying faeces in the air of the bedroom. These are inhaled and land on the moist warm lining of nose or bronchial tubes, and the allergen is dissolved off the surface of the pellet. The result in sensitized people is an allergic reaction where the pellet struck, setting off mediator chemicals which produce the symptoms. Also, tiny amounts of allergen get into the circulation, and may cause reactions in distant organs such as the skin, where eczema may be produced.

Why is the house-dust mite so common in western countries?

The introduction of fitted carpets in the majority of western homes has provided the mite with the perfect habitat. Carpets used to be taken outside and beaten, but fitted carpets are undisturbed year after year. The mites can survive sweeping, vacuuming and insecticides. They cling to the fibres even in a washing machine, but dryness and sunshine will kill them.

Mite allergy is therefore uncommon in countries where the climate is warm and floors seldom need carpets, so the mites have nowhere to live. Immigrants from such countries frequently become allergic to the dust mite and grass pollen, these major allergens being encountered for the first time when they come to Britain. The Mediterranean countries also have dust allergy, but it is not such a problem as it is in the UK. The mite is also a major cause of allergy in the USA and Canada. Dust-sensitive Britons frequently get dramatically better on holiday, only to relapse on their return home. Obviously, the absence of carpets and other soft furnishings in warm climates is important.

The reverse of this situation was highlighted by a boy at an English public school who was very allergic to dust mites, and who went home every vacation to a very lavishly furnished air-conditioned house in a tropical African country. He always had dreadful asthma there, but recovered on returning to the spartan public-school environment. In his case wealth and expensive tastes contributed to his dust-mite allergy.

Where are mites found in the home?

Mites in your bed are the most important because nearly a third of your life is spent there with them. Symptoms in dust allergy are usually worse at night, worse in bed and worse on rising. Mites are mostly found on the mattress round the buttons, and can multiply even on an unused mattress, for example in winter in an empty caravan. They thrive best in a bed used by somebody with eczema who is shedding skin profusely, and may sweat, scratch, and even bleed. Mites prefer damp humid conditions, provided for example by perspiration in bed and by damp housing conditions.

Wool blankets, because they cannot be washed frequently, tend to harbour many mites, and should be avoided in favour of light cotton cellular blankets or a synthetic duvet. Cuddly toys and old feather pillows have been found infested with mites, and should not be in the bed. In the living room overstuffed furniture, especially the nice comfortable old-fashioned sort, may harbour many mites. Thus, the inhabitants of the relatively prosperous developed nations seem to have given the dust mite the ideal environment for survival and multiplication in the carpets, soft furnishings and soft beds of the affluent society.

How can mites be eliminated?

Sadly, even the most intensive cleaning campaign will not necessarily help patients. Some mothers become very discouraged, while other cases definitely benefit as shown in Figure 4.2, which is a rare example. The explanation probably depends on the intensity of the allergy to mites, because it may be practically impossible to reduce the mite population of the home to a low enough level to make a real difference to an ultrasensitive sufferer. When the victim is only slightly sensitive, this objective may be less difficult to achieve.

Mites are very resistant to insecticides, but in the past few years their ecology has been studied more closely and two new methods of destroying them have been found.

The excreta contains guanine, like birds and spiders, and a simple test anyone can do will show how much mite excreta there is in house dust. This test can pinpoint the most contaminated areas of the house, furniture or bedding. It is also possible to measure very accurately the amount of mite allergen in a sample of dust using an immunological method.

An aerosol spray for bedding and moist powder for carpets, called Acarosan, which kills the mites and makes the particles of excreta stick together so they are no longer small enough to get airborne, has been developed in Germany. It is on sale in Europe and will be available soon in the USA and the UK. This product is toxic only to mites, and a most important feature is that one application may get rid of them for a year. The author has used it with great success on cases of rhinitis, asthma and eczema, and feels that it is a real advance in management, requiring much less treatment, or being able to stop treatment altogether without relapse.

Another agent has been found in Australia, and is simply a 1% or 3% solution of tannic acid, which is sprayed on soft furniture, bedding and carpets. The tannic acid denatures the allergen in the excreta, but the effect is not so long lasting. Tannic acid is harmless, and will also denature pollens and animal allergens. Hence both agents may be required in a case of combined dust mite and animal allergy.

Once the house of the patient has been decontaminated the eczema or asthma may disappear, but sleeping in a bed which has not been treated will soon cause a relapse of the allergic problem.

An amusing and instructive case history is relevant here. A very dust mite allergic patient was supplied with Acarosan to treat her bed and bedroom, but she returned it unused because she had bought a water bed, which has no place for mites. Soon she no longer needed treatment for her asthma, and as a bonus her husband's chronic eczema also cleared completely . . . yet he was not a patient!

Plastic covers on the mattress may be practical but tend to be sweaty and uncomfortable. Fitted wardrobes, especially if on an outside wall, tend to promote moulds and mites on clothes seldom used, especially if in the spare bedroom.

The author has recently devised a simple method of making an extract of house dust or animal hair which can be used for skin testing in a few minutes. In this way the role of pets and dust from bed, mattress, and other parts of the house can be rapidly assessed.

A recent case illustrates how much can be accomplished by investigation of the home environment. He was a man of 48 who had had asthma as a boy, and had begun to have severe night attacks once more during the previous 3 years. Testing his skin against an extract of the dust from his own mattress produced a

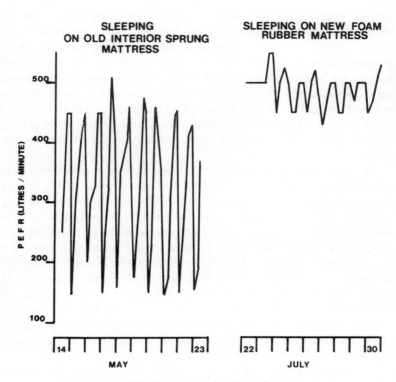

Figure 4.2   The importance of mites in the mattress.

huge reaction. His wife reminded him that that particular mattress had been in store for years until just before his asthma relapsed. A new mattress effected a cure without drugs. Another case where the peak flow readings improved dramatically is illustrated by Figure 4.2.

What other allergens are found in house dust?

A minority of dust-sensitive patients react on skin testing to crude house-dust extracts, but not to pure mite extracts. A main ingredient of the bag of the vacuum sweeper is wool, which may be the cause of the symptoms in cases who react only to house dust. Wool is a very complex animal product found all over the house, which can be a major allergen in some cases, but it is difficult to confirm this without special tests. A characteristic story suggesting wool allergy is often the only guide. For example, sufferers may give a history of being affected by a new wool carpet, or by going into carpet shops, or of having been forced to give up knitting with wool years ago and having to use synthetics instead because the wool provoked asthma or rhinitis. Rarely some people react to sheepskin coats, and heavy wool jerseys, but woollen clothes rarely cause problems because they are not fluffy.

Feathers can be most important but allergy to feathers is often confused with dust-mite allergies and can present great difficulties in diagnosis. It is not a common allergy but sometimes very serious as in the case of a 10 year old boy who had been given steroid drugs for several years for severe asthma. As soon as he was taken into hospital his asthma disappeared, suggesting an environmental cause, which proved to be the family budgerigar, because every time the bird was brought into his cubicle in the hospital he had a severe attack of asthma. Fortunately the bird flew away and the boy remained well for 2 years with no treatment until he had a sudden attack in bed in a hotel on holiday. His parents removed an old feather pillow from under the bottom sheet, and he had no further trouble.

Another example was a 10 year old boy whose asthma was very difficult to control, yet got even *worse* on admission to the children's hospital. Investigation revealed that all the pillows in the hospital were filled with feathers. He was not much better at home, but was always completely well on holiday. The next time the family went away his mother hid an old feather cushion in the lavatory before departure. On arrival home from a perfect holiday he was told to go and sit in the lavatory until sent for, but had severe asthma after 10 minutes, although unaware that there was a concealed cushion. This case was being investigated by the daily use of a peak flow meter, and the dramatic and lasting improvement resulting from removing every feather from the house is illustrated in Figure 4.3. He now has no significant asthma, and is a good athlete.

The diagnosis of feather allergy can sometimes be made by a patient getting much worse in countries where feather beds are still common, or following purchase of a feather duvet. A synthetic duvet is relatively inexpensive and a good substitute for

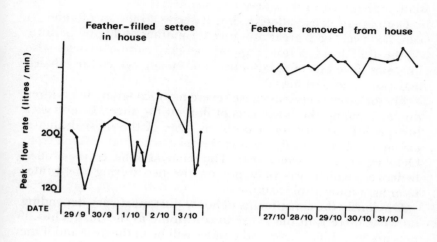

Figure 4.3   Asthma caused by feathers.

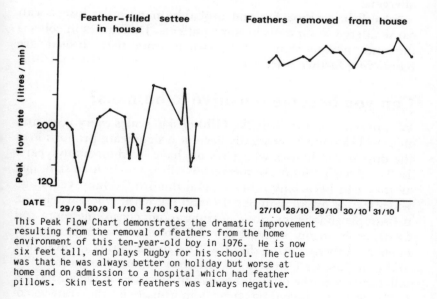

This Peak Flow Chart demonstrates the dramatic improvement resulting from the removal of feathers from the home environment of this ten-year-old boy in 1976. He is now six feet tall, and plays Rugby for his school. The clue was that he was always better on holiday but worse at home and on admission to a hospital which had feather pillows. Skin test for feathers was always negative.

Figure 4.4   Effect of ducted air central heating on allergic asthma.

blankets, feather duvets and eiderdowns, all of which are potentially dangerous to the allergic subject.

Cotton can cause allergies but it seems to be uncommon. It can, however, be a great nuisance for mother and baby because of the fluff from cotton nappies. Ironing cotton articles also liberates little bits of cotton fibre into the air, which are inhaled and can cause asthma.

Flannelette sheets can cause severe night coughing in children due to inhaling the little balls of fluff off the sheet. Candlewick bedspreads can also be a problem. One of the most dramatic examples of cotton allergy was the man who had asthma from October to March every year. The removal of his cotton-stuffed bedcover, which was only put on the bed during the winter months, removed his asthma.

Obviously the constituents of house dust must vary depending on what there is in the house to contribute to the dust. Thus, if pets are kept bits of hair and dander will be in the dust and if the house is damp mould spores may also be present. There are many other possibilities in dust and it is sometimes necessary to take samples for microscopical examination to identify possible allergens.

Silverfish, cockroaches and probably many other insects can cause allergic symptoms in some patients. Difficulties in collecting and making skin-testing extracts from these insects are hampering further research.

Can you become sensitive to humans?

We are estimated to shed 2kg (4lb) of skin scales every year, and this shed skin must eventually become a significant proportion of the dust in old houses where people have lived for many years. In fact, a few patients are specifically allergic to human skin, just as they can be to any other animal dandruff. Many years ago when testing an air sampler, I found unidentifiable particles on the sample slide in my clinic, waiting room, consulting room and finally even in my home, but none from samples taken in the open air. I then realized that I was looking at human skin scales, and that they were to be found in every human habitation. The full story about the importance of human scales in the air has yet to be written, including their importance in the transfer of infection from one person to another, the bacteria and viruses hitching a ride on the floating scales.

Audrey was a case of severe chronic asthma. Provocation tests showed that she reacted with asthma to inhaling extracts of house dust and of human skin scales, but did not react to mites. Injection treatment with mite extracts was ineffective, but she was greatly improved by injections of crude dust which contains extracts of human skin.

Human skin scales in the indoor environment are unavoidable, and may be an important allergen, but further research is required. So far they appear to be a weak allergen compared with mites. Allergy to discarded skin may be a form of auto-immunity because the reaction is against a 'self' protein from the body.

Why are animals a major cause of allergic disease?

All animals produce skin scales (the main source of allergen), hair and characteristic smells. The urine also contains potent allergens. Many of us share our homes, and sometimes even our beds, with pet animals. Children are exposed to pets in an intimate way which is fundamentally insanitary, and the closer the contact the more likely is the child to be sensitized. Potentially allergic humans are exposed to sensitization to a much greater extent than seems to have been the case a hundred years ago. In Britain and other western countries millions of animals are kept as pets, and schools often keep them in the classroom. In the last 30 years horse-riding has become extremely popular, and developing allergy to horses can be a disaster for some keen young riders. It is almost impossible to escape traces of animal allergens for even if we do not have pets in the house ourselves, it is difficult to avoid friends and relations who do. It is common to develop allergy to several animals, making avoidance a very difficult problem. Many of these cases are also sensitive to dust mites and pollen.

Animal proteins are definitely 'non-self'; therefore sensitization of individuals prone to develop allergic problems is very common. The allergens are inhaled directly into the nose or bronchi, causing respiratory symptoms, but once absorbed into the bloodstream may also affect sensitized skin or other organs. Direct contact can cause local symptoms; reactions in the eye are often caused by traces of allergen transferred from hands which

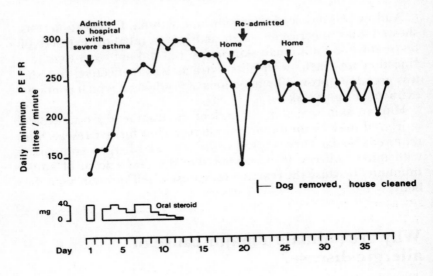

This boy was first seen because of incessant cough, night and day, for weeks on end, even when asleep. The cause was the development of allergy to the dog, which had been in the house for only six months. He had a severe attack of asthma which recovered quickly in hospital and relapsed at home until the house was cleaned.

Figure 4.5   An example of dog asthma.

have touched the animals or by airborne particles of animal dandruff.

Domestic pets often pose a great problem, because the obvious answer is to get rid of them if they are clearly the cause of the allergy, and for many families difficult decisions may have to be made. Even short exposures to cats and dogs can have prolonged effects. A weekly visit to a granny who has a cat or dog can be enough to cause asthma which is only improving just before the next visit. Thus it is always worthwhile considering the pets of the relatives and friends as well as those of the household itself.

Sensitivity to animals can be extreme. I have known people who would definitely react to a horse 20 yards away, or to a dog shut away in the back room of the house. Some react violently to even the smell of tomcats' urine in a garage. The reason is that the animal skin scales and smell molecules travel considerable distances on the air currents. I have sometimes had to request that school-teachers put all pet-owning children on one side of the room because animal traces on their clothes were enough to cause symptoms in those children allergic to animals. For example, serious asthma in a brother was caused by traces of horse on the clothes of his horse-mad sister who violently wished her brother dead so that she could carry on riding her beloved horse.

Allergy to animals can also be an occupational hazard, particularly affecting farmers, veterinarians, jockeys, animal breeders, scientists working with experimental animals, and so on. Serious career difficulties may arise for which the only adequate alternative answer is change of job, change of animal, or desensitization, which has now become impractical in the UK except in hospital (*see* pages 219 to 220).

What advice can be given regarding animal allergies?

If there is a strong family history of allergic problems, especially on both sides of the family, never risk having pets in the house and discourage riding horses. If you *must* keep a dog, keep it in a kennel outside, as warm air from the kitchen will carry traces to every part of the house in minutes. Allergic children and animals just do not mix. Never give in to entreaties and demands to admit any pet to the home as there is a serious risk that even if allergic symptoms are not caused at once, the child will have become sensitized after 6–12 months. By that time the pet may be beloved by the whole family and parting with it will be much worse than if there had never been a pet at all. Nevertheless, it must be said that people prone to allergies do not invariably become sensitive to their pets. But sometimes an animal can be kept for 20 years and then suddenly its owner will become acutely sensitive to it.

Intermittent contact can cause increasing sensitivity and create a serious problem between childhood friends. The best compromise is for the child who owns the pet to come to your house to play, as it ought to be free from animals. Sometimes an adult reacts violently to the contaminated clothes of a boyfriend or girlfriend so that a difficult choice has to be made. I once successfully immunized a girl against her boyfriend's cat, but by the time she ceased to react to the cat the affair had come to an end.

Anyone allergic to animals who is contemplating the purchase of a house should enquire regarding previous occupancy by dogs and cats. The best answer in very sensitive cases is to buy a brand-new house, avoiding old ones with the residue of many families and their pets in accumulated dust. If any members of an allergic family ride horses, they must undress in an outhouse or porch and never bring contaminated clothing inside. Even if they themselves do not react to horses, they can cause serious problems for other members of the family that can baffle diagnosis for a long time, as in the case of the woman who had suddenly developed asthma 3 months previously. There was no clue to the cause except a violently positive skin test for horse, though she' had never been near one. The reason was that her 10 year old daughter had been grooming her friend's pony for about 6 months, in exchange for riding, and had thrown contaminated clothes in the wash basket, thus sensitizing her mother.

What other allergic problems can be caused by pets apart from sneezing and wheezing?

Pets can also be an unrecognized cause of eczema, as exposure for an hour or two can result in a flare-up which can last a week. Thus a visit to granny once a week can be the cause of a troublesome chronic skin problem, and sometimes asthma can last just as long. The eyes can be the main area sensitized, and care may have to be taken to avoid contaminating the eyes from hands which have been licked or otherwise contaminated by pets.

Unusual allergens associated with keeping pets, such as daphnia fish food and bird seed, may cause trouble, but the most serious disease of the allergic type is alveolitis arising from bird-fancier's lung from caged birds or from pigeons.

What are moulds and can they be allergens?

Moulds, or fungi, are simple microscopic plants which act as nature's scavengers and, with bacteria, convert both live and dead material into basic chemicals, such as amino acids, which can be used as building blocks to make proteins.

They have no chlorophyll (the green colour of plants), grow in long branches called mycelium, and reproduce by spores. Some prefer room temperature for growth, others blood heat, while a few will grow in the refrigerator. There are at least 100,000 known species, but fortunately only a few are common allergens. Some moulds can cause disease in man, animals and birds, and can destroy crops, stored food, wood, paper, leather and so on. Others are beneficial, producing antibiotics, alcohol enzymes and many other products.

Moulds can cause allergic problems in those who inhale the spores. If the environment of the house becomes contaminated with moulds, perennial allergies may be caused. Moulds also grow outside on all vegetation and become airborne in enormous numbers in the summer and autumn, causing seasonal allergies.

What we can see with the naked eye on a mouldy piece of bread is mainly the branching mycelium, but the part which causes allergic problems is the spores, which are so small and light that they can be carried very quickly and for long distances in the wind. For this reason mould spores from the cellar can be all over the house in minutes. These spores correspond to the seeds of plants, and just like pollen are essential for procreation. Being sexual material the spores are very allergenic, but some allergen is also found in the mycelium.

What are the main moulds which cause perennial allergic problems?

The commonest are *Aspergillus*, *Cladosporium* and *Penicillium* in this country, and occasionally other fungal spores associated with damp houses, such as dry rot. These spores are also found outside near rotting vegetation (such as a compost heap), which is being broken down by the moulds. They are more prevalent in warm humid weather conditions, and in farms, particularly in barns and cowsheds.

Dry rot is an uncommon cause of allergy in the indoor environment, and will only happen when there is a fruiting body present shedding untold millions of spores. This can be seen as brown dust resembling instant coffee which appears round the skirting boards day after day. Microscopic examination will soon show that it is composed of dry rot spores, which may sensitize the inhabitants of the house, causing asthma.

Yeasts are also found in houses and occasionally cause allergic problems. For example, amateur wine-makers or bread-bakers have more contact with yeast, but it is much more likely to cause trouble when eaten or drunk. It is, therefore, dealt with in the food section of this book. Some yeasts cause problems in the late summer and autumn, and are covered in the seasonal allergens section.

Where are moulds found in houses?

Old property with rising damp and no damp course is the major source of allergenic perennial moulds. Renovation of old houses and the installation of central heating can cause an outbreak of mould growth or dry rot because some moulds, such as *Aspergillus* and some varieties of *Penicillium*, grow much faster at higher temperatures. Conservatories with their plants and inevitable damp will increase the mould contamination of any house, as every leaf has moulds growing on it, especially the underside. Well-heated but badly ventilated rooms full of pot plants are also a source of moulds, especially if the pot is placed on a saucer to catch the surplus water in which moulds grow profusely. The wet-blotting paper type of humidifier which is sometimes hung on a radiator is an excellent way to grow moulds.

Cellars, unless bone dry, are a fruitful source of mould spores which are rapidly distributed throughout the house. It is common for cellars to be closed up or even forgotten, and if the ventilation is interfered with an expensive outbreak of dry rot may result. At the same time the occupants of the house, if they are allergic persons, may become sensitized to the spores.

In newer or new houses moulds may cause problems if they are occupied for the first time in the winter, and excessive heat is used to accelerate the drying out of the plaster. Careless builders leave piles of shavings under floors and the relatively unseasoned wood used today may develop rot remarkably quickly. Clothing bedding or boots brought in damp and put in a fitted cupboard especially on an outside wall, will soon have a good growth of moulds.

Foliage, particularly Christmas trees, have dormant moulds on the leaves, and when they are brought in from the cold and placed in a warm room the fungi think that summer has come and will spore so profusely that sensitive people may suddenly complain of symptoms they usually get only in the summer.

What can be done to get rid of moulds?

Measures to improve housing conditions such as damp courses, improved ventilation and warmth are obviously necessary. Warmth alone simply causes moulds to grow, and ventilation to carry away the surplus water is essential.

Antique houses with packed clay or quarry-tile floors and no damp course often cause problems in those who live in them. I have known fitted carpets to be laid on quarry tiles, and after a while *Aspergillus* will grow under the carpet causing it to rot away. Fungicides are only effective in conjunction with long-term measures to reduce damp. Mould-sensitive people should not rake up the autumn leaves, turn over the compost heap or clear out the greenhouse because in all this vegetable material the moulds are thriving by the billion.

5 The seasonal allergens

What is meant by seasonal allergens?

These are allergens that appear in the air during the summer months only, so that a person sensitive to them has symptoms only when that allergen is present in the air.

The main seasonal allergens in the UK are grass, tree and weed pollens, plus the moulds *Cladosporium, Sporobolomyces, Botrytis, Diddymella, Alternaria* and *Phoma*, when the weather conditions are correct for shedding of their spores into the air. The Midlands of England, with large areas of grassland, many trees and a fair rainfall, is probably one of the worst areas in Europe for seasonal allergies.

This section deals with the various factors which are known to affect the seasonal allergic. It is clear that there are many aspects about which we know very little, especially in late summer and autumn, when a great many people have acute attacks, particularly children. The picture is rendered more complex by the fact that many sufferers have multiple sensitivities and skin tests for diagnosis are often very unsatisfactory.

What are the main symptoms of seasonal allergy?

Seasonal allergic rhinitis or hay fever is extremely common, there being at least 4 million sufferers in Britain. Perhaps one in ten of these may also have severe seasonal asthma, and intense irritation and itching of eyes, ears and palate is frequently experienced in addition to wheezing or sneezing. Contact with grass pollen produces rashes on the legs resembling a skin test in some cases, and seasonal eczema, kidney problems, or even colitis, may occur but are uncommon. The clue is the seasonal recurrence of the symptoms.

What is the annual cycle of seasonal allergy?

The year can be roughly divided up as follows. In January, February and March there are very few mould spores in the outside air because it is so cold. Indoors, however, there may be a good many *Aspergillus*, and *Penicillium* spores, particularly if the house is damp and well heated.

In March trees begin to pollinate, depending on the weather. By April growth is rapid, the leaves are on the trees, and the tree pollen season is in full swing. Tree pollens have a short season and usually cause slight problems of short duration. The exception is in London, where there are so many plane trees that some allergic people have a very difficult time for about 3 weeks in April each year. Birch pollen is a big problem in Scandinavia and other countries with large forests.

The author has recently shown that the cause of symptoms near grass cutting, which may become troublesome long before the pollen season in June and July, is due to the dissemination of particles of grass sap into the air, especially when using hover type mowers. Extracts of sap give skin reactions in these patients and detailed investigations of this new allergen are proceeding.

Meanwhile the grass has been growing rapidly and by the end of May a few grasses are actually pollinating but in insufficient numbers to cause more than a sniffle in very sensitive persons. In June the pollen count begins to rise slowly until one day, when conditions are just right, a large amount of pollen is shed suddenly. This date varies from year to year. In the Midlands it is usual for sudden pollination to occur between 10 and 16 June, after which the pollen counts remain consistently high until the second or third week in July.

Grass pollen is the most important and commonest cause of seasonal allergy. The amount of air inhaled by a sedentary person in a day is about 20 cubic metres, and on the very worst day of the pollen season, this amount of outdoor air will contain a total of about 10,000 grains of grass pollen. This amount will certainly upset anyone who has the slightest sensitivity, but the severity of the reaction always depends on the amount of allergen and the sensitivity of the person.

Around mid-June the mould-spore counts, mainly *Cladosporium* and *Sporobolomyces*, are slowly rising, but do not really cause problems until about the third week in July (depending on the weather), when there is often a simultaneous sudden outburst of different mould spores. This occurs because the weather conditions required for the spores to fly are identical for several species, for example *Cladosporium*, *Botrytis* and *Alternaria*, so they are all released on the same day in enormous numbers. This is important for diagnosis because patients who have a severe problem on that particular date must be mould sensitive.

Weed pollens are seldom important except for nettle, which tends to cause problems in July and August. Nettles produce large quantities of the smallest and lightest pollen in the world. Mugwort (*Artemesia*) sheds a very potent pollen and is now growing profusely on the central reservations of motorways, and on vacant lots. This may well be a future cause of trouble when the population becomes sensitized to it, as it is very allergenic and is a close relative of ragweed, the major cause of allergy in the USA.

In August the mould-spore counts of most species are often very high at the beginning of the month, but vary strictly in accordance with weather conditions. The *Alternaria* counts continue high due to harvesting operations because this mould is a parasite of grain. In September the *Cladosporium* begins to subside about the first or second week, to be replaced by the mould *Phoma* which is associated with wet weather and can cause quite serious problems. The count for *Botrytis* is often high at this time, perhaps because of the falling leaves, and then as we move into October the counts begin to drop. Wild yeasts are common in September.

During July, August and September enormous numbers of basidiospores from toadstools and from the fungi that grow on trees become airborne. In fact they outnumber all other spores and constitute a great unexplored area in late-summer allergy in this country. This is because although we can see and count them we cannot grow them or test patients with them, so we do not know how many people are affected.

As we move into November and December the spores subside with the coming of the frost, but if the season is very mild a fair number may persist up to Christmas.

How can the cause or causes of a seasonal allergic problem be pinpointed?

By asking the right questions in the right order the trained allergist can suggest the most likely causes. For example, is the complaint only in summer? How many years? Is the seasonal pattern the same every year? Which months are involved? Which is the worst month? Awareness of the months when the counts for the various airborne allergens are at their highest will suggest the most likely cause or causes, according to the seasonal cycle (Figure 5.1). Skin tests may or may not confirm this impression, as they tend to be unreliable for moulds, but if the history is convincing it may be possible to challenge the patient with the allergen in winter. If a mild wheeze is produced this will confirm the diagnosis and may have lead to specific treatment by desensitizing injections (before 1986) until a negative challenge test is achieved, followed by a clear season.

It is important to know exactly when sneezing or wheezing starts and stops because if the sufferer does not get better until September or October, moulds must be involved. Some people sneeze in June and July when grass pollen is in the air, but in late July, August and September they have asthma. This means that their noses are sensitive to pollen and their bronchi to mould spores.

Most of the answers are there if asked for. For example, some cases are worse in wet weather, and others improve. Many can predict rain accurately because they are sensitive to the spores which are disseminated into the air before rain, while other spores and pollens are washed down by rain so symptoms disappear. During heavy rain other spores become airborne. Hence, it helps to know how victims are affected by wet or dry summers, in humid warm weather, heavy rain, and so on.

What are pollens and why do they cause so many problems?

In plants and flowers pollen is the equivalent of male sperm. It is a very potent sensitizer, presumably because it is very definitely 'non-self' and of a sexual nature. Many flowers and shrubs

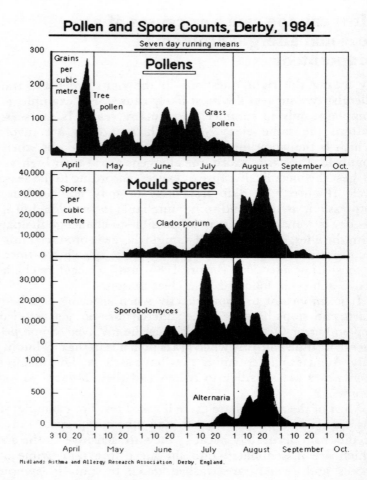

These graphs of the numbers of pollen grains and mould
spores in each cubic metre of air illustrate the
seasonal patterns of the summer allergens. Only the
most important have been shown.

Figure 5.1   The pollen and spore calendar.

depend on bees or other insects to cross-pollinate them, but grasses and trees rely on wind, so the pollen grains must be ripe, dry, and fertile before they can become airborne.

About a week of warm dry sunny weather is necessary to bring the grass pollen to the point where it is ready to be released. The time of pollination depends entirely on sun, rain, temperature, humidity, wind and the species of grass. These complex influences culminate in a sudden explosion of pollen grains one day in June when the weather conditions are just right. In the few days before that date early pollen grains may cause a mild sniffle in a few very sensitive people, but nothing more.

A pollen grain resembles a collapsed football until it is wetted by contact with the moist lining of the nose or bronchi, when it absorbs liquid and becomes spherical. The allergen is in the outer coating of the pollen and is dissolved out in less than a second.

The first wholesale shedding of the ripe grass pollen into the air has spectacular effects because all over the country up to 4 million people will start to sneeze violently, sometimes at the same time on the same day. This sudden epidemic of sneezing represents a simultaneous allergic reaction by all those who have become sensitized to grass pollen. It is really a remarkable phenomenon, and is followed by a dramatic increase in attendances at doctors' surgeries the next day.

After that date the pollen season has begun in earnest, and the large quantities of pollen will continue to fluctuate, at the whim of the weather, until the end of July, when mould spores take over as the main causes of seasonal allergic problems.

Why is hay fever so common?

The available evidence suggests that seasonal hay fever was quite *uncommon* a hundred years ago, when there was a great deal of established meadow undisturbed for centuries, but most has since been ploughed and planted with other grass species which give more nourishment for cattle. Sixty or seventy years ago Timothy and Cocksfoot were the popular grasses, but in the past twenty-five or thirty years Italian rye grass has been preferred. This species produces large quantities of very potent pollen, and Yorkshire fog and meadow grass are also extensively planted, often by the motorways.

Obviously, with the increase in the population over the last hundred years the number of hay-fever sufferers has also increased, and intermarriage of families prone to allergy has probably increased the tendency to allergy in the population. Improved diagnosis seems unlikely to be the cause of an increase in seasonal allergy.

When are seasonal moulds found in the air?

Moulds prefer warm humid conditions for growth and setting off their spores. Some yeasts actually spore at night instead of during the day, so that a damp night can set off enormous numbers of spores which may persist if the following day is humid or wet. The mould spores are controlled by the weather, and the peaks of mould-spore concentration are never the same 2 years running.

In the colder climates the summers are often wet; however, when there is an exceptionally long and dry summer, many people who usually have problems right through up to September or October have no symptoms at all until the rains in late autumn. This experiment of nature identifies many people as having a mould-spore allergy where it had not been suspected before (*see* Figure 5.4).

Seasonal moulds live on the leaves of every tree, and on every blade of grass or cereal. Moulds are also found in large numbers on fallen leaves, cut grass and other crops, and breaking down organic matter in the compost heap. There are also many parasites of cereals and grass such as *Ustilago* or barley smut, but their place in the causation of allergy in this country is unknown. Yeast is found in the air in July and August, but the prevalence cannot be counted because the simple round yeast cells cannot be accurately identified. Wild yeasts are very common, as many a winemaker knows to his or her cost, but it is very difficult to pin down a seasonal yeast allergy (*see* Figure 5.5).

One yeast-like organism which grows on the leaves of trees, *Sporobolomyces*, shoots its spores off into the air at 4 am, just when many asthmatics are hanging out of the bedroom window to get breath. Enormous numbers of spores are found in humid weather, when they can be present right through the day. *Sporobolomyces* is very prevalent in the Midlands, the counts often exceeding half a million at the peak of the season, so this allergen can be important.

The first patient I ever found sensitive to this allergen once had an attack of asthma with loud wheezing, and finally fell asleep exhausted. Her husband noticed that she had suddenly ceased to wheeze, and feared the worst, but heavy rain had commenced, stopping the release of spores. No psychological factor could be involved as she was asleep.

Other yeasts are also possible causes of seasonal allergic symptoms, but apart from my own work on this subject during the 1970s, insufficient research has been done to assess their importance.

How are pollen and spore counts carried out?

In order to find out which seasonal allergens predominate at any particular time, and in what quantities, it is necessary to use a special air sampler called a spore trap. Ten litres of air a minute are sucked through a narrow slit, and the pollen grains and mould spores are caught on the surface of a microscope slide coated with greasy Vaseline, which is moving very slowly past the slit. This slide is changed daily, and the pollen grains and mould spores are identified and counted under the microscope. A simple calculation gives the average number of pollen grains or mould spores present in a cubic metre of air on a particular day, and this is the figure which is recorded. The pollen count is published in the press every day, but the mould-spore counts are distributed to interested doctors only. Full counts of this type are carried out only in Derby, London and Cardiff.

It is important to realize that the pollen and spore counts for the day are an average figure, and that the actual count fluctuates continuously according to the weather conditions (*see* Figure 5.3). Thus, the count for any allergen at one moment in time may be a great deal higher than the 24 hour average, and thus cause sudden and severe symptoms. There is little or no grass pollen at night, and from dawn to dusk the count varies with the weather and the wind.

In the last three years in Derby it has been shown that taking air samples for five minutes in the hour gives useful information on the peaks of the pollen count, which can be as much as ten

INSTRUCTIONS FOR FILLING IN YOUR

Allergy Symptoms and Treatment Chart

Name .... Address ....

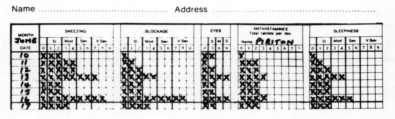

Chart of a hay fever sufferer The pollen count was very high on the 13th and 16th, confirming that the cause is grass pollen

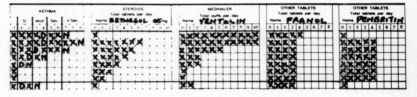

Chart of an asthmatic, showing recovery from an attack with the aid of steroids and antibiotics (Prednisolone, Prednisone. Medro.ie. Ledercort, Prednelan. Betnelan, Sintisone, and many others are 'steroids').

This is a new type of symptoms and treatment diary and we hope you will help us to help *you* by filling it up every day with great care.

We want you to decide how severe your symptoms are on a number scale from 0, meaning no symptoms, to 9, meaning very, very severe symptoms. As long as you do not change your mind every day, it should make sense when it is analysed by the laboratory.

For example, 1 or 2 would be slight, 3 or 4 moderate, 5 or 6 severe and 7, 8 and 9 very severe. This rating is deliberately biased to exaggerate the bad patches and enable us to compare your symptoms with the pollen and spore counts. It is even more helpful to use a coloured pen and put 'D' for severity in the day, and 'N' for severity at night, as illustrated.

Put crosses in the correct squares every night before bed, and please remember to mark the '0' squares if you have *no symptoms* or are having *no medicines*. Please keep on filling it up on holiday. The NOTES section is for entering where you are, or if you have a cold, bronchitis, etc.

> You should take this chart every time you visit your doctor, so that he can see at a glance how you are getting on, and what treatment you are having. Your doctor can also enter any changes in treatment, injections, etc.

Figure 5.2   Allergy symptoms and treatment chart.

times the daily average. This information is much more relevant to hay fever victims than the average.

What do the pollen or mould-spore counts mean to the seasonal allergy victim?

Whatever the allergen, if the amount in the air increases sensitized people will get worse according to how sensitive they are. Pollen counts help sufferers by explaining why they were worse or better yesterday, but are of little value after the event. Prediction of the pollen count would obviously be more helpful but has not yet proved reliable.

The counts can be very useful in diagnosis, because careful daily recording of symptoms may demonstrate a clear relationship between symptoms and pollen or spore counts. The daily symptom record is most useful when recorded on a chart similar to that illustrated in Figure 5.2. Such records can be a great help in identifying the cause, as shown by Figure 5.5 where it is obvious that this person was affected by one allergen but not by the others.

Some seasonal allergic patients have very long seasons, and are allergic to several allergens. Careful record-keeping is essential if there is to be any prospect of identifying the cause and giving this sort of patient positive help.

What happens if you are sensitive to more than one seasonal allergen?

To be sensitive to more than one allergen complicates and lengthens the seasonal pattern because there is overlap between the seasons of one allergen and the other. It is common to be sensitive to perennial allergens such as house dust as well as to seasonal ones. When this happens the seasonal problems are superimposed on the perennial ones, and for these people the summer can be a very difficult time. Cases where the symptoms get worse in late July and carry on in to September or even October are almost certainly being caused by mould spores, but it is often extremely difficult to find out which spores are involved. These patients sometimes do not improve until the first frost in the late autumn.

Does where you are and what you are doing influence the symptoms as well as the season?

Yes, your location is most important. For example, the amount of allergen may be negligible in a closed room, low if the window is open, higher in the garden or on the golf course, very high in the countryside and extremely high in a hay field.

Physical work or vigorous exercise in the open obviously requires the inhalation of larger quantities of air, so that more allergens are taken in. This means that allergic athletes performing in the summer require more intensive treatment. Nowadays the grass beside the trunk roads and motorways is seldom cut, so people sensitive to pollen are actually driving along an elongated hay field with the pollen being dislodged by the passage of the traffic. In fact, enough pollen may be inhaled on the way to work to ensure the persistence of symptoms all day. Keeping the car windows shut will help, and it is ideal to have air-conditioning or filtration in the car.

Mould-spore counts are much higher around houses surrounded by trees or on the edge of a wood. Town is to be preferred to country for pollen-sensitive people – the pollen count in Derby, for instance, is often about four times the highest counts in London. Obviously a farm surrounded by hay fields is a bad situation for the pollen-sensitive person, and houses in the suburbs often have large areas of grass nearby.

The seasonal cycle also varies according to your geographical position: the pollen season gets later the further north you go, and there are other more local variations. The data suggest that spring marches north at about 3 miles per hour, so that the pollen season in Spain and Majorca is in May, England's is in June and July, and it is September in the Shetland Islands.

Observations in Derby over the last 15 years show that it is best to have holidays on the British west coast where the prevailing wind is off the sea. Counts are higher on the east coast where patients are often severely affected on holiday.

Can seasonal allergens cause psychological problems?

I first became aware that grass pollen can cause extreme sleepiness, confusion and lethargy when I found that a patient had

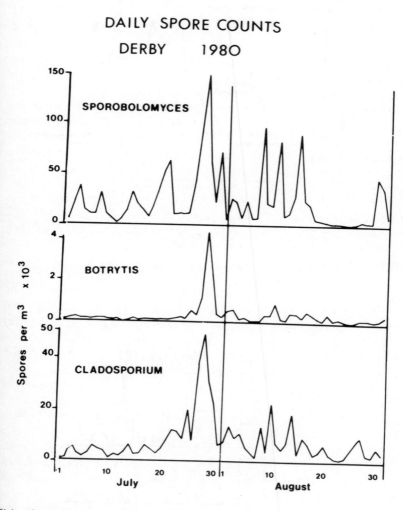

This shows how several moulds spore profusely on the same day when conditions are right, so that it is sometimes impossible to know which allergen causes the symptoms.

Figure 5.3   Effect of weather on the shedding of mould spores into the air.

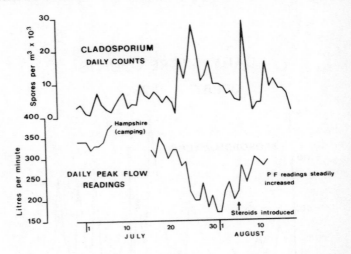

This peak flow chart shows how his young man's peak flow readings decreased when the spore counts for <u>Cladosporium</u> increased, until he was given steroids to rescue him.

Figure 5.4   Seasonal moulds causing asthma.

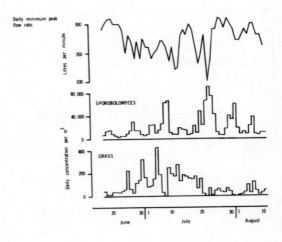

A good example of a clear response of the peak flow rate to the spore count for <u>Sporobolomyces</u>, but not to the grass pollen count.

Figure 5.5   Seasonal yeasts causing asthma.

recorded these symptoms on his chart, and that the severity closely corresponded to the pollen count. The patient denied taking any antihistamine tablets but added that he always felt stupid, bad-tempered and irritable in the pollen season. Many other patients confirmed that they had similar symptoms in the pollen season.

Summer is not only the time for the pollen but also for examinations, and for many young people failure in their examinations may blight a promising career because they were not in good physical and mental health at that time. Some remarkable cases of what might be termed 'mid-summer madness' have been seen and because there might be many others who have not been recognized, it seems reasonable to describe one such case.

A teacher of 42, for example, had such obvious emotional problems in July, August and September for 3 years that she was labelled a neurotic and almost lost her job. Her best friend was a nursing sister with an interest in allergy who noticed that emotional symptoms disappeared when they boarded a plane for Australia in mid-August and promptly recurred when they came back in mid-September. In her case emotional symptoms could be reliably reproduced in winter by nasal provocation tests, given so that the patient was unaware as to which test was active. This person was successfully desensitized by injections with mould vaccines in the winter, but these often triggered some emotional reactions. By the following summer, however, she no longer reacted to the tests, her emotional problems did not recur, and she kept her job.

Can you avoid seasonal allergens?

This is practically impossible, but some suggestions are as follows:

1.   Take a holiday in a suitable country to avoid the season, or go on a long ocean cruise. The latter used to be popular before the war when there was much less that could be done about hay fever and asthma, but sometimes a cloud of pollen grains would be blown far out to sea and affect susceptible individuals on a liner.

2.   Installation of air filtration in the house is one answer, but you would have to stay inside all summer, or arrange to have an air-conditioned car to get to your air-conditioned office. This is

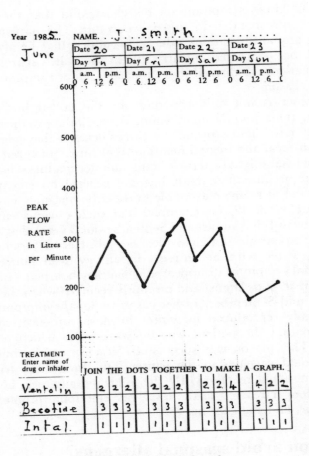

Figure 5.6 A peak flow chart.

because exposure to the outside air full of pollen grains can cause delayed symptoms. However, air filtration can be helpful with the smaller spores, particularly those which predominate in the early hours of the morning. An air filter can be placed in the window as an alternative to keeping it closed.

3. You could wear an air-filtered helmet when outside, but I doubt if this solution, which is now available, will ever be popular. The pollen count indoors with the windows shut is practically zero, so if you never go out unless it is pouring with rain you can avoid the pollen.

6 Occupational, drug and insect allergens

OCCUPATIONAL ALLERGENS

Many allergens can be found in all kinds of different environments and may not be exclusively related to the workplace. There are, however, some allergic problems caused by substances that people are exposed to most frequently in certain occupations and working environments. Particularly common occupational allergens are organic dusts generated in factories, chemicals and fumes, and moulds and mites in stored foods and on farms.

What circumstances would suggest that an allergy has an occupational cause?

Asthma, or indeed any other allergic symptom possibly caused by one's occupation, should improve at weekends, recur on Monday, and become progressively worse until Friday. Obvious improvement should occur on holiday followed by equally obvious recurrence on return to work. Sometimes the association is less obvious as there may not be enough time at weekends or on holiday for full recovery to take place. Figure 6.1 is a good example – cure was effected by the patient changing his job.

The pattern of response outlined above should always suggest occupational allergy, particularly if several workers are involved simultaneously, but it does not indicate the cause. The amount of potential allergen inhaled is important because massive quantities tend to sensitize even those who are not easily rendered allergic.

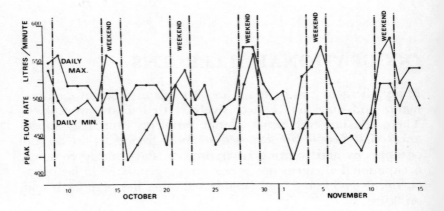

The increase in the peak flow rate at weekends suggested that this man's job was the cause of his asthma. Changing to an outside job effected a complete cure. The cause was a chemical he was exposed to in the factory.

Figure 6.1 A good example of occupational asthma.

The following case history is a good example of how complex the relationship between possible occupational allergies and the symptoms of allergy can be. A man who worked in a chemical plant making an antibiotic now used only in animal feeding stuffs developed asthma. It was proved by controlled exposure that the cause was the antibiotic powder he handled at work, so he gave up his job. Unfortunately, his asthma was not completely better, except when he was on holiday, because his wife had continued to work in the office at the factory. Although she had no contact whatsoever with the antibiotic, the husband did not become completely free from asthma until his wife also gave up her job. Some time later, he began to have asthma every time he ate an egg, yet he was not sensitive to eggs. The reason was that the antibiotic had been added to the hens' food, so that the minute trace in the egg was enough to trigger off his asthma.

What are the most common organic dusts causing occupational allergies?

Exposure to organic dusts of vegetable origin, especially if mouldy, can cause severe allergic problems in susceptible people. For example, sensitization can be caused by sawdust, vegetable matter, flour particles or chemicals and fumes in the air – in fact anything inhaled. Mouldy materials may cause allergy to the moulds which grow on the dust rather than the dust itself.

The source of the dusty material can be important as in a recent outbreak of asthma in a factory making felt for hats out of assorted rags, including old sacks previously used to contain castor beans, one of the most allergenic substances known. The use of these contaminated sacks as a source of fibre was enough to cause an epidemic of asthma in the workers. The dusts listed in Table 6.1 may cause the immediate type of allergic reaction in the respiratory system with the weekly patterns described. In such cases, removal of the cause of the problem from the workplace or of the worker from the workplace as an avoidance measure will result in relief and no permanent effects will remain unless the process has been going on for a very long time so as to damage the alveoli.

Are there any particular chemicals at work which can cause allergies?

At work there are innumerable possibilities for sensitization, some known, many unknown. Examples are in the manufacture of plastics, polyurethane foam, enzymes, antibiotics, and sometimes vegetable powders of all types. A reliable blood test has been devised to check for sensitivity to one of the chemicals used in making polyurethane foam. This is one of the first reliable tests for chemical sensitivity. No doubt others will follow, but the pattern of work-related symptoms will always be the initial clue.

To give an example, workers assembling electronic equipment are exposed to pine-resin fumes from the flux used in soldering, and some individuals develop solderer's asthma. Because many of those affected by the fumes simply found another job it was a long time before the relationship was recognized. Occasional cases of allergy to pine resin (rosin) have been reported over the years in professional violinists, where it can be a severe handicap. Small quantities of colophony (pine resin) may also be used in soap, plaster, linoleum, fireworks, glue, car polish, wood varnish, glossy paper, and so on. Thus, somebody who gets sensitized in an electronics factory may have problems which will continue even when he or she leaves work.

Polyvinyl chloride (PVC) is the starting point for the manufacture of some types of plastic. After several years of exposure to the fumes involved in clearing out the retorts in which the plastic mixtures were heated, the operatives developed a most unusual type of disease syndrome which involved many body systems. This reaction seems to be due to the plastic, and can now be avoided by taking care to avoid the fumes. This new disease has something in common with reactions to other chemicals, and demonstrates how warily new chemicals must be regarded.

What should someone dedicated to a career involving animals do if he or she becomes allergic to them?

Desensitization is really the only answer, if practicable. This is always a very difficult situation for both doctor and patient because it is so much easier for the doctor simply to advise avoidance and leave it at that. This is undoubtedly the safest course, but even when all the difficulties and possible problems with injection treatment have been pointed out there will always be those who are unable to avoid the animals concerned. As long as people are made fully aware of all the facts I feel that an attempt to desensitize should be made, but if many species of animals are concerned this can be almost impossible.

Workers in research laboratories often become sensitized to rats, mice, rabbits, etc. A person's career as a scientist can be threatened if he or she becomes sensitized to the animals used in the research. The choice may be a change of job or trying desensitizing injections, but unfortunately suitably active extracts may not be obtainable and as a result treatment may be disappointing just when it is most necessary. Recent research work has shown that the most powerful allergens are present in the urine of laboratory animals, especially the males. The urine may dry out and the allergen become airborne in the air of the animal house. Perhaps more effective treatment may result from this discovery. Strenuous efforts have been made to improve the air conditioning in laboratories, but if someone is very sensitive indeed it is almost impossible to remove all traces of allergen from the air.

Can injections given to prevent or combat disease cause allergic reactions instead?

Anti-serum containing specific antibody against potentially lethal infections is produced by immunizing animals. If someone is already sensitive to the animal an injection of serum can produce all kinds of allergic reactions from a slight rash to anaphylactic shock, or serum sickness, which may occur 7–14 days after an injection of anti-serum or other treatment material which is derived from animals. The clinical features are fever, enlarged glands, rashes, kidney damage, and swollen joints, and the cause is an immune reaction against the foreign protein from the animal which was used to produce the anti-serum.

Anti-tetanus serum derived from horses is perhaps the commonest cause of these problems. If an individual known to be allergic to horse requires anti-serum today, bovine or human anti-serum can now be used instead. In people with allergic tendencies the first injection of anti-serum will give no problems, but can sensitize them so that a subsequent injection may cause a serious reaction.

Virus vaccines such as measles and many others are grown in chicken embryo and sometimes cause problems in egg-sensitive individuals. The allergy may be directed against egg, but it can be specifically against chicken. This was clearly illustrated by a man who began to have severe asthma for the first time after an influenza vaccine injection. The asthma only occurred on Sundays, when he had chicken for lunch, and he ate eggs every day without any reaction.

What allergens cause occupational allergy on farms?

Farmers as a group are exposed to a very wide range of potential allergens. For example, they may be exposed to large numbers of mites in grain stores and in animal feed. Recent surveys have shown that farmers are more frequently affected by these storage mites than was thought. Farm animals are, of course, an obvious source of trouble, but their surroundings such as cow sheds and hay lofts are also grossly contaminated with mould spores in enormous quantities. In summer a combine harvester, grain dryer or similar machine creating a lot of dust exposes the farmer to vast quantities of spores to which he or she may become sensitized. Harvesting machines are frequently fitted with air-conditioned cabs nowadays to prevent sensitization of farm workers. Pollen is, of course, stirred up in very large quantities when harvesting the hay.

Stored grain is particularly liable to contamination with moulds and mites while stored, so the dust from this when feeding the animals can also cause problems. Another possibility is presented by broiler-houses, but experience has shown that feather allergy is not as common as one would expect. Cleaning out broiler-houses may be a risky occupation also because of the faecal dust and the powerful chemicals used for sterilizing the houses.

The overheating of hay which has been harvested damp encourages the growth of *Aspergillus fumigatus*, one of the nastiest and most allergenic of the moulds. This can cause very severe asthma, and may also take root in the bronchial tubes and grow there, causing bronchial damage. The very severe asthma

Table 6.1 Possible causes of alveolitis

Disease	Cause
Farmer's lung	mouldy hay
Bird-fancier's lung	pigeons, budgerigars and other birds
Cheesewasher's disease	*Penicillium* spores
Suberosis	penicillin in mouldy cork dust
Mushroom worker's lung	mushroom compost
Malt worker's lung	barley and malt dust in breweries
Humidifier fever	organisms growing in hot humidifier water
Grain worker's lung	weevils in flour
Bagassosis	mouldy bagasse – the discarded sugar cane

caused by *Aspergillus* is called allergic aspergillosis. Sometimes a ball of fungus grows in the lung and has to be removed surgically, and x-rays may prompt an incorrect diagnosis of tuberculosis. Table 6.1 lists some possible causes of alveolitis.

What is farmer's lung and how is it caused?

Farmer's lung is caused by an allergic reaction in the tiny alveoli of the lung, where gas exchange takes place. As a result of the reaction oxygen cannot so easily be transferred to the blood, thus causing severe disablement. Farmer's lung is therefore a form of allergic alveolitis, a condition which is caused by other organic dusts as well, as will be mentioned.

If hay is harvested and made into bales when wet or damp it will overheat in the centre of the bale, thus creating ideal conditions for the growth of a microscopic organism called *micro-poly-spora faeni* which will only grow and set off spores at high temperatures. When the bale of hay is opened by the farmer in the winter white powder flies in the air containing billions of spores which are inhaled and sensitize the alveoli. The symptoms occur some hours after exposure and consist of a hacking dry cough, a feeling as if the victim has an attack of influenza, and shortness of breath. There is no wheezing as in asthma. The attack may take a few days to recover from, and will recur every time the sensitized patient is exposed to mouldy hay. Finally the condition becomes continuous and irreversible, but avoidance at an earlier stage may stop the full development of the disease.

What are the other causes of allergic alveolitis?

The known causes are farmer's lung, bird-fancier's lung, humidifier fever, mouldy sugar cane in Jamaica, and mouldy cork in factories in Portugal. They have been tabulated for your information in Table 6.1.

Pigeon breeding is a major cause of bird-fancier's lung in this country, and recent research has suggested that it is not so much the dust from the droppings, as was previously thought, but the bloom on the feathers of the pigeon that is the cause of the problem. This can be a very serious disease which can be quite disabling. It can also be caused by a budgerigar or any other bird, especially if kept indoors. Avoidance is the only real answer but frequently the diagnosis is not made until serious irreversible damage has been done.

Air-conditioning involves humidifying the air, particularly in printing factories and in large hotels and offices, but in the USA refrigerated air-conditioning, which removes moisture from the air, is most common. Epidemics of alveolitis or legionairres disease can result from contaminated humidifier water spreading micro-organisms through the air of the building. These organisms prefer to live at high temperatures in the hot water used in the humidifiers, and can be prevented by attention to the cleanliness of the water. A shop assistant was ill for several days every time she served for a few hours in a baker's shop where a humidifier behind the counter had been installed as part of a modernization programme. She had symptoms similar to those caused by farmer's lung and the cause turned out to be the humidifier water which was full of fungi.

ALLERGY TO DRUGS

This aspect of allergy is ill defined, because there are no tests yet to show clearly whether drugs or chemicals in the environment are causing allergic reactions.

Any simple chemical can become an allergen by combining with a large molecule of body protein to form a 'hapten'. Reactions can occur locally, as on the hands in contact dermatitis, or the hapten may gain access to the circulation and cause general sensitization.

For many years a few farsighted doctors and scientists have pointed out the potential dangers of polluting our environment and our food with chemicals, but there is reluctance to accept that chemicals can do harm because positive proof of toxic or cancer-producing effects is often lacking.

Allergic reactions which occur only in a minority of individuals are obviously much more difficult to identify and to prove, in the absence of specific tests. The result is controversy and disagreement regarding the importance of chemical contamination of the environment. On the other hand the slightest suspicion that some chemical in food or environment could cause cancer may quickly cause the banning of that substance, even on scanty evidence, but regulatory authorities seldom appear interested in allergic reactions to additives, preservatives and dyes.

How can drugs be administered?

Drugs can be given orally (by mouth), applied to the body surface externally as ointments or internally as aerosol sprays (topically), injected under the skin (sub-cutaneously), injected into a muscle (intra-muscularly), injected into a vein (intra-venously), injected into the heart (intra-cardiac), injected into the rectum (intra-rectally), placed in the rectum (suppository) and administered by tube to the stomach (intra-gastric).

Reactions can occur at the site of contact (topical drugs), or oral or injected drugs can cause a reaction in any distant organ or system of the body which has become sensitized.

Does the route of administration affect reactions caused by drugs?

Injection is a very important route, as it is used in emergency treatments. Obviously injections into a vein (intra-venous) go directly into the circulation, so if the patient is allergic to the drug, the reaction can be very rapid. If there is any possibility of an allergic reaction it is safer to perform skin tests with the drug first.

Injections into muscle (intra-muscular) get into the circulation quite quickly, as muscle is full of blood vessels. Injections into the loose tissue under the skin (sub-cutaneous) gain entry into the circulation more slowly, unless a small vein has been entered accidentally. This is why the plunger of the syringe is pulled back before injecting, because blood will come if a vein has been entered.

Contact sensitizers, such as ointments, creams or sprays used on the skin or in the nose or eyes can cause local allergic reactions to the treatment which can be worse than the condition for which they were given. Once sensitization has occurred an allergic reaction will follow every time this medication is used. Some antibiotics (such as neomycin) are included in nose sprays, skin creams or eye drops. These may cause local sensitization which can be quite troublesome.

Where drugs are given by mouth, vomiting and diarrhoea may signal intolerance or allergy. Skin rashes are a common manifestation of drug allergy, but any part of the body can be affected. Photosensitivity is an indirect effect, not really an allergy, which can result from certain antibiotics. This reaction to sunshine on the exposed skin can be a serious handicap on holiday.

How do people become allergic to drugs and what can be done about it?

Previous exposure to the drug to induce sensitivity is essential, but sensitization may occur when taking a drug continuously for 7–14 days. It may be difficult in such cases to distinguish the symptoms due to the disease for which the drug is being given from those caused by the treatment.

Alternatively, a drug may be tolerated for weeks, months or even years, before sensitization develops. This can happen where drugs are necessary for long periods, as for tuberculosis. Recognition that the drug is causing the symptoms is vital, as stopping the drugs stops the symptoms. If alternative drugs are available avoidance is the answer, but the allergy often extends to similar drugs. Desensitization can be accomplished if there is no alternative drug and the disease a serious one. The offending drug cannot usually be taken ever again, so it is important for the victim to know what it is. The full explanation of why and how such sensitivities occur is often incomplete.

What form can drug reactions take?

Sensitization to drugs and vaccines can affect any part of the body, and reactions can vary from very fast to very slow, from a trivial nuisance to a threat to life.

Immediate reactions include fatal anaphylaxis, which can occur when a drug is injected, especially intra-venously. This is why anyone who knows that they are very allergic to a drug or other injected substance *must* tell the doctor about this allergy. Most doctors ask about allergies, but this precaution can be forgotten in a crisis situation. Wearing a bracelet or necklet giving this information can be life-saving if unconscious. It is best to join the Medic-Alert Foundation (*see* Chapter 7).

Less serious immediate reactions may occur with certain foods and sometimes aspirin. A sudden attack of nettlerash or hives (urticaria) or angio-oedema (very severe urticaria) can cause much alarm, but is not usually dangerous, unless there is swelling of tongue or throat, causing choking and suffocation.

Some of the *slow reactions* are controversial, and their inclusion as allergic phenomena disputed. I feel that they should be mentioned to show the scope of drug-induced allergy. Sulphonamide drugs (M & B), for example, were introduced before the war, and were the first antibiotics. By 1940 it was recognized that these drugs could cause severe delayed reactions in the smaller arteries (vasculitis or periarteritis). Since then many other drugs have been thought to produce similar problems in some subjects. If the cause is recognized in time and the drug stopped no permanent harm results. This class of reaction is closely related to the serious auto-immune diseases in which the immune system of the body is reacting against one of its own body proteins.

Which drugs are most likely to cause allergic reactions?

Penicillin is one of the commonest drugs to cause dangerous allergy. Many different types of penicillin have been developed, but sensitized patients cannot tolerate any of them. Special tests for penicillin allergy have been developed, but today these tests are seldom relevant as there are so many alternative antibiotics. Tests often show that patients who reacted to penicillin many years before are no longer sensitive.

Another drug which often causes allergic reactions is aspirin, usually including many similar anti-rheumatic drugs. Patients with nasal polyps are particularly likely to be aspirin-sensitive, and may get very severe asthma without warning. Thus, there may be hidden menace in a seemingly innocent headache powder. People aware of aspirin sensitivity must *never* take any medication without reading the label to check for acetylsalicylic acid (aspirin).

There is no drug which does not cause problems for somebody – so it is really impossible to provide any sort of list. It is important to realize that an allergic reaction is always possible, and those from allergic families are most liable to develop drug reactions.

What non-allergic side-effects can be caused by drugs?

Direct toxic reactions of all sorts may occur if the drug does not agree in some way, e.g. vomiting, diarrhoea, bleeding from the stomach (aspirin), liver damage (paracetamol excess), drowsiness, palpitations, and so on. These are really intolerance or toxicity, not allergy, and mean that the drug does not suit the recipient for some reason. Effects on blood production in the bone marrow may cause serious anaemia, or stop production of the white cells essential for defence against infection (agranulocytosis). This is usually a direct toxic effect on the bone marrow. Some people, for example, may have an enzyme deficiency which renders them more susceptible to a drug, or perhaps to damage to the liver, but these effects are not due to allergy, but to specific intolerance of the drug.

Drugs can also cause skin rashes, purpura (bleeding capillaries under the skin), vasculitis in skin vessels, reactions in the tiny blood vessels of the kidney, periarteritis in larger arteries, liver damage, and many other problems. For example, the very first 'beta-blocker' drug for heart disease and hypertension caused a delayed immunological reaction in some patients, which caused thickening of the membranes in the abdominal cavity, lungs, and so on.

INSECT ALLERGENS

Can one be allergic to insects?

Yes – Table 6.2 gives a list of insect allergens. The mating seasons of insects can fill the air with wing scales and other parts, and sensitization may occur.

Can one be allergic to wasp and bee stings?

Yes – dangerously so! It has been known for thousands of years that sudden death may result from a wasp or bee sting, but the knowledge that a previous sensitizing sting is necessary, and that death is due to anaphylactic shock is comparatively recent. Less serious allergic reactions to insect stings resemble those to injections given by doctors or nurses. Perhaps it is true that the insects are statistically the lesser danger!

In recent years a great deal of research has been carried out, the venom collected and analysed, reliable RAST and other tests established, and many people who have survived a sting reaction have been immunized so that they no longer are at risk to their life in the event of a further sting. Desensitization against wasp and bee venom is the only injection treatment for allergy which is still carried out in this country.

Table 6.2 Insect allergens

Source of allergen	Effects reported
Maggots for fishing	asthma and contact, causing swelling of penis
Moulted skin of mayflies in mating season	mostly in season in Canadian Great Lakes – asthma and rhinitis
Insect wing scales – moths, butterflies	asthma and rhinitis
Weevils in flour	asthma and alveolitis
Storage mites	asthma
Nemeti flies	Egypt, by the Nile – severe asthma
Silkworms	rhinitis and asthma
Silverfish in house dust	asthma and rhinitis
Locusts, fruit flies	asthma and rhinitis in laboratories
Cockroach	rhinitis and asthma
Bees (not venom)	airborne particles can cause rhinitis, or asthma
Hairy caterpillars	irritation of skin and sometimes allergic skin reaction
Daphnia as fish food	rhinitis and asthma
Bee and wasp venom	anaphylaxis

Details of centres for treatment in Britain should be available at any doctor's surgery, in the *GP Guide to Emergency & Medical Services*.

PART 3

How Allergens Cause Allergic Disease

7 Effects of allergic reactions on the circulation

By now the reader should have a fairly clear concept of the holistic approach to allergic disease which is the guiding principle of this book.

Now it is necessary to be more specific, and to attempt to describe how allergic reactions in any special part of the body will produce effects which will vary according to the function of the affected organ. Further reference to the holistic diagram (Figure 3.1) will show how the allergen is distributed throughout the body fluids so as to reach the areas of the body which are hypersensitive. In this chapter we are dealing with allergy in a broad sense as previously defined, including all kinds of hypersensitivity reaction.

When allergens are distributed by the blood and tissue fluids to the sensitized areas (Figure 7.1), the blood vessels themselves may also become sensitized, and thus take part in allergic reactions. Damage to a vessel must affect the tissues which normally receive their blood supply from that vessel, thus producing effects secondary to the allergic reaction.

Similar changes can be produced by many ordinary diseases, especially infections, so it is difficult to define where the role of the allergic reaction begins and ends.

Reactions in the blood vessels are discussed first because of the great potential importance of hypersensitivity in the vessels as a cause of disease. If a cause/effect relationship can be repeatedly demonstrated, it may be possible to identify a causative factor and avoid it. This concept is controversial, but seems more attractive than the alternative – suppressive drugs which themselves have been known to cause widespread vascular reactions.

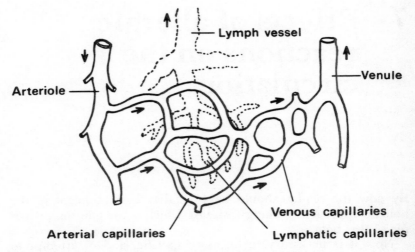

Capillaries have thin walls composed of flattened cells, so as to
allow fluid, but not large protein molecules or blood cells, to pass
easily into the tissues.

Figure 7.1   The microcirculation.

What can be the effect of an allergic reaction in a blood vessel?

The tiny vessels can become sensitized and thus be involved in
long-lasting allergic reactions which seriously damage the vessel
wall, and have secondary effects on the tissues which the vessel
should be supplying with blood. A reaction taking place in a tiny
vessel usually begins with swelling of the lining, which causes
leakage of fluid into the tissues to produce swelling or oedema. If
the reaction continues, white cells from the blood may leak
through into the tissues. If the process continues and becomes
more severe there may be a tiny burst in the wall, allowing blood
out into the tissues, producing what seems like a bruise. Finally,
the vessel may become completely blocked and a considerable
inflammatory reaction takes place which finally heals to leave a
scarred vessel.

These changes take place partly as a result of the liberation of
mediator chemicals, but are mainly immunological reactions of
hypersensitivity in the cells of the vessel itself. The effects and

symptoms vary depending on which part of the body has sustained the most damage to the vessels and what size of vessel is involved. These reactions often take place in the vessels of the skin, thus presenting us with the opportunity of observing these reactions and their effects. For example, a little blood leaking out of a tiny vessel may produce a tiny red spot, while blood from a larger vessel will look like a bruise and there may even be a small lump to be felt. This type of reaction is called vasculitis.

What causes vasculitis?

Reactions in the small blood vessels have been extensively studied and many possible causes have been incriminated, including infections, and injections of foreign proteins and drugs. Reactions in the blood vessels of the affected tissues may also complicate ulcerative colitis or rheumatoid arthritis. In fact, this field of research is littered with discarded theories, but it does appear clear that various drugs are associated with this type of disease.

There are also claims that cases of recurrent vasculitis, where there is no evidence for a cause, have recovered when isolated in special accommodation where the food, water and the air are completely free from chemical pollution, and further exposure to chemicals has led to relapse. Similar claims have been made in relation to disease of the coronary arteries and to irregular action of the heart. These claims are controversial and confirmation is urgently required in view of their possible importance, but is not forthcoming.

Can larger arteries be affected by allergic reactions?

The medium-sized arteries are sometimes involved in periarteritis nodosa, so called because the reactions take place at intervals along the artery causing little lumps (nodules) which can be felt with the finger. The cause is usually unknown, but certain drugs and perhaps some chemicals may be associated with the disease. Steroids by mouth are helpful treatment, but not curative.

The very large arteries, like the aorta, require tiny arteries to supply blood to the wall of the artery itself. Thus, allergic reactions in these tiny vessels can damage and weaken the walls of the larger arteries themselves.

Can spasm of arteries be caused by allergies?

Arteries all have smooth muscle, which can become sensitized or can react to mediator chemicals liberated from mast cells near the vessel. Spasm of an artery cuts down the blood supply to the area which the artery supplies with blood. The effects of a sudden reduction in blood supply are sometimes obvious, as in cases where spasm affecting the coronary arteries causes anginal pain, but often there is no obvious effect to be seen.

There have been many reports in the past 60 years of various foods and tobacco causing coronary spasm, and more often irregular or fast heart beat, but this possibility is not widely known or considered.

Spasm of arteries to the brain may be involved in migraine and other effects of allergy on the brain.

What is anaphylactic shock?

Anaphylactic shock is the most dangerous and frightening allergic reaction. Any substance injected will be distributed to the whole body through the circulation of the blood and extracellular fluids. A subcutaneous injection will not reach the general circulation so quickly as one into muscle, and an intravenous injection will be distributed to the whole body in seconds. Hence, a reaction to an injection directly into a vein, accidentally or on purpose, or to a sting by a bee, wasp or other venomous insect, can be very sudden and severe.

Because the whole body is exposed to the allergen at the same time every sensitized cell reacts simultaneously, especially in the walls of all the blood vessels, liberating large amounts of mediator chemicals which cause all the blood vessels to open up to their fullest extent. The blood fills up these dilated vessels with the result that there is very little venous blood returning to the heart, and the blood pressure falls very rapidly. The victim may collapse if shock is severe and may die if immediate treatment is not available to combat the shock and restore the blood pressure.

The sensitized cells in the skin react a little later, causing itch and giant weals all over, and other symptoms due to liberation of histamine and other chemicals.

What causes anaphylactic shock?

The first step in explaining how this dangerous allergic reaction is caused was taken in 1903 by a French scientist called Charles Richet. He was attempting to immunize a dog to the poison of a jelly-fish by injecting the unfortunate animal with increasing doses of the poison. The first injection caused no problem, but the second injection, although small and apparently harmless, caused the death of the dog in a few minutes. This was a great surprise, because what he was trying to do was to induce protection, or 'prophylaxis', against the poison. As the result was exactly the opposite of the expected, he called it 'anaphylaxis', and went on to be one of the very first immunologists and won a Nobel prize for his discoveries. Today it is obvious that the dog was sensitized by the first injection instead of becoming immune to the poison, and that the second injection caused a catastrophic allergic reaction.

In the course of evolution insects developed hollow stings and poison sacs so as to inject venom to paralyse and kill other insects for food and as a means of defence or attack. Just as in the dog of Richet, the first sting may inject enough venom to sensitize, so that a second sting some time later may cause anaphylactic shock. The first recorded sudden death from a sting of a great wasp or a hornet was King Menes of Memphis in Egypt in 3000 BC, but death from insect stings is really quite rare, and desensitization with venom is a very successful treatment today.

The commonest cause of anaphylactic shock today is not insect stings but allergy to drugs, such as penicillin, or to horse serum in anti-tetanus serum, local anaesthetics, and desensitizing injections for allergies, and so on. Shock from an oral dose of a drug is very rare.

What are the symptoms and emergency treatment of anaphylactic shock?

The person who is having an acute anaphylactic reaction rarely falls down dead immediately. First there may be an obvious reaction at or near the site of the injection or sting, and then the patient feels generally flushed and itchy all over, faint and dizzy, with some palpitations, shortness of breath and a sense of constriction in the chest. Cramps, vomiting, wheezing and a widespread itchy rash may also occur. The biggest danger is a sudden drop in blood pressure, and the patient must lie flat so that the blood supply to the brain is maintained. If the site of the injection or sting is to be seen on a limb it may help to apply a tourniquet above the site to prevent more venom or drug being absorbed into the general circulation. Of course, if there is obvious trouble with breathing then the 'kiss of life' may be necessary, or – if the pulse stops – external cardiac massage. Dial emergency and get the patient into hospital as soon as possible.

If the victim has an 'Ana-Kit' (*see* below) with an adrenaline syringe but has been overcome before he or she had time to use it, inject it at once subcutaneously, or even inject it into the thigh through the clothes, because time is running out.

Adrenaline is life saving, and must be given as soon as possible, to constrict the blood vessels and restore the blood pressure. It works dramatically if given in time. Later on injections of antihistamines and steroids may be given, but they do not act quickly.

How can anaphylactic shock be prevented?

Attempts to prevent anaphylactic reactions can be made by both patient and doctor. For example, always tell a doctor or nurse about any previous reaction to any drug, serum, vaccine, allergy extracts or other medication, even if they do not ask you. Also, it is a good idea to have a Medic-Alert bracelet on your wrist or round your neck. If you are involved in an accident or are unable to speak for yourself for any reason your bracelet could save your life.

People who have had a severe reaction to a sting by a bee or wasp, may be advised to carry a special 'Ana-Kit', which contains a syringe already filled with adrenaline. This is so that an adrenaline injection can be self-administered, or given by anyone present at the time. These special emergency kits are not available on prescription.

If you have had a severe reaction to any food, particularly egg, fish or shellfish, for example, it is good sense never to eat that food again because the second reaction can be catastrophic or fatal because of choking due to very sudden swelling of the throat. Though this is rare, it can and it does happen, as in the case of the woman who nibbled one sesame seed, and died in seconds. Sometimes fish can be a serious menace, because a trace of fish in a canapé can be enough to cause a dangerous reaction, so the only safe advice for such patients is to eat only recognizable food. Choking because of a local reaction in the throat is not anaphylaxis but can be as dangerous.

What is the Medic-Alert Foundation?

This charity organization was founded in 1956 by a doctor whose daughter nearly died of anaphylactic shock when given an anti-tetanus injection without being asked if she was allergic to it. To prevent another such incident he placed a bracelet on her arm with this information engraved on it.

Medic-Alert, founded in 1956 in the USA and in London in 1963, is now an international non-profit-making organization, with many thousands of members throughout the United Kingdom and the Republic of Ireland.

The Medic-Alert Foundation is now operating in the United Kingdom, the Republic of Ireland, the USA, Canada, Holland, South Africa, Zimbabwe, the Philippine Islands, West Malaysia, Australia, New Zealand, the Fiji Islands, Zambia, Jamaica, Iceland, Japan, Cyprus and Israel.

Willingness to act as organ donor can also be indicated on the disc. Thus, you may be able to save the life of another if your luck runs out!

What does Medic-Alert do?

The organization provides, for any person with a hidden medical problem, the protection of an emblem which gives an immediate 'warning' to hospitals, doctors, police or other agencies who might attend such individuals at a time and in circumstances when they are unable to speak for themselves, for example following an accident or collapse.

The Medic-Alert Foundation provides a stainless-steel bracelet or necklet with medical insignia engraved on one side and on the reverse the appropriate medical warning, a serial number and the emergency telephone number. The organization maintains a central file in London recording any further information regarded by the applicant's doctor as essential for adequate protection. In an emergency this information can be obtained by a doctor or other authorized person on making a reverse charge telephone call from anywhere in the world. The telephone is manned day and night.

Allergy is not by any means the only reason to carry a warning bracelet or disc. For example, it is vital for a doctor to know if the unconscious patient is a diabetic, epileptic or asthmatic, and if steroids, blood-pressure drugs, anti-coagulants or anti-convulsants are required.

Accidents can happen at any time in any place, and seizure, unconsciousness, shock or delirium may result in the inability of a victim to tell the attending doctor, or others, of a hidden medical condition. Those with hidden conditions always present a problem in an emergency, but knowledge of the problem ensures correct emergency treatment.

8 Effects on the nervous system and the eyes

It is clear that what we eat and drink can affect the functioning of the brain. Examples of obvious effects are sleepiness after a heavy protein meal or the consequences of too much alcohol. Poisonous substances in the food will have affects on anybody, but in allergic disease only certain sensitized individuals will react to specific foods or other allergens.

The effects of allergic reactions on the brain are either secondary to reactions in the vessels supplying blood to the nerve cells, or due to a direct effect on the cells of the brain itself.

Allergens gain access to the brain through the circulation, the most common route of entry being absorption from the gut. Recent research has shown that many proteins being digested in the gut are not broken down completely to amino acids, and that quite large molecules of protein can pass into the circulation and be detected in the brain.

Schizophrenia is a serious and common mental disorder. The possibility that diet could play a part in its causation was suggested by the fact that it became much less common during the last war in countries affected by shortages of food, particularly cereals, and the disease is more common in countries where the staple cereal is wheat, barley or rye. The possible association between diet and serious mental disorders should stimulate further research, but so far has received little interest. Perhaps it is too optimistic to expect that a significant proportion of serious psychiatric disorders could be attributed to dietary factors, but it is difficult to understand why a cereal exclusion diet should not be tried for a few weeks in these patients, for there is nothing to be lost. This idea is not accepted by psychiatrists at the present time and is most controversial.

The role of foods and dyes in behavioural disorders, especially hyperactivity and tantrums in children, is dealt with in some detail in the food section. My experience has suggested that food allergy and intolerance is a cause of behaviour problems to which more attention could and should be given, especially as diagnosis can lead to cure by avoidance.

Can organic neurological disease such as multiple sclerosis be caused by allergy?

Immunological reactions can occur in the central nervous system and its blood vessels, just as in any other tissue of the body. Several American allergists have produced evidence that dietary factors can cause neurological disorders and have written a great deal regarding the possible role of allergy in diseases of the central nervous system. The author's personal experience is limited to only four cases of firmly diagnosed multiple sclerosis where dietary factors have been identified and shown to have repeatable effects.

It is possible that there are several causes of multiple sclerosis, one of which may be reactions to food. Certainly it would seem sensible to consider dietary factors as a possibility in a disease with such a sad outlook where conventional medicine has little to offer. A trial of a restricted diet may be worthwhile, if only to make sure that food plays no part in the illness.

Unfortunately some practitioners, both qualified and unqualified, pursue this aspect to a dangerous extent, and use most dubious methods of 'diagnosis'. This is a very controversial field, and one should beware of raising false hopes, but it is possible that this factor could be important.

How common is migraine?

Migraine headaches are very common, and have been said to affect 10 per cent of men and 20 per cent of women. They tend to run in families and are commoner in younger people. Headaches are also commonly caused by tension in the muscles at the back of the neck, a sinus infection, and sometimes high blood pressure. Obviously there are some very serious causes of persistent headache which should be excluded by full investigation when necessary.

What are the symptoms of migraine?

Books have been written describing the many forms of migraine and the bizarre ways in which it may present itself. It would be inappropriate to attempt a detailed description here, except to emphasize that the diagnosis often depends on the recognition of a repeatable pattern of symptoms in each attack, and perhaps a recognizable trigger factor.

Almost any bizarre form of alteration in vision, usually one-sided, may be experienced. Flashing lights, zig-zags, or temporary loss of part of the vision is common, sometimes with weakness, numbness of part of the body, or difficulty in speaking. Intense one-sided headache then commences and can be so severe as to necessitate retiring to bed in the dark. Vomiting is common in this phase. Attacks of stomach ache and incessant vomiting in children are sometimes considered to be a manifestation of migraine localized to the abdomen. The interval between attacks may vary from days to months.

What happens to cause migraine?

The fundamental cause of migraine is instability of the blood supply to the brain. In the premonitory or warning stage of an attack (the 'aura') some arteries of the brain constrict and reduce the supply of blood, and therefore oxygen, to the part of the brain which they supply. The effect depends entirely on what function the part of the brain starved of oxygen performs.

What are the main trigger factors in migraine?

Many non-specific factors can trigger off an attack of migraine, including bright lights, weather changes, travel, premenstrual tension, oral contraceptives, coffee, hunger, emotional disturbance, infection, alcohol, and so on. Even this abbreviated list illustrates the confusing nature of the disorder, and why there are so many opinions regarding its causation.

Sensitization of the blood vessels of the brain to allergens undoubtedly occurs, but the place of food allergy in the causation of migraine has been the subject of much disagreement, and is discussed further in Chapter 22. It seems most probable that an unrecognized food allergy, plus non-specific trigger factors, will often produce a confusing pattern. Recognition and avoidance of the food may give cure, as the trigger factors no longer provoke the attacks.

What are the most useful drugs in migraine?

Obviously all kinds of common drugs for headaches are used by sufferers, and it was discovered many years ago that ergotamine, which causes contraction of arteries, could relieve the pain in a number of cases. This drug can be used under the tongue, taken by an aerosol spray or injected, but excessive use can cause side-effects. The number of remedies is a clear indication that many do not work.

More recently Intal by mouth in large doses has been found to block the reactions in *some* cases of food allergy associated with migraine, and others have been helped by antihistamines.

Can epileptic fits be caused by food?

In the past 50 years food has sometimes been reported as a possible cause of epilepsy. Recent research has confirmed beyond doubt that food is the cause in three-quarters of a large group of epileptic children. This has been accomplished by using the same double-blind methods used in the migraine and hyperactive groups at Great Ormond Street Hospital, London. Similar trials must now be carried out in adults suffering from these conditions as soon as they can be organized.

It is worth mentioning that one boy with epilepsy almost stopped having fits as a result of changing his suppressive drug to one containing no azo dyes. Some of these children were suffering from migraine, misbehaviour, *and* epilepsy, linking all these problems with food, and showing how diseases of the nervous system can be cured by avoidance of causative foods or chemicals.

How often is food the cause of emotional or functional disorders of the brain?

The answer will not be clarified until more trials are organized, but the Great Ormond Street findings should stimulate further research. A warning must, however, be given yet again against overenthusiastic dieting and altering drug dosages without medical permission. Phasing out suppressive drugs *must* be under medical supervision, particularly in epilepsy and emotional problems. Test feeds can be dangerous and totally unsuitable to be done at home if the consequences can be a fit or an emotional crisis.

In the author's experience, wheat, banana and rice respectively caused overwhelming drowsiness in these individuals. One was a civil servant who needed dexedrine for 20 years to do her job at all, another was an apprentice chef who had to take to bed for 3 days after eating one banana, and also after ginger, which is in the same botanical family. The third was an executive who fell asleep in board meetings if he had rice at lunch.

9 How allergy affects the respiratory system and the ear

HOW ALLERGY AFFECTS THE NOSE

What is allergic rhinitis?

Allergic rhinitis is the medical name for an allergic reaction in the nose. Seasonal allergic rhinitis is hay fever, which occurs only in the summer, while perennial allergic rhinitis produces symptoms all the year round. As the nose is the upper part of the respiratory tract, allergic reactions in the nose are often associated with allergic reactions in the bronchial tubes. Many asthmatics also suffer from allergic rhinitis, but it is often overlooked or forgotten.

What are the causes of allergic rhinitis?

Seasonal or perennial allergens, or both together, cause allergic reactions of the upper respiratory tract, so the causes are just the same as for the lower respiratory tract, the bronchi.

Diagnosis is by the same methods as for asthma, and in older patients the cause is often completely unknown, just as in many older asthmatics.

What are the symptoms of perennial allergic rhinitis?

Sneezing, often paroxysmal and sometimes difficult to stop, stuffiness, blockage, or constant running 'like a tap' are the main symptoms. Attacks of sneezing are often unpredictable and embarrassing, but it is also common to have a permanently blocked and stuffy nose, which the patient may eventually accept as usual.

Sometimes there are no clear-cut symptoms suggesting nasal allergy but if a person has frequent colds which are here today and gone tomorrow, or a constant 'cold' for months on end, the cause is likely to be allergy. Sneezing on rising is usually an allergic reaction because throwing back the covers stirs up the dust mites and their excreta, which become airborne and the sensitive person will then react. This also applies to pets, especially when they share the bed!

What can be the consequences of perennial allergic rhinitis?

Sometimes people have chronic nasal catarrh (which is probably perennial allergic rhinitis) for many years, and then develop asthma in middle life. What has happened is that the allergic process has extended to the lower part of the respiratory system as well as the upper. Sometimes when this happens the nose suddenly gets better when the chest gets worse, but nobody understands why.

Sinus infection is a common complication, and chronic infections may dominate so that it may not be realized that there is an underlying allergic problem. As a result, patients often have extensive surgery to the nose, but without more than temporary benefit.

A yellow or green discharge, especially on rising, is the sign of sinus infection, and quite intensive antibiotic treatment may be necessary.

Can perennial allergic rhinitis affect the sense of smell?

The tiny organs responsible for the sense of smell are tucked away deep in the nasal cavity, and if nasal congestion or polyps prevent the air from reaching them then the sense of smell becomes lost.

What are polyps?

Polyps resemble little grapes which grow in the nose. They can be removed surgically, but often grow again quite quickly. They are a common cause of extreme obstruction and loss of smell and taste. Many patients have their polyps removed surgically ten or even twelve times. Surgery can be a distressing experience and it is often possible to use medical treatment instead to control the situation. They are allergic, not malignant, but the causative allergens can seldom be defined.

Can animals cause perennial allergic rhinitis?

Swelling of the eyes and sneezing on contact with dogs, cats, rabbits, gerbils and other pets is a sure sign of allergy. If all further exposure is avoided then so may be a lot of trouble. Unfortunately, it may be 6–12 months after a pet has joined the household before anyone begins to react. By this time everyone has become fond of the animal, making the situation more difficult when removal becomes essential.

Can nose drops make rhinitis worse?

Powerful nasal decongestants will clear the nose at first but become less and less effective. The period of relief becomes less, and excessive use may finally result in actual harm to the lining of the nose and 'rebound' congestion.

Can perennial rhinitis be treated surgically?

Nasal blockage, chronic infection and nasal polyps, are often treated surgically. The swollen lining of the nose, and often the turbinate bones, may be removed to improve the airway. The nasal septum, which separates one side of the nose from another, is often straightened. The drainage of the chronically infected sinuses is improved surgically, so that pus no longer becomes locked up in the sinus cavity.

Unfortunately, after surgical procedures, which can be very distressing, improvement is often only temporary. This is because allergy cannot be cut out and thrown away, and after an interval it usually recurs as before. Also, nasal surgery will sometimes trigger off severe asthma for no obvious reason. Medical treatment with drugs, plus identification or avoidance of allergens, should be the initial approach, with surgery being kept in reserve. Many doctors are unaware that nasal allergy cannot be cured surgically, and that effective medical treatment is available.

How does allergic rhinitis affect children?

The child with allergic rhinitis often rubs his or her nose in a typical way, is always sniffling, often snores, is a mouth breather, and frequently has a crease across the tip of the nose as the result of constantly pushing it upwards with the heel of the hand in the so-called allergic salute. These children often have dark shadows under the eyes which are due to chronic allergy, not insomnia or television.

Blockage of the Eustachian tubes is common, and may result in deafness from fluid in the ear. The child with severe allergic rhinitis presents a miserable picture, which may become even worse in the summer if summer allergens such as grass pollen are also involved.

Chronic or latent asthma may be another part of the picture, overlooked because of attention to the nasal problem, and sometimes only recognized when the child is referred to the ear, nose and throat department because of fluid in the ears causing deafness. Children do not wish to be different, or be fussed over, so they do not complain, and eventually adjust to their condition.

HOW ALLERGY AFFECTS THE LUNGS

How serious is disease of the airways?

The basic physiology of the air passages and lung has already been dealt with in Chapter 1. At this point the reader is reminded that gas exchange is the most important function of the lung, and affected by any disease of the alveoli. Disease of the airways may often spare the alveoli completely, and if allergic in causation may be reversible. Chronic bronchitis, on the other hand, is often quite irreversible and is also associated with emphysema.

What is asthma?

This disease was known to the ancient Greeks, the word 'asthma' meaning panting or gasping for breath – a good description of the main symptoms. The causes are obstruction of the bronchial tubes by swelling of the lining of the bronchus, by excessive thick mucus which it may not be possible to cough up, and by spasm of the bronchial muscles.

In an acute attack the difficulty in inhaling enough air to oxygenate the blood may be extreme. This is because the stale air already in the chest cannot get out through the restricted bronchi, and so very little fresh air can be inhaled. As a result the chest becomes blown up like a balloon with air from which the oxygen has already been removed. The appearance of the chest of the sufferer, especially a child, undergoes a change. The shoulders go up and a pronounced stoop appears to accommodate the trapped stagnant air until relief is obtained. Neck and chest muscles strain and struggle to move some air out so that fresh air can get in, and feelings of suffocation may lead to panic which makes the situation worse and sets up a vicious circle.

In a person suffering from allergic asthma the particles of allergen are either inhaled with the air, or reach the bronchi via the blood. The sensitized mast cells are triggered off by contact with the allergen to liberate chemical mediators which initiate an allergic reaction in the bronchus. This results in swelling of the bronchial lining, hence some restriction to the passage of air, and the mucous glands produce more thick mucus, which makes matters worse. In addition, some of the mediator chemicals which are liberated cause the bronchial muscles to go into spasm, causing further narrowing of a tube already partly blocked by swelling and mucus.

Asthma is frequently mild, but can also be disastrously severe and quite unpredictable, or so fluctuant that patients are mistaken for neurotics or malingerers. Death is unusual, but can occur unexpectedly with overwhelming suddenness, so it can be dangerous to underestimate asthma.

What can trigger an asthma attack?

Specific allergens to which the bronchi are sensitive may be present constantly, intermittently or only in season. When sufficient allergen is inhaled an attack will occur, but when not exposed, as in seasonal or intermittent asthma, the patient will be quite normal.

Constant exposure to an allergen, such as to house-dust mite, causes a completely different situation to arise, because the bronchi become irritable and may go into spasm when contacted by a wide range of non-specific triggers as well as responding to the specific allergen. Some of these non-specific factors are very common, as in the case of exercise asthma, which seems to be attributable to the drying effect of large volumes of air passing through the bronchi. Swimming does not trigger asthma because of the high humidity of the inhaled air near the surface of the water. Cold dry air, as on a frosty morning, can have the same effect as exercise.

Other examples of non-specific triggers, of which there are many, are sulphur dioxide preservative in fizzy drinks, or in the fumes from power stations, air pollution in general, smoke from bonfires or in pubs, bacterial and virus infections of the bronchi. Emotion or panic can also cause non-specific spasm by acting as a trigger in a situation which is already unstable.

Thus the possible effects of all these non-specific factors, in addition to the specific reactions to the perennial allergen to which the patient is sensitive, makes a very complicated and confusing picture. The asthmatic condition may be put down to shortness of breath due to exercise alone, or to emotional instability.

What is the difference between chronic asthma and chronic bronchitis?

In asthma, sputum coughed up contains a great many cells called eosinophils, the dye eosin staining them red. Eosinophils are usually found where an allergic reaction is taking place so their presence in sputum indicates allergic asthma. Some patients with asthma cough up tiny blobs of sputum which feel quite firm between the tongue and the roof of the mouth, or produce stringy solid pieces which resemble tiny worms or plugs. These 'worms' are actually casts of the smaller branches of the bronchial tree and often indicate allergic asthma. All these facts were described 150 years ago by Laennec, the French physician who invented the stethoscope, but today the character of the sputum attracts little attention or enquiry, so the significance of what is expectorated may often be missed.

Asthma, being due mainly to an *allergic* reaction in the airways (the bronchial tubes), responds dramatically to oral steroid treatment.

Chronic bronchitis, usually the end result of smoking, pollution and chronic infection of the bronchi, differs in many ways from chronic allergic asthma, but can also resemble it closely to the extent that a trial of the effects of steroids is often worthwhile. One outstanding difference is that eosinophil cells are not found in the sputum, but instead there are many scavenger cells (macrophages) which engulf and remove carbon particles derived from cigarettes or air pollution.

The airway obstruction in allergic asthma usually varies markedly from day to day, but though it is responsive to steroid treatment it can sometimes be severe and unvarying. In bronchitis there is much less variation in the degree of airway obstruction, and no response to steroids. Frequent infection, with production of nasty yellow or green sputum, is more commonly a feature of bronchitis, and responds to antibiotics.

Asthma often gets better on holiday away from the home environment, or abroad in a good climate with tiled floors and no house dust, while bronchitis does not improve as dramatically, or relapse so obviously on return home.

Although still frequently diagnosed, chronic bronchitis is now quite uncommon in childhood, and the symptoms are usually caused by asthma. This also applies to many young adults, but in older people with severe airway obstruction it is usual to find a varying proportion of reversible allergic asthma and chronic bronchitis, as shown by the extent to which the condition can be reversed by treatment.

How can the severity of asthma be monitored effectively?

The task of the lung is to transfer oxygen to the blood, and to do so for life. Gas exchange takes place in the countless millions of alveoli, and to measure the efficiency of this process in any patient requires sophisticated and expensive equipment. Gas exchange also depends on the supply of air through the bronchial tree to the alveoli. The capacity of any patient to inhale or exhale air is quite easy to measure, but the equipment is bulky and expensive, and only found in hospitals and clinics. Thus, their use is limited to patients able to go to the pulmonary function laboratory in working hours.

The obvious need for a simple, cheap and portable device to measure the severity of the asthma anywhere at any time has been met by the peak flow meter. This British invention has made it possible to monitor the severity of any case of asthma as many times a day as necessary, so that treatment can be adjusted according to the readings.

The peak flow meter measures the amount of air which can be blown out in a hundredth of a second. The meter is set to zero, the patient inhales as full a breath as possible, places the mouthpiece between the teeth and blows out as hard and fast as possible. The result is then read off on the scale in litres per minute. Normal values have been established for all ages, and are influenced by sex and height, as shown in Figures 9.1 and 9.2.

In asthma the peak flow rate can vary from day to day, from hour to hour or even less, so occasional tests in hospital or clinic may be of little value, but any individual patient with his/her own meter can now take several readings per day and chart them on a special graph (on which the treatment is also recorded) so that both patient and doctor know exactly what they are doing. Daily peak flow graphs can also give information which can point to the cause of the asthma. This can be particularly important in seasonal cases.

Is asthma 'all in the mind'?

Many doctors still believe that allergy, particularly asthma, eczema and severe urticaria, is 'all in the mind'. Many sufferers

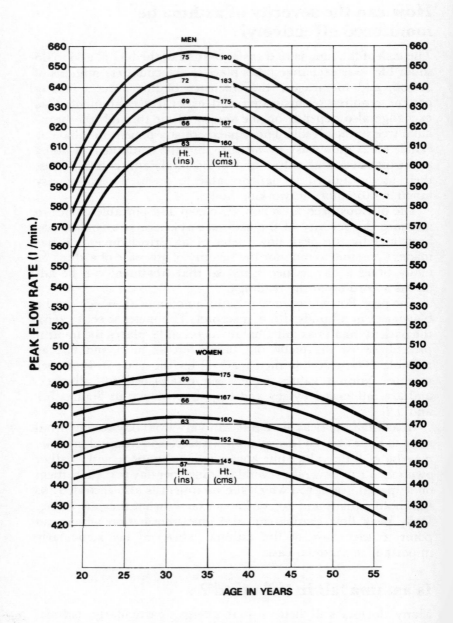

Figure 9.1 Peak flow rates for normal adults.

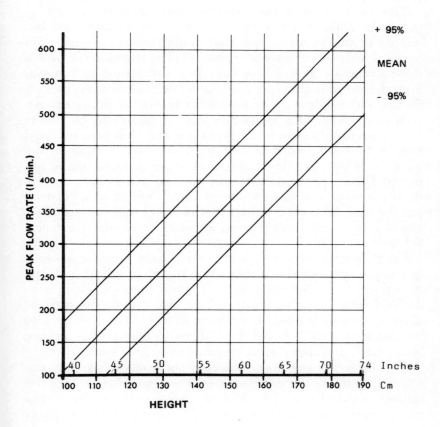

Just as in adults, the peak flow rates for children are related directly to the height, so *both* must be measured. Most children (95%) will achieve a reading between the outer pair of lines, but the range of normal is very wide, and readings below the average line may indicate mild asthma.

Figure 9.2   Normal peak flow rates for children aged 5–18 years.

have also accepted this concept and are most difficult to convince otherwise, yet actually it is exceptionally uncommon for psychological factors to be dominant in allergy.

The origin of this fallacy was probably observations such as that many children get better when sent to boarding school, but relapse in the vacation, and that many patients get better in hospital without any special treatment. The effects in the first of these examples have erroneously been attributed to removal from the stressful atmosphere of the home, with anxious parents fussing and coddling the victim, to the spartan environment of a boarding school. One instructive case is illustrated by Figure 9.3. A more likely explanation is that the child has been removed from a house full of dust and pets, and that relapse in the vacation is due to being exposed to these allergens again, not parental anxiety. In adults, where removal to hospital may also mean entering a relatively allergen-free environment, experts put forward the bizarre notion that recovery without treatment was due to relief at finally being admitted to hospital for expert help!

Up to 25 years ago these ideas were usually accepted without question, to the extent that they were taught to medical students. As a result these outmoded views are still common, along with the odd idea that the word 'asthma' must never be used to parents, because it would upset them so much. On the contrary, parents are usually relieved that a definite diagnosis has, at last, been made, and that correct treatment can now begin.

The correct answer to this clash of opinions is that the physical distress of repeated attacks of asthma, often striking the sufferer suddenly at the most inconvenient time, inevitably causes anxiety and often fear of suffocation. The worry aggravates the asthma through the nervous system controlling the bronchi, further increasing anxiety and fear, and thus setting up a vicious circle. The anxiety, fear and panic are not causes of the asthma, but effects, though they will also aggravate the condition. It is a common observation that both asthma *and* anxiety promptly disappear as soon as *effective* treatment is introduced.

Asthma is the best example of confusion between effect and cause which has plagued allergy sufferers. Thus, anxiety from any cause can set off an attack of asthma, but only in a highly allergic individual who is easily triggered off. A very rare but most instructive example is illustrated in Figure 9.4 showing how a bullying teacher could set off an asthma attack.

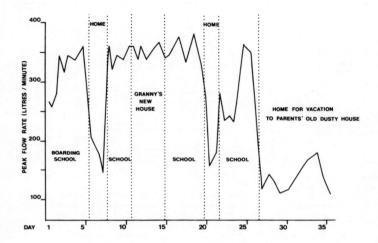

This peak flow chart of a schoolboy shows the influence of the environment on his asthma. He was slightly allergic to dust mites, and it is very obvious that only the old house affected him.

Figure 9.3   Effect of different environments on an asthmatic boy aged 12.

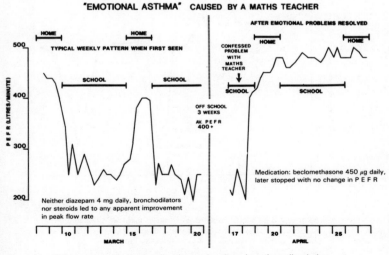

This example of emotionally triggered asthma in a dust allergic boy of thirteen is shown to emphasize the extreme rarity of this type of asthma.

Figure 9.4   'Emotional asthma' caused by a maths teacher.

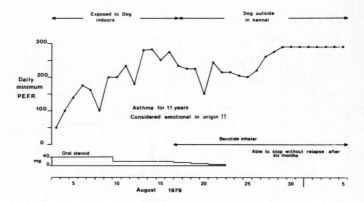

This girl of twelve had been confidently diagnosed as 'emotional' asthma for 11 years, because her father was always in trouble with the law. In fact, her asthma was due to the dog. She needed three weeks on oral steroids before she came under control (from 50 to 300 litres/minute). She changed from an introverted cripple to a fun-loving extrovert.

Figure 9.5   Chronic asthma due to dog mistaken for 'emotional' asthma for 11 years.

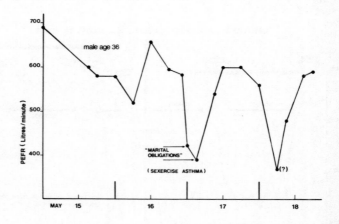

This house dust allergic patient was told to take extra readings if he got asthma, and to note what he was doing at the time. This is a form of exercise-induced asthma not usually reported.

Figure 9.6   Sexercise-induced asthma.

The cardinal error of blaming emotional factors alone for severe asthma is well illustrated in Figure 9.5. In this interesting case the fact that the child's father was frequently in prison was assumed to be the cause, and the dog was not even suspected.

Figure 9.6 illustrates a most unusual combination of asthma due to house dust, and to the trigger factor of the physical and emotional stress of sexual intercourse. This problem may not be uncommon, and causes great anxiety to both partners, who may feel too embarrassed to talk about it to their doctor. Situations such as this may arise out of mutual unspoken concern, and if allowed to persist might result in the breakdown of an otherwise satisfactory relationship. Under these circumstances it would be more practical to seek the advice of the family doctor to improve medication and management of the asthma, rather than to resort to psychiatry or a marriage guidance counsellor.

What is emphysema?

Patients or their relatives are often told that they have emphysema, but the meaning of the term is seldom explained clearly, and it is quite often employed loosely. Remember that the smallest bronchial tubes, the bronchioles, lead into a small cluster of alveoli, which resemble a bunch of grapes except that they must be visualized as being hollow, the twig being the bronchiole. The air passes down the bronchiole so that the oxygen can pass through the wall of the alveoli into the blood, while the carbon dioxide can come out of the blood and be exhaled.

Gas exchange depends on the alveoli being healthy, and will be interfered with by any disease which affects the alveoli. If the alveoli become overinflated they may burst to form one big space, with only destroyed blood vessels in the walls instead of lots of tiny alveoli exchanging the gases efficiently. The result is a small number of large, inefficient alveoli which take up more space, so the chest of the patient becomes permanently blown up with stale air, and assumes a barrel or balloon shape.

Thus, emphysema is a process which is permanent and irreversible, caused by the destruction of the alveoli. Similar effects can be produced by allergic disease of the bronchioles, resulting in spasm, swelling of the lining, and secretion of thick mucus which cannot be got rid of. Overinflation is again the result, but fortunately does not result in the destruction of the alveoli because the disease is affecting the bronchioles and bronchi only. With efficient treatment the obstruction in the bronchi can be cleared to a variable extent, and often completely in younger patients. In older patients the degree of reversibility tends to be less, as might be expected, and chronic asthma may lead gradually to irreversible bronchitis and emphysema, unless recognized and treated effectively.

In allergic alveolitis, as in farmer's lung and similar conditions, the alveoli are affected directly and the airways remain completely clear. In chronic bronchitis with emphysema both airways and alveoli are affected, and the main causes of this very common condition are smoking, air pollution in general or at work, chronic infection, and the dust diseases. The extent of the emphysema in any case of chronic chest disease is very difficult to measure, cannot be diagnosed from a chest x-ray, and cannot be accurately assessed until after death.

HOW ALLERGY AFFECTS THE EAR

Allergic reactions in the lining of the nose and at the back of the throat frequently cause problems with hearing because of blockage of the tiny Eustachian tubes.

What are the Eustachian tubes?

They run from the back of the throat on each side to the internal ear, which lies behind the eardrum. The function of the tube is to ventilate the inner ear and equalize the pressures on each side of the eardrum (Figure 9.7).

What are the symptoms of Eustachian blockage?

Slight blockage causes popping and crackling and intermittent slight deafness. Swallowing and blowing the nose may produce loud noises in the ears.

Many people become acutely aware of blockage in their Eustachian tubes when travelling by air. This is because after

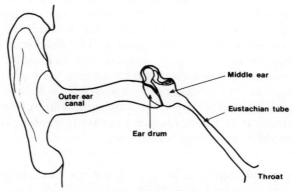

Air cannot pass through the ear drum. Blockage of the Eustachian (auditory) tube prevents the air pressure on each side of the drum remaining equal. Persistent blockage may result in fluid in the ear, which causes deafness.

Figure 9.7   The ear and Eustachian tube.

taking off the air pressure inside the plane drops rapidly, even when the cabin is pressurized. The air trapped in the inner ear behind the drum is at the higher pressure pertaining at ground level, and cannot escape if the tube is blocked. As a result the eardrum is pushed outwards and causes pain. Swallowing and yawning may help, but if the tube is more or less completely blocked equalization of pressures will take place very slowly during the flight.

By the end of the flight the air will have escaped from inside the ear, the pain will have disappeared, and at last the pressure inside the ear has become the same as the pressure inside the plane. On landing the situation becomes reversed, because the air at ground level is now at a higher pressure than the air inside the ear. Because of the blockage of the tube readjustment cannot take place quickly, so this time the eardrum is pushed inwards, again causing pain.

Can deafness result from Eustachian blockage?

When the end of the Eustachian tube is permanently blocked all the air becomes absorbed from the middle ear. Something has to take its place, the result being the secretion of a thick fluid which gums up the delicate works of the ear and causes deafness. This can happen quite insidiously, especially in children. The condition is called secretory otitis media. The fluid can be drained surgically but it will simply reaccumulate, so in order to equalize the pressures between the air surrounding the body and the air inside the ear a tiny plastic device with a little hole in it (called a grommet) is inserted into the eardrum. This gives relief, but swimming has to be prohibited because infection can penetrate to the middle ear through the hole.

What part does allergy play in causing secretory otitis media?

In a recent investigation in Derby 40 per cent of children with deafness due to fluid in the ears had good evidence of nasal allergy as a continuing cause. This would suggest that attention to the allergic factors as well as or instead of using grommets may be necessary to achieve a really good result.

Medical treatment can also relieve the fluid in the ear by releasing the blockage at the inner end of the Eustachian tube, and treatment for the nasal allergy might prevent a recurrence. Allergy as a cause of fluid in the ear has been accepted for a long time in the USA but not in Great Britain.

Do seasonal allergies affect the ear?

Seasonal allergies can cause all the problems just described, plus more intense nasal symptoms. These are often accompanied by intensely itchy ears and palate.

10 How allergy affects other parts of the body

HOW ALLERGY AFFECTS THE GUT

In the alimentary tract allergy can cause all manner of complaints from lips to anus. Foods as a possible cause of problems may not be considered seriously because satisfactory proof may be difficult to obtain, and food allergy is a controversial subject. Food allergy is dealt with in a separate chapter, so it will be sufficient here to indicate the type of problem which may be encountered and to give occasional examples.

How can allergy affect the lips, mouth and throat?

Allergy on the lips can be very obvious and simple, as when due to lipstick for example, or when a violently fish-sensitive man kissed a girl who had been eating fish and chips. Another patient reacted with huge swollen lips to chips or sausages which had been fried in fat previously used for fish, a very powerful allergen, the mere smell of which can cause reactions in some patients.

Mouth ulcers can be due to foods, but this can be difficult to pin down because the effects of a food may be delayed by several hours or even into the next day. One of my cases who had migraine due to milk had persistent mouth ulcers for 18 months before it was found that the cause was milk casein in so-called non-dairy milk substitute. Another was due to additives in white flour.

Acute swelling of the throat can be caused by an allergic

reaction. There may be a danger of choking and an emergency tracheotomy may be necesary to save life.

Can the stomach be affected by allergy?

Special diets high in milk and eggs are usually prescribed for ulcers, but in a few cases the diet seems to make them worse. The medically qualified wife of a solicitor who had a duodenal ulcer noticed that after meals containing eggs he had symptoms suggesting mild allergic shock. When they were avoided the symptoms disappeared and the ulcer cleared up within a matter of a few weeks. Perhaps this happens more often than we think, as Professor Romanski in Warsaw has shown that allergy of the stomach is a common cause of ulcers.

What allergic problems affect the gut?

A variety of problems in the small intestine can be due to allergens, and chronic allergic reactions can cause such damage to the lining of the gut that food is not properly absorbed and goes practically straight through. This happens in coeliac disease, and can also occur in infancy with milk allergy, sometimes associated with lactase deficiency. A person allergic to a food may reject it upwards by vomiting or downwards by acute diarrhoea, but may also absorb the food into the general circulation and thus the allergen gains access to any sensitized organ in the body without any local disturbance in the wall of the gut.

There are a great many causes of colic or intermittent diarrhoea and other abdominal complaints, food allergy being only one of them. In the absence of reliable laboratory tests there are difficulties in picking out the cases where food allergy is important and may be a major cause. Severe intestinal symptoms can have so many causes it is unwise to assume that the cause is allergy to food unless every other possibility has been excluded.

Acute allergic reaction to foods may cause severe abdominal pain leading to surgical operation, which fails to discover any obvious cause. The father of modern food allergy, Dr Albert Rowe of California, became interested in food allergy because he often underwent surgery for acute abdominal pain yet nothing was ever found to account for it. He finally diagnosed the causative foods for himself and thus began his own life's work on food allergies.

In the small intestine a condition known as Crohn's disease may cause severe thickening and eventual blocking of the gut. This is usually dealt with surgically and it is seldom recognized that it can be attributed to food allergy in some cases. If the food can be identified a recurrence can be prevented by avoiding it, as in a case of a girl who got asthma and eczema from egg as an infant which gradually passed off. When she was 11 years old she developed abdominal symptoms which were eventually found, at operation, to be due to Crohn's disease. After she had had her operation, abdominal pains and diarrhoea could still be reproduced reliably by taking some egg, and if she avoided egg she remained well. Her case is particularly interesting because the target organ changed from the skin and bronchi to the gut yet the allergen was the same.

Can ulcerative colitis be caused by allergy?

Ulcerative colitis is a most distressing disease which often responds to steroids orally or locally, suggesting an allergic factor in causation. It is over 50 years since it was first shown that some cases are caused by milk and that avoidance of milk products may give a complete cure. At the present time, surgical removal of the colon has become quite a popular approach to treatment in a severe case and gives good results. Many specialists fail to consider dietary manipulation in the treatment of ulcerative colitis, but there can be no good reason for failure to experiment with diets in the early stages of the disease, or in the so-called spastic colon or irritable bowel syndrome. There may be much to gain by a trial of the dietary approach before accepting major surgery, but all depends on the condition of the patient at the time. Rarely, patients are afflicted with seasonal colitis in June due to allergy to grass pollen. If diagnosed this can be treated and cured by desensitization but this treatment is no longer available in this country.

HOW ALLERGY AFFECTS THE GALL-BLADDER AND KIDNEY

Can allergy affect the gall-bladder?

The gall-bladder acts as a reservoir for the bile from the liver and is situated under the right side of the lower ribs. It is common knowledge that the gall-bladder can cause problems and severe colicky pain, and that this is usually due to stones in the gall-bladder or bile ducts. However, acute muscle spasm can produce the same symptoms. In fact, gall-bladder colic caused by food allergy was first reported in 1924, and allergic reactions were demonstrated experimentally in the gall-bladder of sensitized monkeys in 1943. No doubt this research has long been forgotten but may be worth further enquiry.

Can allergy cause kidney disease?

The significance of allergy in causing kidney disease is ill defined. Occasionally quite severe kidney disease occurs in the pollen season only. If it is noted that this is a *seasonal* affliction it may well be a kidney reaction to grass pollen. This should lead to successful prevention by desensitization against grass pollen.

In non-seasonal problems, especially in kidney disease in children which is steroid-responsive, further research is needed. Some investigators have shown milk to be associated with kidney disease but confirmation is lacking. If identification and avoidance of a specfic cause could be accomplished then suppression could be replaced by a possible cure.

The urinary bladder can also be affected by food allergy. Its function is to hold the urine until it can be excreted, thus exposing the bladder to everything in the urine for long periods. If the bladder becomes sensitized it may be so irritated as to get rid of the urine in small instalments, producing a picture usually mistaken for infection. It is interesting that in some children food allergy is definitely associated with bed wetting, milk being the most usual cause.

HOW ALLERGY AFFECTS THE JOINTS

Can arthritis or rheumatism be caused by allergic reactions?

The joints are temporarily affected in many illnesses, particularly serum sickness due to anti-sera raised in horses. This demonstrates that the joints can react to foreign substances.

Rheumatoid arthritis and rheumatic pains in the muscles can, in my personal experience, occasionally be attributed to food, particularly milk. This is probably quite uncommon, but there is nothing to be lost by trying a milk-free diet in an early case of joint problems because there is no *specific* treatment anyway. A clue may be provided by sudden relief of joint pains and swelling when unable to eat because of a stomach upset, but more convincing evidence can be produced by controlled dieting.

In cases of established rheumatoid arthritis of many years duration improvement is unlikely. Sufferers hearing of dietary cures naturally attempt to carry them out but usually become discouraged and disillusioned. In any event the best they can hope for is a decrease in pain and in progression of the disease.

HOW ALLERGY AFFECTS THE SKIN

The skin is one of the largest organs of the body, its function being to separate us from our surrounding environment. It is not a passive envelope, but a living layer of cells, blood vessels, nerves and sweat glands. It is tough, flexible, waterproof and sensitive, with a dead, horny layer on top to give durability, and it will stand up to a great deal of abuse without complaint, especially on the hands and feet. The skin also regulates temperature by controlling the blood supply and by sweating. The horny layer is dead and insensitive, and is formed constantly from the cells of the living skin just underneath the horny layer, which evolve into the horny layer as they die off.

The living skin is liberally supplied with tiny capillary blood vessels surrounded by many types of specialized cells. The most important cells for allergy are the mast cells, already described briefly in the introductory chapters. They lie near the blood vessels, contain large amounts of toxic mediator chemicals such as histamine, and become sensitized by specific IgE (*see* Chapter 1).

It is difficult to understand why these cells are present in such abundance, but they are certainly a great convenience to the allergist. This is because if a tiny amount of allergen is pricked into the skin through the horny layer it will contact the living mast cells. If the mast cells are sensitive a reaction will occur, telling the allergist that the patient may be sensitive to that allergen. Prick skin testing will produce results within 15 minutes, thus detecting the immediate-type allergies usually associated with allergic rhinitis or asthma, but not necessarily allergies affecting the skin itself.

Local skin allergy, such as to nickel, affects the lymphocyte type of cells, and is slow to develop. The patch test is used for diagnosis, taking 48 hours of contact before a reaction becomes obvious. This reaction has occurred because inflammatory cells have accumulated in the provoked area, and because the tiny vessels of the skin are irritated and dilated.

In what ways can skin react to allergens?

The skin can only react in a limited number of ways, no matter what the cause. Disease of the skin is usually obvious to everyone, and it can be observed and photographed, and a biopsy sample can easily be taken for microscopical examination. In spite of the ease of observation and sampling, and the skin's accessibility for the application of ointments and creams, very little was known about the causation of skin disease until immune reactions began to be understood, and there is still much controversy regarding which skin problems can properly be regarded as of allergic origin.

Allergens may act by affecting tiny blood vessels in the skin which have become sensitized, so that any changes are secondary to damage to these vessels. Alternatively it is the mast cells and other reactive cells lying in the tissues outside the vessels which are sensitive, and which react by producing mediators. Rashes from infectious diseases or drug sensitivity are mostly due to damage to tiny vessels by a sensitivity reaction to the infection. Effects on the skin itself are mostly associated with reactions in the cells in the tissues outside the tiny vessels. In eczema this leads to the formation of tiny blisters deep in the skin which itch and irritate, leading to scratching, which causes trauma and infection. There is also redness, itching, swelling and scaling of the skin, and tiny blisters which burst and weep, then crust over, so that the skin becomes thick, scaly and cracked.

HOW ALLERGY AFFECTS THE EYE

The eye offers a unique opportunity for the observation of allergic reactions, particularly in the tiny blood vessels. Serious allergic reactions can occur in the interior of the eye, but we need not discuss these here, as obvious reactions usually concern the external eye only.

The inside of the eyelids are lined with a thin loose membrane, the conjunctiva, which also covers the eyeball except for the clear cornea in the middle through which the coloured iris and pupil can be seen. The eyes are protected and wiped by the blink reflex, and are lubricated and kept clean by the tears.

Allergens reach the eye in the air, as dusts, pollens, spores, cosmetics, flakes of dandruff from animals, or from rubbing the eye with hands contaminated with allergens.

The tears immediately dissolve out the allergen, which causes an intense reaction in the sensitized eye, but none in the normal person. This is called conjunctivitis, and can be caused by allergy, irritation, infection, and small particles of grit. Congestion of the tiny blood vessels can easily be seen, hence the term 'pink eye'.

The tears contain the anti-bacterial substance lysozyme, immunoglobulin A and antibodies. Thus we all have built in wash/wipe mechanisms, with special additives!

The cornea is made up of a lattice of collagen fibrils arranged in such a way as to be transparent. There is no blood supply, so antibodies cannot reach the cornea. This partly accounts for the fact that the cornea can usually be transplanted without any rejection problems.

How serious is allergic conjunctivitis?

Seasonal conjunctivitis is associated with hay fever or asthma. It can be so severe that children playing in long grass may have problems in finding their way home, as their eyes have become swollen and closed. It can be avoided as a rule, or treated by eye drops, and so on.

Chronic allergic conjunctivitis may cause chronic inflammation of the eyelids, with itching, watering and soreness. Sometimes the inside of the lids becomes covered in tiny red lumps, described as like cobblestones. Asthma or eczema may also be present. A diagnosis of allergy can often be made by microscopical examination of a smear of the eye secretion.

What allergens affect the eye?

The short answer is anything which is airborne or which can contact the eye directly. Contact-lens plastics, but more commonly the antiseptics in the solutions used with the lenses, cause difficulties. It is important to be aware of these possibilities so that expert guidance can be obtained.

Very rarely, a food can be identified as the cause, the clue being when the conjunctivitis clears up when nothing has been eaten because of a gastric upset.

How can allergies of the eye be treated?

Direct medication can be effective using decongestants, antihistamines, Intal, local steroids, and so on. However, these are all suppressants, and for pollen or dust the only real cure is desensitization, if the symptoms are severe enough. With modern drugs this is less often necessary.

Can allergic reactions affect the structures in the interior of the eye?

If any of the blood vessels or the delicate structures of the eye become sensitized allergic reactions can occur. These can be very serious and damaging to the parts of the eye affected.

PART 4

How Causative Allergens Can Be Identified

11 The many faces of allergy

Have you really got an allergy?

While many people have symptoms recognized as allergic, a great many others suffer from unsuspected allergic problems. For example, their cough may be blamed on cigarettes, their stuffy nose on sinus trouble, and their headaches on stress, while the true cause may be allergy. The importance of recognizing allergies is that if the cause can be identified and removed or avoided, considerable improvement or even 'cure' can be obtained – but if the problem is not known to be allergic there is no such prospect, nor will the correct treatment be given. A number of pointers suggest allergy, several of which may be present at the same time, for example:

Family history

If many members of the family have or have had allergic problems of any kind, especially if close relatives on *both* sides of the family are involved, allergy is more likely.

Cause/effect relationships

If there is a history of fairly clear-cut symptoms after exposure to, for example, dust or pets, or problems immediately after one particular food, then allergy is likely.

The nature of the problem

Rhinitis, asthma and eczema are usually allergic in causation, but other problems can only *sometimes* be put down to allergy, such as rheumatoid arthritis, miscellaneous digestive and gut problems, ulcerative colitis, behaviour problems in children, emotional difficulties in adults and children, migraine, and so on. This is a grey area where only a certain proportion of these problems appear to be 'allergic' in the light of today's knowledge, but there is nothing to be lost by investigating the possibility. If the allergen is intermittently present the reaction will be intermittent. Constant exposure causes constant symptoms which may not be recognized by either doctor or patient as being of allergic origin.

Hoarseness and a night cough is an uncommon presentation of asthma. A severe attack can occur in the night but the patient is so well in the day the attack may be discredited. Wheezing may not be obvious.

Gut problems associated with cow's milk formula in infancy, such as diarrhoea, constipation, malabsorption, failure to thrive, pyloric stenosis and projectile vomiting, all suggest that allergy should be considered. Obviously any gut problem can be due to allergy, but the big difficulty is demonstrating clear association of cause with effect, and that avoidance brings a cure. Chronic problems caused by a daily food are more difficult to recognize.

Is it possible to tell if a person has allergic problem from facial appearance and other obvious characteristics?

It is not generally known that allergic patients often have a characteristic appearance, which can help in the diagnosis of allergic problems but is often attributed to other causes. Why not try looking closely at your children and relatives to find out if they display any of the following signs? One small patient surveyed his classmates with new eyes, and reported that six out of thirty had allergy! Hence, if the observer knows what to look for, the sufferer from a chronic respiratory allergy is often easily recognized, even from a distance. The following observations apply mainly to children but are also found in many adults.

Allergic shiners

The appearance of heavy shadows under the eyes is typical of an allergic patient, but is often attributed to television, dissipation or insomnia. People displaying this sign are quite often food allergics and shiners sometimes appear in several members of the same family. They may disappear when the correct food is removed from the diet.

Extra eye creases

Some children, especially those with eczema, tend to have extra creases under the eyes which are again associated with allergy.

Nasal blockage

Blockage produces a pinched nose with small nostrils, mouth breathing, sometimes nasal polyps, and nasal speech. Constant mouth breathing, snoring and apparent inability to blow the nose effectively may be the result of chronic nasal allergy rather than adenoids. Also, grimacing and wiggling the nose like a rabbit is to relieve the allergic itch, not to annoy parents.

Constant or frequent colds which tend to be here today and gone tomorrow are often caused by allergy. A true cold lasts for days and often ends with a thick yellow nasal discharge. Frequent sneezing fits with a copiously running nose are usually due to allergy.

The nasal crease and allergic salute

An allergic nose is an itchy nose, and children relieve the itch by pushing the nose upwards. Eventually this results in a tiny crease across the tip of the nose, sometimes accentuated by a little line of blackheads. This cannot be caused by anything but allergy. The characteristic gesture of rubbing the nose with the heel of the hand is known in the USA as the allergic salute. Once seen always recognized!

Ear symptoms

Noises in the ears on blowing or swallowing may be caused by swelling and blockage of the end of the Eustachian tubes. This may cause fluid in the ear (serous otitis media) and deafness. Itchy palate, throat and ears usually indicate allergy.

Small stature

The chronic allergic child may not grow as fast or be as robust as other children in the family, and be smaller than a brother or sister who is a year or so younger.

Faulty posture

Chronic asthmatic children develop a stoop resulting from curvature of the spine to accommodate the over inflated lungs. The upper spine bends backwards, the lower spine forwards, producing an S shape, thus pushing out the stomach and giving a pot-bellied appearance. Adult chronic asthmatics often have a similar appearance.

Pigeon chest

The breast bone is unduly prominent, and the lower ribs are pulled inwards, producing an appearance resembling the breast of a bird. This can also be a family characteristic, but it is usually the result of uncontrolled chronic asthma which is sometimes not diagnosed at all.

How can a cause/effect relationship be established?

The observation that symptoms always occur after an encounter with a specific substance is crucial to the establishment of a cause/effect relationship. The potential allergen may be inhaled, ingested or contacted, and the interval between the encounter and the symptoms may vary from seconds to 24 hours, rarely longer.

The cause of a perennial allergy may lie in the home environment, occupation, hobbies, food, drink or pharmaceutical or cosmetic preparations. Daily symptoms imply daily exposure or contact, and rapid improvement on holiday with relapse on return should direct suspicion to environmental factors. If one is not better on holiday in this country, but symptom-free in a high or dry climate, both dust and pets are suspect, especially if the pets are taken on holiday in this country. If one is neither better nor worse in the Mediterranean area or on a cruise, foods or the yeast in wine and beer may be important. The elucidation of such information patterns by persistent enquiry may provide significant clues to the cause or causes, but these patterns must be reproducible. For example, asthma every Sunday in men can be due to more beer on Saturday night, or in working women to doing all the housework on Saturdays.

Should allergy sufferers try to find the cause of their own allergic problems?

It has been said that the doctor who chooses to be his or her own physician has a fool for a doctor, so to suggest that someone suffering from an allergic problem might, by applying the information in this book in a common sense way, have a chance of finding the cause without further help could be considered a much more serious heresy. All I will say is that in my opinion there can be nothing wrong in sufferers trying to help themselves as long as they do not do anything foolish or dangerous.

It is advisable for anyone contemplating such a course to remember that every symptom caused by allergy can also be caused by a medical condition unrelated to allergy. To consult with your medical adviser to make sure that some serious problem is not being overlooked is a wise precaution. This done, I see no good reason why self-help should not be encouraged. It might be said that some people could become obsessional and neurotic, but my personal experience has been that the patient who develops emotional problems usually does so because of fear born of ignorance, and that the more patients understand about the problem the more confident and the less anxious they become.

It is for these and other reasons that I produced a 'multiple-choice' questionnaire for recording case histories before the first interview, which is designed to establish whether the symptoms fit any special pattern, and whether any avoiding action has a chance of giving relief or reducing medication requirements. This way of presenting such information is, I think, a new idea, and it will be interesting to find out if it will be successful.

How is an allergic problem investigated?

The investigation of an illness suspected of being caused by an allergic reaction should proceed along broad guidelines which have been very slowly established as a result of both clinical and scientific research over many years. A doctor deeply involved with allergic patients receives a great deal of information from their observations on their own symptoms. Although such evidence is subjective, cannot be measured, and may be biased or incorrect, it may also be relevant, accurate and important. It should never be disregarded or dismissed, especially if many patients report symptoms in similar circumstances, because they may be providing a significant clue to the cause of their problems. The reports often describe the effects of reactions which are imperfectly understood, but an attempt at interpretation in the light of current knowledge can be attempted. Human patients are unique because they can communicate with the investigator, if he or she will listen. It is often as a result of this kind of feedback that the clinical investigator has ideas which are years ahead of his or her scientific colleagues, who may eventually provide scientific proof. The clinical investigator can thus play the part of a centralized clearing depot where information is sorted, integrated, and analysed, rather like a computer, but much more discriminating.

The first step is for the investigating doctor to elicit from the patient the full story of the illness, and by skilful informed questioning to gain a fairly clear idea as to whether the problem is allergic in causation or not. If the evidence is in favour of allergy, the questions must be structured in such a way that the patient's responses suggest first the broad category of likely cause, and then, by a process of narrowing down the possibilities, the correct answer or answers.

How should the history of an allergic problem be obtained?

Taking the case history should enable the doctor to obtain the maximum information in the minimum time, but is a neglected art today. Patients cannot possibly know which symptoms are significant because they lack the knowledge. Leading questions are essential lest the more odd-seeming items of information are held back because the patient fears ridicule or disbelief. It is of paramount importance to listen to the patient because, even though a statement may not make sense now, it might do so in future. An unusual observation by a patient has often proved significant when followed up. Taking the case history is an acquired skill. I can recall that 25 years ago to interrogate and investigate only two allergic problems in an afternoon was completely exhausting.

What are the important facts in an allergy case history?

Listed below are the important areas which should be covered when an allergy case history is taken. You may like to go through them with reference to your own case – you may find a clue to your problem.

Basic details

Age   Indicates general trends. For example from birth to 2 years is most likely to be a food problem, from then to 40 inhalant allergies are more likely, and over 40 there are often no clues.

Sex   More boys develop allergies than girls, but more boys get better spontaneously (though not enough to justify waiting to find out if the problem is a serious one).

Race   Ethnic origins can have some effect. People from Asia tend to get mite and pollen allergies when they come to the West, but seldom keep pets. Those born here are just as likely as the rest of the population to develop allergies.

Family history   History of allergic or possibly allergic problems in both sides of the family for at least three generations should be taken into account. The information may be incomplete, and the effects of heredity difficult to assess, but as a rule the more allergics there are, the more likely it is that the subject in question is also suffering from an allergic problem, especially if both sides of the family are affected. Eczema and urticaria are allergic, and they count even if the trouble did not persist for long. Migraine, colitis, and arthritis are only sometimes associated with allergy.

Key questions

Is the complaint present:

All year? Suggests that the cause is always present at home or at work or both.

Summer only? Indicates purely seasonal problem excluding home/work.

All year, worse in summer? Indicates presence of both perennial and seasonal factors as above, hence a more complex problem.

All year, worse in winter? Indicates bronchitis rather than allergic asthma, especially if chronic cough, spit, and frequent infection in winter.

What is the:

Age of onset? Onset in infancy, perhaps as eczema or gut problems, may suggest a food background, most likely to be milk. Onset in childhood or early adult life usually due to inhalants such as dust or pets. Onset for first time in middle or later life, often with rhinitis and polyps, is usually a mystery, sometimes the person is allergic to aspirin.

Duration of allergic problems? Very recent onset may cause difficulty because there has been no time for a pattern to form. Longstanding problems suggest that there may be some permanent damage, but younger patients usually respond well to treatment no matter how long the duration of the complaint.

Is the asthma/rhinitis:

Worse at weekends? Sufferers may do most of the housework at weekends, thus concentrating the dust exposure. The weekend may be a time for getting out into the country, exposing oneself to pollens and animals, or it may be a time for indulging in hobbies. More beer may be drunk at weekends.

Worse at home or worse inside, better outside? Suggests environmental factors such as dust or pets.

Worse on rising? Typical of house dust or other bed allergen.

Worse at night? Suggests environmental causes such as dust, pets, bedding, ducted air heating, and old damp houses with no damp course, or with cellars, and perhaps dry rot.

Perennial chest symptoms

Production and character of sputum Yellow or green and thick usually, but not always, indicates infection. Hard lumps like string or worms, or little hard lumps like sago, are due to asthma. Asthmatic sputum is sticky, gelatinous and very difficult to get up.

Wheezing, coughing, shortness of breath Unvarying symptoms every day suggest bronchitis rather than allergic asthma, but *not* always. Obvious improvement on holiday in the sun suggests asthma. Varying from one day to the next, worse at night and on rising favours asthma strongly, and allergy investigation desirable.

Worse at work The typical pattern of worse at work, better at the weekend and on holiday, with a relapse on return to work, suggests an occupational cause. However, the weekend may not be long enough to give relief, so that prompt relapse after a longer absence may be a better pointer to occupational asthma. Can be proved by an individual peak flow meter used over several weeks to show the pattern.

Asthma on exercise or from cold air, fumes or smoke Mostly children and younger people. The amount of exercise required to provoke asthma may vary a great deal. Shortness of breath *without* wheezing is a normal response to exercise. Allergy, usually to dust or pets, is often present, especially in children.

Easily suppressed with drugs, but full investigation for allergy advisable, because drugs do not cure. Removal of cause will eventually cause decrease in irritability of bronchi. Desensitization can be very effective.

Nasal symptoms

Chronic nasal symptoms Chronic nasal allergy, may be the unrecognized cause of chronic nasal problems, such as chronic nasal catarrh, frequent sinusitis, sinus washouts, or nasal polyps. Polyps are nearly always allergic, associated with chronic rhinitis and sinusitis. Rhinitis often produces disproportionate disability. Blockage, stuffiness, inability to smell, attacks of incessant sneezing and running nose, can be so distressing that concurrent severe chronic asthma may be completely overlooked because it is not the main complaint.

Severe seasonal hay fever and asthma Severe seasonal hay fever causes symptoms which can be more obviously troublesome to the patient than seasonal asthma, which may not be recognized if the patient is sedentary.

Severity of past asthmatic attacks

Unable to get out of bed, walk or dress This is very important for assessment. To have been so bad, even once, is a sign that the asthma is severe, potentially dangerous, and should have specialist attention. This degree of seasonal asthma can be very dangerous indeed.

Unable to walk up a slight hill or a flight of stairs If this is occurring constantly or frequently, investigation and assessment is desirable or essential. If seasonal asthma is of this severity medical help *must* be obtained.

Home environment

How long in present house? The house is suspect if the problem began soon after moving in, e.g. moving from modern dry house to old, damp, larger house.

Is house damp? Old houses, and some new ones too, may be damp and mouldy. Cellar/lack of damp course are bad features. Surveyor may have missed dry rot, which may follow flooding.

How is house heated? Recent installation of central heating in an old house may produce mould growth if ventilation is inadequate. Ducted air heating keeps dust moving and is the *worst* for allergic families. Gas fumes from improperly installed flues for fires or boilers, and pilot lights, can affect certain people severely.

What about floor coverings and furnishings? The ideal is polished wood or tiled floors throughout – normal is fitted carpets, sometimes even in the kitchen! Carpets provide the perfect habitat for mites. Some patients are affected by new wool carpets until they settle down. Furniture may have feather cushions (which are important to a minority only).

Bedding? Synthetic bedding on a rubber foam mattress may be best, but feather pillows and eiderdowns are only sometimes important, and experimentation is necessary.

Pets? Dealt with elsewhere – a realistic approach is an essential. Pets and allergy do not mix, especially in the bedroom or the bed. Sensitivity can be extreme, and the pets of previous owners of the house can cause serious problems.

Affected by housework? Activities such as bedmaking, dusting, spring cleaning, shaking blankets and emptying vacuum-cleaner bags all involve exposure to the flying excreta of the dust mite, which is by far the commonest perennial allergen. Faulty vacuum-cleaner bags will disseminate this excreta.

Cleaning out the house of a deceased elderly relative? The exposure to the dust of ages can awaken a latent allergy to dust or feathers, in the relatives of the deceased, and sometimes this will not stop once it has been triggered off.

Holidays

Britain Seasonal cases tend to be worst on the East and South

Coasts, and better on the West due to prevailing westerly winds – but this is a general trend only. Perennial cases may be worse if the dog goes too, and is in closer proximity in a caravan or tent. Dogs and cats may be encountered in hotels.

Northern France, the Low Countries, North Germany There may not be much difference, as climate, vegetation, and housing are quite similar. Pollen season May – June.

Southern France, Spain, Italy and around the Mediterranean, the Canaries Warm dry summers, tiled floors, sand, sea and sun will usually be beneficial to asthma, eczema and rhinitis.

The USA and Canada A wide range of allergens, so it depends where and when you go. In winter the mould-sensitive patient will be happy because of the intense cold.

Hot dry countries Beneficial to most asthmatics and rhinitis sufferers, and some cases of eczema.

Returning home Seasonal allergies may have had complete relief, but slowly relapse on driving north as the climate changes and seasonal allergens reappear in the air. Returning by air can produce dramatic relapse at the airport or on the way home from there. Perennial environment allergies do not relapse until home is reached, and will have returned as usual by the next day.

Hobbies and home improvements

DIY All kinds of DIY activities can cause exposure to toxic fumes, chemicals and various dusts, often under conditions which would not be tolerated in industry. Sanding exotic woods and repairing old furniture may cause problems. When painting and decorating, cleaning down exposes to dust. Fumes of paint thinners and drying paint often cause a flare-up of asthma, some paints being worse than others. The skin may suffer too.

Knitting Asthma and rhinitis can be caused by sheep wool, angora (rabbit) or by mohair (goat), but not by synthetics.

Electronics   Asthma may be provoked by resin-cored solder fumes or violin bow resin.

Alterations to house   Often causes asthma for the first time by gross-exposure to old dust triggering off a latent dust allergy.

Household cleaning agents

Enzyme washing powders, household aerosols, air fresheners, spray polish, fabric softeners, and detergents, are all chemicals which may be present in the home environment and can cause allergic problems.   The quickest way to find out if they are causing trouble is to stop using everything.

Cosmetics

Deodorants, aftershave, talcum powder, hair lacquer, shampoos, hair dyes, scent and cosmetics can all cause allergic problems with the skin, or by inhalation may trigger asthma.   Pinpointing the cause often entails stopping everything then trying them out one by one.

Chemicals in the air, water or food

It is believed by clinical ecologists that these factors are important in the causation of many diseases. Some people recover in a special environment free from pollution, and it may be very important to assess the role of chemical pollution as a cause of disease. This is discussed elsewhere.

Occupational allergies

Occupational allergic problems have already been discussed. All that is necessary here is to draw attention to the high-risk occupations. Those most affected are animal breeders, jockeys, veterinarians, farmers and scientists.

Problems caused by foods

These are dealt with in greater detail in the chapters on food allergy.

Birth weight   Useful to know, especially if premature and had intensive care in the first few days. May have had bank breast milk, or cow's milk formula.

Duration of breast-feeding   Even 3 days helps by supplying maternal antibodies. Eczema on breast suggests a revision of maternal diet to exclude egg, milk, cereals, nuts, and so on, and it may be helpful to do skin tests. Colic often means allergy to cow's milk.

Start of bottle-feeding   Bottle-feeding from the start may mean trouble from the start. If problems began when changed from breast to bottle, this is an important pointer to cow's milk allergy.

Start of weaning   Problems such as eczema or gut upsets beginning at this point or within a few months suggest new foods added are suspect. Colic, diarrhoea, vomiting and skin problems may start now.

History of infant feeding problems in adults and in several blood relatives   Cow's milk should be considered as a possible cause, no matter what the age or complaint of the sufferer may be. Milk- and beef-free diet is always worth a try.

Dislike or craving for specific foods   Children should never be forced to eat foods they dislike, as they may know instinctively that they will react in some way. Craving for certain foods is also an indication of a possible allergy to that food, and suggests that it should be avoided for a trial period.

Cream and butter   Some milk allergics can tolerate cream and butter but in unusual cases the milk fat is the cause, not the milk protein.

Cheese   This is a very variable product which may not be tolerated by milk allergics, and sometimes seems to be a very potent cause. Cheese is an amazing mixture of biological products. Mould-sensitive people cannot tolerate mould blue cheeses.

Beef With the cow being the main source of milk, beef is frequently overlooked as a cause of allergy. Many milk allergics cannot tolerate it. Steaks are often treated with papain enzyme tenderizer, sometimes injected intravenously before slaughter.

Eggs, nuts, fish and shellfish Effects are often dramatic, affecting lips, throat, chest, gut, and skin. Extreme sensitivity is common, and sufferers have usually found out by bitter experience. Sometimes a hidden factor, e.g. fish oils in margarine, can flare up eczema caused by fish. Also, peanut oil used in cooking can be a hidden source of trouble (arachis oil is peanut, and nut oil may be found in vegetable oil).

Yeast Yeast is full of B group vitamins, is a flavouring agent, and is added to all manner of foods and spices, e.g. Oxo, Bovril, Marmite. It seldom produces a skin test but undoubtedly causes many allergic problems. People sometimes take yeast tablets to get better, but get worse instead! Symptoms may be put down to wine, beer, and so on, but avoidance of fermented liquors *and* other sources of yeast are essential for success.

Wheat, oats, barley, maize, and so on Allergic problems, such as eczema, which begin when wheat is introduced to diet, may be due to allergy to wheat or other cereals. Rice can usually be tolerated. Any age is susceptible.

Syrups and sugars Honey, beet sugar, cane sugar or corn syrup may be involved. Total exclusion followed by controlled reintroduction may indicate whether a certain type of sugar is causing problems. Saccharine can be used meanwhile and lack of sugar will be good for the teeth. Allergy to sugars is quite often diagnosed in the USA but is a controversial area.

Problems when food is being prepared Even the smell of an egg can affect sensitive subjects. The person preparing the food may not react, while a child in the house does. Licking out the bowl which has contained an egg mixture can cause obvious problems. Scraping new potatoes causes a fine spray in the air which can cause reactions in the eyes, nose or chest. This is surprisingly common, and a good indicator of an allergic tendency, but easily avoided. The actual cause has never been isolated, but must be in the skin of the new potato only.

Food dyes, additives and preservatives   This subject is dealt with in detail in the chapter on foods.

Alcoholic drinks and yeast

Beer and cider   All alcoholic drinks are fermented with yeast, traces of which remain to cause allergies. Sometimes one type of beer causes asthma or rhinitis, while others do not. Reactions can be to alcohol, yeast or the many additives. There are many additives to beer, many of which are secret, so that the only tests are by trial and error.

Sherry, Martini, Port, Champagne, and so on   Made with special strains of yeast, and can cause runny nose and sneezing every evening. Martini is a secret formula containing all sorts of ingredients, champagne has high yeast content, due to the way it is made. Can cause acute asthma at weddings.

Wine   Effects variable and can be quite specific. Some people can drink only cheap wine, others only vintage, some white, some red. As with beer, there are many possible additives and it is impossible to know all of them. Reactions can be to alcohol, yeast or the many additives, and especially sulphites used as preservatives.

Whisky   Traces of the barley and yeast can set off the susceptible patient.

Brandy liqueurs   Allergies uncommon – links with wine allergy.

Gin, vodka   These are relatively pure alcohol, with no trace of yeast, so yeast allergics can tolerate these, but true alcohol allergics cannot.

Soft drinks, ice lollies, sweets, chocolates, aerated waters, and so on   Contain preservatives and dyes and may cause respiratory and other problems. Sulphur dioxide (SO_2) gas is used as a preservative, and can cause bronchospasm in some people just after drinking pop. Sodium benzoate and other preservative chemicals may also cause reactions. Dyes and preservatives are dealt with in the food section, but establishment of a cause/effect relationship is vital for diagnosis.

Problems caused by medicines

Aspirin Will cause severe asthma in many people who have nasal polyps. Contained in many mixed preparations – always check label (proper name is acetylsalicylic acid). But in rare cases of asthma aspirin will cause remarkable improvement!

Non-steroid anti-inflammatory drugs (NSAID) These drugs are given for rheumatism, and have similar effects to aspirin. There are a great many of these preparations.

Penicillin Allergy can cause fatal anaphylaxis following an injection, but is rare. Cause was often due to impurities in the penicillin, now removed, but can still happen. Anybody who has had a bad reaction should wear a Medic-Alert bracelet. Rashes are the commonest reaction to this drug and its variants.

Other antibiotics Allergic sensitization is possible to any of the antibiotics, which are often extracted from moulds or bacteria. Reactions to injections are potentially dangerous, but most antibiotics are now given orally. Hence, vomiting, diarrhoea and rashes are commonly the result. Sometimes difficult to be sure, but availability of many alternatives has simplified these problems, except that a reaction to penicillin means none of the penicillin group can be taken, and so on. *Always tell the doctor if you have had a reaction.*

Dyes, additives, syrups, flavourings In spite of evidence showing harmful effects, colouring and flavourings are used extensively in all sorts of medicines. The usual food dyes and preservatives are used, but unfortunately these are not listed on the label. Hence your doctor, unaware of the full list of contents, may innocently prescribe for you a medicine containing additives to which you are allergic.

12 Scientific tests which may help to find the cause of your allergy

In the present state of knowledge, the clinical history, and the rare skills and specialized knowledge required in obtaining the information from the patient, are still very necessary. The reason is that none of the results of scientific tests will give a definite diagnosis of the cause of the allergic symptoms, except the rather crude method of direct challenge (*see* later in this chapter). Thus to obtain clear proof requires controlled exposure to produce symptoms, ideally under double-blind conditions where neither patient nor doctor is aware of which testing material is active.

At the end of this chapter, Table 12.1 lists some of the most common fallacies about allergies, including several concerning the various tests you may come across.

Why is the skin used for allergy testing?

The skin grows in layers, the outermost horny layer being dead skin which protects the living skin underneath. This horny layer is being continually cast off, especially in bed. If we wish to test the true skin for sensitivity it is essential to get below the external horny layer to reach the living cells and blood vessels of the skin beneath. If we select a part of the body where the skin is of uniform thickness and easy to get at, such as the forearm or the back, the horny layer is less than 1mm thick. These facts are the basis for skin testing with allergens. The method depends on the introduction of a tiny amount of an allergen into the skin so that it comes into contact with living skin cells.

It is a curious fact that although the skin is not directly involved in the inhalant allergies, such as asthma and hay fever, sensitized mast cells are present in large numbers in the deeper layers of the skin. Thus they are lying there like a microscopic minefield, waiting to be set off by the specific allergens used for skin testing.

What causes a skin reaction to an allergen?

If the mast cells have been sensitized by a specific allergen, such as grass pollen, the surface of the cell will have many molecules of specific IgE developed against grass pollen stuck on it. When grass pollen molecules touch the cell they bridge across the specific IgE stuck on the cell surface. This triggers the break-up of the cell, with the secretion of toxic chemicals, such as histamine and many others. One effect of these chemicals, known as 'mediators', is to damage the capillaries, the walls of which are composed of only a single layer of cells, so that it is easy to cause leakage of fluid, including large protein molecules, from the blood plasma. Furthermore, just as in the case of any inflammation in the tissues, some of the mediators which are released get into the bloodstream to summon other special cells, which rush to the spot to carry out their special functions.

In older people there may be so few mast cells that it is impossible for a skin reaction to occur. Introducing a little histamine into the skin will always cause a reaction if the skin is capable of reacting, so it is used as a control test. If the histamine test is negative the skin of that patient will not react to anything, so testing is a waste of time.

What methods are used for skin testing?

Unfortunately no materials for prick skin testing are now manufactured in Britain, because all three companies who made the extracts have withdrawn completely, since allergy injections became impossible in 1986. As a result there are great difficulties in obtaining supplies.

Table 12.1   Common fallacies about allergies

False belief	Correction
Positive skin tests always give meaningful answers.	Only sometimes, and then only if the clinical history agrees with the positive skin test. Tests carried out inexpertly or using blunt instruments can cause many false positive reactions.
Negative skin tests mean that there is no sensitivity to that allergen, or that the problem is not an allergic one.	Testing extracts may be impotent or tests not properly done. Skin tests are often falsely negative in food allergy. Skin may not react in older people. Anti-histamines can suppress skin tests.
Skin tests cannot be done in babies or below the age of 6 years or in eczema, and are useless in old age.	Prick tests can be done at any age, even on a newborn baby. In eczema there may be difficulty in finding areas of normal skin, but there is no reason not to do skin tests. Skin reactions in old people may be very helpful, if the histamine control is positive.
Food allergies can be diagnosed by blood tests or skin tests.	The clinical history gives the most important information. Positive skin tests may be confirmed by blood tests, but neither skin nor blood tests, nor cytotoxic tests, are reliable for food allergy.
Cytotoxic tests can produce useful answers.	These tests are completely unreliable, and the results on the same blood sample can vary from day to day. Healthy people often give positive results.
Steroids are dangerous.	Steroids should be a crutch when essential, and are not dangerous for short-term use. The danger is in withholding steroids when needed.
Many shrubs and flowers cause allergic problems.	Positive skin tests for insect-pollinated plants may not be significant, as the pollen cannot be inhaled in quantity. Allergy to flowers is rare, and avoidance is the simple answer.

Table 12.1   Common fallacies about allergies

False belief	Correction
Steroid drugs will inhibit skin tests.	Only in huge doses seldom or never used outside hospital. Anti-histamines definitely suppress skin tests but strong reactions still occur to a lesser extent.
Steroids orally will harm the unborn child.	Oral steroids when essential have never been shown to harm the foetus in any way.
Steroids by inhalation such as Becotide or Beconase and Intal, should not be given in pregnancy.	Inhaled steroids have been shown clearly to have no such effects, yet abortion has been advised! Treatment must *not* be stopped in pregnancy – lack of oxygen in an attack of asthma is likely to harm the baby. Hence, it is essential to control asthma properly in pregnancy.

Intra-dermal testing

In continental Europe and the USA intra-dermal testing is popular. A fine syringe and needle are used to inject a tiny amount of the allergen into the deeper layers of the skin. This method is painful, requires skill and expensive syringes, and is not free from risk in very sensitive patients. Although seldom used in Britain for allergy testing, this method is much more sensitive than other methods but is liable to produce false positive reactions.

Prick testing

Prick testing, where a tiny prick is made with a needle through a drop of the allergen placed on the skin, is the method of choice in Britain, Scandinavia and many other countries. A great advantage is that the amount of allergen introduced into the skin is very small indeed, so there is no risk of the most sensitive patient having a nasty reaction to a test.

Separate needles should be used for each test, but this unfortunately is not always what happens. Where the same needle is used for all tests, with only a wipe on a piece of cotton wool between each test, sufficient of the stronger allergens may be carried over on the needle from one test to the next and many false positives may be produced. I have seen many patients tested elsewhere by such clumsy methods, who are said to 'react to everything'.

Patch testing

This type of skin test is usually carried out in the skin (dermatology) department where it is used to find the cause of contact dermatitis.

The patch test is applied to the skin of the back, covered by a patch of special adhesive tape and left for 48 hours, when it is taken off and the site of the test inspected for signs of reaction. A contact allergy is limited to the sensitized skin cells, which react slowly, because this is a cellular-immunity type of reaction as previously described (Chapter 1). Thus it differs greatly from the immediate-type reaction caused by a prick test, which occurs in 15 minutes.

This test identifies the cause of the dermatitis and what to avoid, because once skin becomes sensitized it tends to remain so for many years. For example, builders may become sensitive to the chromium in cement, so they often have to find a job which does not entail contact with cement or chromium.

What does a positive reaction to a prick skin test look like?

The result of this complex explosion of the mast cells with liberation of mediator chemicals is to cause the leakage of so much fluid from the tiny capillaries that the skin becomes raised and swollen, forming a 'wheal'. This reaction begins with itching, within a few minutes, and then the wheal begins to appear, with a raised edge which slowly expands to reach its maximum size in about 15 minutes. Very occasionally the wheal will reach 2.5cm across, and round it is a wider zone of redness and itching, but even a sizeable reaction will fade out within a few hours.

Prick tests introduce such a small amount of allergen into the skin that they are quite safe. Sometimes the reaction subsides normally but returns the following day as diffuse swelling of the forearm, which may last a day or so. This is usually caused by the mould *Aspergillus fumigatus*, but can occur to a lesser extent with other allergens. A delayed reaction should be reported as it is quite important that the doctor should be aware that it has occurred.

What is the significance of positive skin-test reactions?

The interpretation of skin-test reactions to allergens is of the greatest importance, and not a matter to leave to the uninitiated. The presence of a positive skin-test reaction simply means that the *skin* of that particular patient is sensitive to a greater or lesser degree to the allergenic extract being used for testing. It does not automatically mean that this allergen is significant for that patient.

For example, many people have a positive skin-test reaction to grass pollen or to dust mite without ever having had any symptoms whatever. Perhaps this false positive predicts future problems with these allergens. Conversely, patients who have had problems many years ago still have positive skin tests for allergens to which they are no longer sensitive. This means only that they still have sufficient sensitized mast cells in their skin to give a positive test, but in the really important parts of the body, such as the nose or the bronchi, they are no longer clinically sensitive.

In a patient who exhibits obvious skin-test reactions to many allergens and also has symptoms, a decision has to be made as to which allergens are important. This cannot be done unless the physician is in possession of the full clinical details of the case, particularly the history. A positive skin-test reaction by itself is a meaningless piece of information, because it may mean past, present or even future sensitivity to an allergen.

For example a patient may have a violently positive skin test to a cat, yet has never had a cat and never comes close to one, so this skin reaction is not relevant. On the other hand, if the patient has a cat which is clearly the cause, then the cat must go, unless so many friends and relations also have cats that it seems more appropriate to attempt to desensitize the patient against cats, as being unavoidable. Intense reactions to animals in a person who has never had any direct contact with animals should not, however, be lightly dismissed – remembering the mother who developed asthma from her daughter's contaminated riding clothes, her skin reaction to horse being the only clue to the cause.

From the above the reader might assume that skin tests are useless. In fact they are only part of the investigation, and are a guide which should never be taken at face value. Sometimes an unexpected positive reaction, such as to the mould *Aspergillus fumigatus*, may shed entirely new light on an old problem. Skin tests for house dust, house-dust mite, dog, cat, horse, rabbit and grass pollen are the most reliable and significant, and these are also by far the commonest allergens. Prick tests with these allergens alone will often be sufficient to indicate that the patient is an allergic, and to suggest the likely cause. Unfortunately, prick skin testing is often left to nurses or very junior medical staff who are not fully trained in how to do them and how to interpret them.

Ragweed pollen is a very potent allergen in North America, causing severe allergy problems. Different allergens have to be used for testing in different parts of the USA, as the climate and vegetation vary from one part to another.

What is the significance of a negative skin-test reaction?

A negative response to a skin test with an allergen may be brought about in several ways apart from the patient not being allergic to the substance being tested. The skin may not be capable of reacting to anything (as in some old people). The testing extract may be impotent, or the test may not have been carried out properly so that no allergen reached the sensitive cells in the skin. Sometimes the patient is taking anti-histamine drugs, which suppress skin reactions, but this has little effect on really intense positive reactions. Finally, negative skin-test responses may be due to the fact that the correct allergen is not available for testing, or the correct allergen is unknown and is still to be discovered.

Are allergen extracts standardized?

Attempts by international committees to establish international standards for allergens for testing and treatment have not been successful. Comparing the potency of allergenic extracts using sophisticated techniques of assay showed that even when the labels alleged that the strength of the contents was the same, the test results showed that some could be a thousand times stronger than others. Admirable efforts are now being made in Scandinavia to supply pure material to very high standards.

If the testing extracts are inactive, completely misleading false negative results will be obtained. This can be of great importance when there is a suspicion of allergy to a pet. Many doctors may be disposed to accept the results at their face value, not realizing these pitfalls. This recently happened in a case where the patient suspected that the cat was the cause of her almost lifelong asthma. Her general practitioner sent her to have a skin test done, but it was negative, so the cat was allowed to stay. When I tested her she had one of the biggest skin reactions to cats I have ever seen!

Can prick skin testing be standardized?

About 10 years ago, because of the difficulties discussed above, it appeared to me that the least we could do to improve reproducibility of the results was to standardize the injury to the skin, and thus also standardize the dose of allergen which contacts the sensitized mast cells. A special instrument was made which consisted of a steel rod with a flat end from which a needle protruded a measured distance. This was plunged through a drop of testing extract placed on the skin, so that some allergen was carried into the skin on the point of the needle. By experiment it was found that a needle length of 1mm or 1.25mm would produce a positive reaction without causing bleeding, and confirmed that identical results could be produced consistently by unskilled operators. Thus, the injury to the skin, at least, can be standardized, and plastic disposable standard needles have now been introduced. This method is ideal for testing children because it hurts much less, and is not so frightening. Using a standard needle also means that testing extracts of different origins can be compared effectively on the same patient, thus quickly detecting useless materials.

('Morrow Brown' plastic disposable skin testing needles are now being used widely in the USA, France, Spain, Italy and other countries – but there is almost no demand in the UK.)

What are the most important allergens for which skin testing is used?

Environmental

House dust and house-dust mite are probably the most important in this group, along with feathers. Wool, which is so common in our western environment, does not seem to produce much skin reaction to prick tests.

Pets are of major importance, mainly dogs, cats, horses and rabbits, but potent testing material for other popular pets such as hamsters or guinea-pigs is not so easily obtained. Rubbing a small bunch of hair into the skin can be used to produce a significant reaction.

Seasonal

Grass pollen is the most common and important, usually a mixture of the main species. Tree pollen is also used as a mixture, but it is probably better to use only the trees commonest in the area, most often birch, hazel, alder, ash and oak. The only seasonal moulds which give skin-test responses are *Cladosporium, Botrytis* and *Alternaria*, but they are not reliable.

Perennial and food allergens

Perennial mould spores, such as *Penicillium* and *Aspergillus*, which are found in damp houses, are the most important of those giving good skin-test results. Amongst the foods, fish, shellfish, egg and various nuts, especially peanut and hazelnut, seem to give reliable reactions, but milk, yeast, cereals and beans are often most disappointing and unreliable.

Is skin testing dangerous?

The prick method of skin testing has never been found to cause a really severe or dangerous reaction, and this is the method in general use. The intra-dermal test, where a tiny amount of allergen is injected into the deeper layers of the skin, can cause dangerous generalized reactions, but this is exceptionally rare, and this sort of test is seldom used in Britain. Elsewhere, it is usual to carry out prick tests first to identify the persons who might react badly to an intra-dermal test. It is believed that the intra-dermal test may pick up important allergies which might be missed by the less sensitive prick test, but many allergists suspect that the intra-dermal method produces many false positive reactions.

At what age can skin tests be carried out?

There is a common, but completely mistaken, belief that skin tests should not be carried out in children below 5 or in infants. In fact, prick skin tests can be done at any age, especially using standardized disposable plastic needles which are almost completely painless. Skin testing in babies where there are feeding problems, even when wholly breast-fed, may be very helpful indeed, as positive reactions of great significance are seen when there is allergy to items in the maternal diet. Skin testing with standard needles has been used on new-born babies, so as to pick up those who have become sensitized by foods in the maternal diet before birth.

Should skin tests be carried out on eczematous patients?

Prick skin tests can be most informative in patients with eczema, and may alert to avoidable factors such as egg, fish, mites or animals. Some part of the body with a clear area of skin can usually be found, but exceptionally the skin may have to be cleared by a few days on oral steroids before skin tests can be done. Dermatology departments seldom carry out prick tests for allergens in eczema cases and have been known to refuse requests to do so. The reasons for this attitude are obscure.

Does a positive skin test mean that desensitizing injections of that allergen should be given?

Skin testing is only a *part* of the investigation of an allergic problem, which must always be viewed as a whole, and *all* the evidence reviewed and evaluated by the physician. Skin test results by themselves are meaningless, but unfortunately there are certain clinics where skin testing constitutes the major part of the investigation of an allergic case. So-called desensitizing vaccines may be recommended which contain every allergen to which the patient's skin has reacted. Sometimes the numbers of ingredients exceed even the fifty-seven varieties of Heinz & Co.

The hapless patient may be injected by the general practitioner with a jumbled mishmash in which the few relevant allergens will be so diluted with irrelevant ones that the dose will be too minute to achieve any benefit. This sort of 'foreign protein cocktail' simply leads to disappointed patients and disillusioned doctors, who become more firmly convinced than ever that allergy investigation is quackery. This approach has done a great disservice to the speciality of allergy and its treatment, and doubtless influenced the Committee for Safety when they decided to discourage injections.

How useful is the RAST test for allergy?

The story of the discovery of immunoglobulin E (IgE) has already been told. When very sensitive methods of detecting and measuring IgE were invented in 1970 it became possible to measure the amount of IgE in the blood serum. This test uses radioactivity and is called the radio-allergo-sorbent test – the 'RAST' test. This test measures the total amount of IgE, which over a certain figure indicates that the patient has an allergy (or worms) and can also measure exactly how much of the total IgE is directed to each specific allergen to which the patient is sensitive.

This discovery was greeted with great enthusiasm because it held the promise that an accurate diagnosis of the cause of the allergy could be made in the laboratory from a blood sample. This proved an illusion, however, as the results of the RAST test are just as difficult to interpret as skin tests and there is such close correlation between skin tests with the more powerful allergens and the RAST test that skin testing gives the same answers at much less cost.

Experience showed that RAST results did not correlate with the clinical situation any better than skin-test reactions. Nevertheless, attempts have been made to achieve a postal diagnosis and suggestions for treatment, based on a blood sample and a questionnaire. This test has serious limitations, and fails to produce answers just when they are most needed. RAST screening tests carried out in the hope of finding an answer to a food allergic problem are only sometimes useful for the diagnosis of food allergies, and a negative result is usually quite meaningless.

Thus, it is important that those who use the RAST test should become much more aware of its limitations and shortcomings. Results from different laboratories in the USA for strong allergens such as pollen, dog, cat, and mites were found to vary by up to 60 per cent for the same test specimen, so accuracy is also poor.

How is a RAST test carried out?

A blood sample of 5–20ml is taken from a vein and allowed to clot. The serum is separated and tested in the immunology laboratory.

Discs of filter paper which have been coated with pure allergen are exposed to the patient's serum. If the serum contains specific IgE antibody to the allergen which is present on the disc it will stick avidly to it. The disc is then washed and exposed to a solution containing radioactive anti-IgE, which will adhere to the specific IgE from the patient's serum which is stuck to the disc. Thus disc, specific IgE and radioactive anti-IgE are all stuck together so that the radioactivity cannot be washed away. The measurement of this radioactivity which remains is an index of the amount of specific IgE present in the patient's serum.

What has RAST testing contributed to allergy research?

While RAST and many other technical procedures are fascinating research tools, we have only lifted the edge of the curtain which covers the mysteries of the immunology of allergy. There is still no substitute for the careful analysis of the whole case by an experienced allergy specialist, because immunology in its present state of development can only produce crude answers. The complex interplay between the allergen or allergens and the whole human organism seems unlikely to be unravelled by the tests so far evolved. Unfortunately both doctors and patients tend to place undue reliance on test-tube diagnosis, often leading to disillusionment, disappointment or even wrong treatment. Many very severe, but definitely allergic, problems have negative skin and RAST tests and it is clear that at this time the scientific diagnosis of the cause of an allergy is not to be relied upon. Constant efforts are being made world-wide to develop new tests which eventually may be a real help to the clinical allergist.

What is the precipitin test?

In cases who are very intensely sensitive to the mould *Aspergillus*, the serum may contain antibodies against this mould. This is easily demonstrated by putting a mould extract and some blood serum together, in the right proportions, in the laboratory. The presence of antibody can be seen, because when it comes together with the allergen it forms a precipitate. This type of test is used for various conditions, particularly for farmer's and bird-fancier's lung, where the presence of precipitins helps towards a firm diagnosis.

Can living cells be tested in the test tube?

It is obvious that if living cells from the patient could be isolated and grown in a test tube, it might be possible, by exposing these cells to allergens, to find out to which allergens the cells are sensitive. This simple concept has proved most difficult to carry out successfully, except as a research tool. There are many cells to choose from, growing cells in culture is not easy, and these techniques are difficult and expensive.

Stimulating cells to liberate mediators which can be measured is another approach.

Brief mention of these techniques will now be made, mainly for completeness and interest.

What is the Histamine Release test and how does it work?

An important white blood cell called the basophil is present in very small numbers in the circulating blood. This cell is the counterpart of the mast cells in the tissues, and shares in the sensitization of mast cells to allergens. When the basophils are exposed to a solution of allergen to which they are sensitized the cell explodes and liberates mediators, including histamine, which can be measured accurately. The amount released indicates just how sensitive the basophil cells of the patient are to that particular allergen.

This test is complicated, labour-intensive, and somewhat difficult, but it does provide a method of challenging the patient's blood with allergen in the test tube. There is no danger to the patient and much useful information can be obtained. For example, it has been shown that after desensitization a challenge will no longer lead to the liberation of histamine. Unfortunately this laboratory procedure is so time-consuming that histamine release is only a research tool at the present time.

What is the basophil degranulation test?

This test also depends on the basophil cells, which contain very prominent granules and can be separated from the patient's blood so that they can be observed with a microscope. When basophils are exposed to an allergen solution to which the cells are sensitive these granules disappear. This will only occur when the specific allergen to which the cells are sensitive is applied to them. This test provides another way of making a test-tube diagnosis of allergy. A simplified modification of this test has been developed in France and is widely used in continental Europe, but not in Britain, partly because of lack of demand and partly because of high cost. It gives similar information to the RAST.

What is the cytotoxic test and what is its significance?

The cytotoxic test was developed in California in the early 1960s, and consists of exposing cells from the patient to very dilute solutions of the suspected allergens. If damage to the cells occurs on exposure to a specific allergen this is assumed to indicate that this allergen is a cause of the patient's problems. This test has been widely used in diagnosis of food allergy in the USA, but it has never gained wide acceptance or credibility, and it is only carried out in this country in a few private laboratories. In the USA some allergists believe in it, but many do not and medical insurers refuse to pay for this test.

What is sublingual testing?

Drops of an allergen placed under the tongue are absorbed very quickly into the bloodstream. The results are assessed subjectively by the patient and again this is a controversial test. There is much scope for future research, but double-blind testing will be essential to establish the validity of these tests. Trials in the USA have failed to establish their accuracy but the protagonists of the method point out that it was not done according to their rules. This type of test is largely used by clinical ecologists in an attempt to define food and chemical allergies – but it is very controversial.

What does hair analysis tell us?

Analysis of the hair is said to produce useful information regarding lack or excess of minerals, metals and poisons. A high lead concentration could be very important, and excess aluminium and copper may also be significant. However, the value of this test is not yet proved and there seems to be little relationship to the concentrations of metals in the blood. At this present time this area is confused and controversial. The significance of hair analysis is not yet clearly established, and much further research is necessary.

What is the lymphocyte transformation test?

This test is carried out by exposing lymphocyte cells from the patient to diluted allergen in the cell culture fluid. It is a difficult technique used mainly in research laboratories, and has never been developed for routine use. When positive the lymphocyte is stimulated to become a lymphoblast.

What is a challenge test?

A challenge test is carried out by deliberately giving a dose of allergen to a patient in order to provoke the production of allergic symptoms. It is really a controlled exposure, carried out to prove the relationship between cause and effect beyond all reasonable doubt, but even this test may not be absolutely clear-cut.

For example, the testing allergen extract must be potent, and the patient must not be taking drugs which could block the reaction. Also, sensitivity is dosage-dependent, so enough allergen must be given. The dose given to a patient with a seasonal allergy should be approximately that which the patient would be exposed to at the worst part of the season. If the patient subsequently receives desensitizing injections, the challenge test may be repeated at the end of the course of injections, and if no response occurs, then the patient has been rendered immune, and should have no symptoms in the season. If still positive, repeated administration of the highest dose given will eventually give rise to a negative challenge, and a clear season. Thus, challenge tests can be used to assess the results of desensitizing treatment, and to monitor this treatment until a negative response is achieved.

How are allergy challenge tests performed?

There are several methods, which may vary from one investigator to another:

Nasal provocation test

A drop of allergen extract of the right strength is placed in one nostril. A positive response will be obvious sneezing, stuffiness and other symptoms typical of those experienced during the summer months, or a one-sided flare-up of symptoms in a perennial case. The allergen can also be sprayed into the nose.

Eye test

A drop of extract, suitably diluted, is dropped into the eye. If no reaction occurs the strength is increased until a reaction occurs, when the extract is washed out at once. A measurement of sensitivity is thus made (not often used).

Bronchial challenge (bronchotest)

Performed by inhaling an aerosol of the extract, in suitable concentration and quantity, after blowing a peak flow meter or other means of measurement. The meter is blown at regular intervals after the test. If the reading drops by a significant amount, thus causing slight asthma, the test is positive, and the asthma can be stopped easily with a bronchodilator aerosol.

After effective desensitizing injections the test should become negative and, of course, there should be absence of symptoms in the season, or significant improvement in a perennial case.

Occupational challenge

The test is carried out by a controlled exposure in the clinic or hospital to materials used at work, mimicking working conditions as far as possible. For example, antibiotic powders may be poured from one dish to another in a small cubicle, so that some powder gets airborne, or a soldering iron and resin flux could be used in a confined space. The rule is to try to expose the patients to about the same amount of fumes or dust as would normally be encountered, but not more.

Food challenge

This will be mentioned in more detail in the appropriate section. Double-blind challenge, where neither doctor nor patient know if the suspect food is being given or not, provides the most convincing demonstration. Even here there are difficulties, and a slow build-up of the allergen in the body may occur over a period of days.

PART 5

Treatments for Allergy

13   Suppressing symptoms with drugs

It is only since the Second World War that really potent drugs have been available for the treatment of allergic disease. These drugs are effective, even when the cause of the condition is completely unknown, and if the cause cannot be found the whole future of an allergic patient may be bound up in treatment with suppressive drugs. Thus, it is of paramount importance that such drugs are used effectively and to the long-term benefit of the sufferer.

Drugs and their side-effects should be discussed in a detailed manner. Before drugs can be used sensibly, it is essential to know what drugs are available, how they work, how they are used, what side-effects to look out for, and how effective they are.

My views, based on many years of instructing patients how to look after their own problems efficiently, is that as long as the information is correct and easily understood the result should be a patient who is confident and co-operative, and that confusion and panic seldom occur.

The side-effects of drugs are a common subject of features in newspapers or magazines, and on radio and television. It is, therefore, no surprise that doctors and patients alike often become very anxious about possible side-effects of treatment. Sometimes this anxiety is fully justified, but the reverse situation, where steroids are not used when they are desperately needed, is only too common. In this section I hope to give information and reassurance regarding the use of drugs to control allergic conditions which should enable the reader to understand modern methods of management. The remainder of this chapter is concerned with the effects, side-effects, advantages and disadvantages of the various suppressive treatments.

How can the patient suffering from allergic disease make the best of the prescribed treatment?

The medication must be taken as directed by the doctor, and if there is any doubt regarding dosage or administration questions *must* be asked at the time of the consultation. The drugs must then be taken in the right dose the correct number of times a day. Many drugs do not give immediate relief, and hence may be discarded as useless.

If the medication is not taken as directed the doctor cannot be blamed, but if the treatment does not work it is common sense to go back and complain that it is not working. If not told, how can the doctor be aware that the treatment is ineffective or inadequate? Patients may assume that nothing more can be done without giving the family doctor the opportunity to use other treatment or to seek advice from a hospital consultant.

When should drug treatment be given for allergies?

Drugs are required in the following circumstances:

1. To regain control in an emergency situation such as an attack of asthma.
2. When the symptoms are disturbing the quality of life or education.
3. To control symptoms when the cause is unknown or unavoidable.
4. To protect against an occasional unavoidable exposure to a known allergen.
5. For trivial or occasional symptoms not severe enough to justify a full investigation.

How are drugs given for allergies?

When given by mouth and absorbed from the gut into the blood and body fluids, or given by injection, a drug will come into contact with every cell in the body. Thus reactions may be controlled whenever they occur, and whatever the allergic disease may be.

Drugs can also be applied locally, as ointments and creams for skin allergies, as aerosols or sprays for local treatment of the nose and bronchi, and as eye drops for allergic eye irritation, and so on. Local treatment exposes only the affected part of the body to the drug, so side-effects are much less likely.

What types of drug are available for treating allergies?

A great many drugs are used to treat allergic disease. Information on the main categories is given below.

Antihistamines

These drugs block the effects of histamine, which is released as a result of an allergic reaction. A great many antihistamine drugs have been synthesized. Drowsiness is a common side-effect. They help skin allergies by suppressing itching, and are used to treat allergic rhinitis and conjunctivitis. Used as a skin cream antihistamines can cause sensitization of the skin.

Nasal decongestants

Decongestant sprays and drops are freely available, and will clear a stuffy nose rapidly, but not usually for long. They tend to become less and less effective, and if used excessively may damage the lining of the nose. They contain many chemicals which shrink the swollen lining of the nose and improve the airway.

Aerosols

These are perhaps the commonest method of treating asthma today. The pressurized can is filled with liquid gas, which remains liquid under low pressure. Mixed with the liquid are very fine particles of the active drug, such as Becotide or Ventolin, along with an emulsifying agent to keep the particles from settling – so always shake an aerosol before use. The metering valve on the aerosol is a device which restricts the aerosol's output to one measured puff at a time. All kinds of drugs can be given in aerosol form because the gas used is completely inert and does no harm. There was some anxiety that overuse of aerosols might cause side-effects, but it is now accepted that drugs administered in this way are convenient, beneficial and efficient. The amount of gas in a medical aerosol is very small, and is no significant threat to the ozone layer.

Bronchodilators

Drugs such as Ventolin are used extensively in asthma to dilate the bronchial tubes. Modern drugs are much less liable to cause side-effects, especially when used only by inhalation. Tablets or syrups expose the whole body to the drug and can cause an annoying tremor. Aerosols or inhaled powders avoid this, and may also be more effective.

Aminophylline

This is another bronchodilating drug which is used in the form of tablets, injections and suppositories. It has been used for many years, but gastric upset was frequently a side-effect which prevented its full use. Slow-release tablets have been devised recently which are much more satisfactory and have become very popular, but are not always effective.

Adrenaline (called epinephrine in the USA)

Adrenaline can be used as aerosol or as an injection in an emergency. It can be life-saving in anaphylactic shock and other emergency situations in allergy. Ephedrine has similar effects but is not so effective.

Intal (sodium cromoglycate)

This is a drug which was extracted from an Egyptian weed known for many years to help asthmatics, but which has now been synthesized. It is a drug which works by blocking the reaction between allergen and mast cell, so it has many applications in allergy treatment.

Steroids

These, given orally, by injection, by inhalation, or as ointments, are the most important drugs for the treatment of serious allergic problems. They are given detailed coverage below.

What are steroid drugs?

These very important drugs, which are used for the suppression of acute and chronic allergic reactions, in auto-immune diseases, and to prevent rejection of transplants, all have a similar chemical structure and effects. They are referred to as cortico-steroids, or steroids, and have many names. These substances are similar to hormones occurring naturally in the body which are produced by the adrenal glands. To prevent any confusion I shall refer to the artificially manufactured hormones as 'steroids' and the natural hormone produced by the body as 'cortisol'.

The story begins in 1949, when chemists first succeeded in making the first synthetic steroid compound, cortisone. The dramatic effects on rheumatoid arthritis, severe asthma and related allergic problems made cortisone seem a wonder drug, but it was not long before it was evident that the price for miracles was the side-effects. Fortunately new steroid compounds were soon produced which were much more powerful, but with fewer side-effects.

So that the reader may understand the effects and the side-effects of cortico-steroids it is necessary to give a simplified explanation of the system of endocrine glands, which pour their hormones into the bloodstream to act as chemical messengers which stimulate distant organs to perform their special functions. A complicated and delicate balance of many hormones is essential for normal growth, health and response to the stress of illness or accident.

How does the pituitary-adrenal system work?

The pituitary is a tiny gland not much bigger than a hazelnut attached to the underside of the brain by a slender stalk which carries its blood supply. It is so important that it has a special socket in the base of the skull completely surrounded by bone to

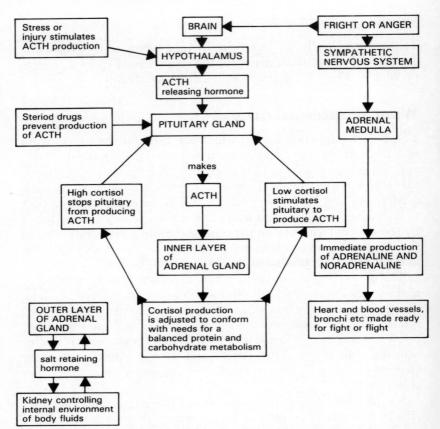

An attempt has been made to show how the adrenal medulla (the middle of the adrenal gland) provides an instant emergency system, while the outer layer looks after the internal environment as an independent system. It can be seen that the pituitary-adrenal system is really three systems working as a closely integrated whole alongside each other.

Figure 13.1   How the pituitary-adrenal system is controlled.

keep it safe. The pituitary controls most of the important glands of the body, to such an extent that it has been described as the leader of the endocrine orchestra (Figure 13.1).

One of the hormones made by the pituitary is called adreno-corticotrophic hormone, usually referred to as 'ACTH'. When this hormone is poured into the blood by the pituitary it reaches the adrenal glands – one above each kidney – and stimulates them to produce cortisol. This causes a rapid increase in the amount of cortisol in the blood, but when it reaches the correct level the secretion of ACTH by the pituitary is stopped, and the blood level falls again until it reaches the level at which ACTH is again switched on. This type of control arrangement, very common in the body, is referred to as a 'feedback' system.

Thus, the secretion of cortisol by the adrenal gland is controlled by the pituitary, but the pituitary gland itself is controlled by the part of the brain just above it called the hypothalamus, which is influenced in turn by bodily activity as a whole, with particular reference to any acute emotional or physical stress. Thus, the chain of command is from acute stress to hypothalamus to pituitary, to adrenal glands, which produce cortisol which gets back to the pituitary, which shuts off ACTH when the level is correct.

How do the adrenal glands work?

The adrenal glands are each three glands in one. The outermost layers of cells control the salt and water balance of the body fluids, being a very powerful guardian of the internal environment, as described in Chapter 1. This layer of the adrenal is essential for life, produces a hormone (aldosterone) which controls blood pressure and kidney function, is not controlled by the pituitary, and is not affected by long-term steroid treatment.

The centre of the adrenal gland, the core or medulla, is a huge nerve centre which produces yet another hormone, adrenaline, held ready in the cells to be released into the circulation at a moment's notice. This provides the fastest system of emergency adaptation, because the whole body can be made ready in an instant for fight or flight. This part of the adrenal gland also is not affected by taking steroids.

We have all experienced a really nasty fright and remember the dry mouth, the sinking feeling in the pit of the stomach, the racing, pounding pulse, and the feeling of alertness, or the sensations of rage. This is due to the release of adrenaline, which also causes other effects such as relaxing the bronchi, shutting off the blood supply to the digestive organs, narrowing some blood vessels and opening up others. All these events are directed at placing the body in the best possible position for emergency action – fight or flight.

Adrenaline is also used by injection as emergency treatment

for severe allergic reactions, and was one of the first drugs used by inhalation for asthma. For example, wasp and bee stings can cause a sudden anaphylactic shock in sensitized persons, and such people can now be supplied with a special ready-to-use syringe full of adrenaline to use on themselves (Ana-Kit).

The middle layer of the adrenal is the part which produces cortisol, under the control of the pituitary. Cortisol and related hormones control the metabolic balance of sugars and proteins. Disease of the pituitary gland prevents production of ACTH, hence no cortisol is secreted by the adrenal, causing widespread effects. Sometimes the pituitary goes out of control, producing too much ACTH, which causes the adrenal to produce too much cortisol, or the adrenal itself can go out of control with the same result. Diseases causing excess cortisol secretion bring about all the side-effects also caused by steroid drugs. All these uncommon disease situations occur naturally, so their study has contributed greatly to the unravelling of the way the endocrine system works as a team, and how steroid side-effects are produced.

In the normal person the pituitary-adrenal system provides one of the major defences against extreme physical stress such as injury, accident, surgery or disease. The pituitary-adrenal system is capable of great flexibility, so that very large amounts of cortisol can be produced when required in an emergency. Hence, it is important for the adrenals to be in good working order as all these emergency systems are intended to ensure survival under the most adverse circumstances, as part of the arrangements built into the body for emergency adaptation to environmental stress.

Is it possible to measure adrenal function?

The response of the adrenal to stimulation can be measured by giving an injection of synthetic ACTH (synacthen test), followed by blood samples to find out if the adrenal has responded by producing cortisol. Sometimes the pituitary gets tired so there are also other tests to find out if stress will make the pituitary produce ACTH to stimulate the adrenal to produce cortisol, which is then measured in the blood. Insulin is used for this test because the results show how the patient will respond to surgery, accident or illness. However, it is seldom done because it causes very low blood-sugar levels (hypoglycaemia) which are rather unpleasant.

Some people have more robust pituitary-adrenal systems than others, so there is great variation in the degree of adrenal suppression caused by oral steroids, and in the rate of recovery of full responsiveness after stopping steroids.

These tests of the capacity of the pituitary-adrenal system to respond to a stimulus will predict the response to physical stress.

What are the beneficial effects of steroids?

One of the major functions of cortisol as it occurs naturally in the body is to control carbohydrate and protein metabolism, but when synthetic steroids are used as a 'drug' the level of hormone in the blood is much higher than normal, so the effects are quite different.

Thus, a normal body hormone is acting as a drug when given in high dosage. Very high doses of oral steroids will suppress the immune system and prevent rejection of transplanted organs. Lower doses suppress auto-immune diseases, and the allergic reactions causing asthma, eczema and other allergic diseases. Steroids also suppress inflammation, hence their use by local injection for joint and muscle injuries.

Severe stress, such as is caused by severe injury, operation, or serious illness stimulates the production of very large amounts of cortisol by the adrenal. This is because the cortisol is required to combat shock and thus ensures survival. If the response of the pituitary or the adrenal to stress is inadequate then too little cortisol will be produced, but a large injection of synthetic steroid will be life-saving. Steroids are now some of the most powerful and essential drugs available for the treatment of acute and chronic problems.

Are oral steroids dangerous?

Patients often ask this question, as both family doctors and their patients seem to have acquired a genuine fear of these drugs. The short answer is that dangerous short-term side-effects are exceptionally rare, and that the use of oral steroids in fairly high dosage for up to 3 weeks does not cause significant side-effects either. The only clear contra-indication to using oral steroids is the presence of an active stomach ulcer, which might bleed severely, or severe diabetes, which might get out of control.

Severe asthma is the commonest reason for giving fairly high doses of oral steroids. There is much more reason to fear the asthma than the steroids as mortality surveys have repeatedly shown. I have so often seen the disastrous effects of timidity in the use of adequate doses of oral steroids, and only once in 35 years seen serious gastric bleeding from an unsuspected ulcer.

Steroids, because they suppress the immune reaction of the body, can lower the resistance to infection, but the dosages used in allergic diseases are not high enough to have this effect.

What are the side-effects of 'steroids' and how are they caused?

So many patients are worried about side-effects that it seems worthwhile to devote a special section to describing what they are, how they are caused and what they mean.

Now that we know how the pituitary-adrenal system works, it is possible to explain how steroids produce side-effects. Taking oral steroid drugs keeps the blood level of steroid continuously high, so the ACTH is turned off, and the adrenal gland stops producing cortisol. Eventually the adrenal gland becomes lazy from disuse and the metabolism of the body comes to rely completely on the steroid drugs supplied from outside. If the drug is stopped suddenly the adrenal cannot make cortisol immediately, so that the patient is suddenly deprived of both cortisol and steroid drugs. This causes the troublesome withdrawal symptoms of lassitude, tiredness, weakness, aches and pains, headache, depression, low blood pressure and, very rarely, collapse. Thus, long-term steroid treatment leads to dependence on steroid tablets, because production of cortisol cannot restart at once.

Short-term steroid therapy

Dosages of 40mg a day of prednisolone (or equivalent in other steroid preparations) can be given for 3 weeks, after which adrenal function will return to normal in less than a week. Indigestion is an uncommon problem, which can be controlled, but the presence of an active stomach ulcer is an absolute contra-indication to the use of steroids orally. As long as the steroid drugs are stopped as soon as possible and alternative methods of control introduced there should be no danger of steroid dependence and production of long-term side-effects.

Heavy doses of steroids for acute situations may cause temporary diabetic problems. Thirst and passing a lot of water are the features which may suggest this complication, which is uncommon with the newer steroid drugs. Oral steroids given to a diabetic will inevitably cause imbalance, which has to be controlled.

Long-term steroid therapy

By 'long term' is meant over 3 months continuous oral treatment, which inevitably has many effects on body systems. The longer the treatment and the higher the dose the greater will be the side-effects. They are listed in Table 13.1.

Side-effects on body metabolism

Because of the effect of the extra steroid on metabolic processes the blood sugar tends to rise, and so latent diabetes will be unmasked or existing diabetes made worse, but all this can be dealt with quite easily as a rule.

The commonest side-effects, especially unpopular with women, are obesity, the moon face so characteristic of steroid therapy, and extra facial hair. These effects are caused by upsetting the normal metabolism of carbohydrate and protein, resulting in virilization and an increase in appetite.

Destruction of collagen tissue

We all know how tough the outside covering of a steak, or a tendon or sinew of an animal, can be. This is largely due to a substance called collagen, which also gives elasticity to the skin, and is the substance in the joints which is affected by rheumatoid arthritis. In fact there is a whole group of diseases which affect the collagen tissue, and in all these diseases steroids have been most helpful.

Taking steroids for years destroys collagen, causing a whole

Table 13.1 Long-term side-effects of oral steroids

Side effects	Comments
Obesity, moon face, facial hair	common; obesity, partly caused by increase in appetite, partly by metabolic changes – causes all the problems usually associated with obesity
Bruising, thin skin, slow healing of wounds	common, but not usually until after a year or two; caused by collagen destruction; mainly nuisance
Ruptured Achilles' tendon	uncommon; caused by loss of collagen
Osteoporosis	uncommon; usually only after years on steroids; causes back pain and tendency to fractures of ribs, vertebrae, and other bones; women over 50 more prone to this problem
Stretch marks on skin resembling those seen in pregnancies	uncommon; caused by sudden increase in weight – skin is unable to stretch quickly enough and therefore splits
Muscle weakness	uncommon
Diabetes mellitus	uncommon; will make existing diabetes worse and will unmask latent diabetes; some steroid drugs are more liable than others to cause this
Peptic ulcer	very uncommon with soluble or enteric-coated steroid preparations
Salt (sodium) and water retention	swelling of ankles etc not common with modern steroid drugs
Irreversible shock from surgery or accident	carry steroid card and a few emergency tablets at all times or Medic-Alert bracelet

range of side-effects. The most obvious is thinning of the skin, which loses its elasticity and becomes very easily bruised, often with the formation of blood blisters under the skin or stretch marks. Wound healing becomes very slow, and sometimes a comparatively trivial injury on the shins may require a skin graft. Women who have this problem should wear trousers, and if necessary a roll-on gauze called Tubigauze or crêpe bandages to give extra protection.

It is possibly relevant that severe lack of vitamin C (ascorbic acid) causes scurvy, a disease which used to afflict sailors on long voyages because they had no fresh fruit or vegetables for months. This deficiency disease has similar effects on collagen tissue and easy bruising is also a feature. Large doses of ascorbic acid given to some patients afflicted with easily bruised shins gave some encouraging results, but further studies are required to ascertain whether extra ascorbic acid would *prevent* damage to collagen in patients on long-term steroids.

The Achilles' tendons at the back of the heels have to be very strong, as each of them has to be capable of supporting the weight of the whole body. When the tendon has been weakened by loss of collagen even slipping from a step on going upstairs has been enough to cause a rupture. Thus, anyone taking long-term steroids for any reason whatsoever should avoid putting violent strains on the Achilles tendons.

Myopathy

Muscle weakness is another side-effect which is uncommon but can be troublesome. It is sometimes associated with potassium deficiency within the cells, made worse if the patient is taking diuretics to get rid of excess fluid. Potassium supplements are easy to take, and may remedy feelings of weakness quite dramatically. Rarely, the muscle weakness is due to a direct effect of the drug on the muscles.

Effects on bone (osteoporosis)

One of the most troublesome, but fortunately uncommon, steroid side-effects is thinning and weakening of the bones. Women who have passed the menopause tend to lose calcium anyway, so if they are also on steroids bone problems are more likely to occur. Hormone-replacement therapy for the menopause sometimes helps to reverse the calcium loss.

A severe bout of coughing in a patient on long-term steroids may cause a painful rib fracture. The best treatment is the old-fashioned method of applying strong adhesive strapping (Elastoplast), fully stretched before application, to an extensive area of the chest. The modern teaching is to leave well alone because of a theory that preventing the chest wall from moving may promote pneumonia, something which I have yet to see. Strapping properly applied will splint the side of the chest affected and prevent the ends of the cracked rib from rubbing against each other and causing intense pain. Incidentally, x-rays may not show the fracture as the cracks are very difficult to see, but there is always intense local tenderness, and after some months a lump may be felt where healing has taken place.

The vertebrae of the spine also lose calcium and tend to collapse, causing severe backache, but this is also uncommon. Although the x-rays of the spine may look most alarming I have yet to encounter any severe spinal nerve complications. Extra calcium, vitamin D, and oestrogens for older women may be helpful, and it is obvious that heavy lifting and other strains should be avoided.

In the USA measurements of bone density to monitor the effectiveness of this treatment are now quite common, but only available at special centres in Britain.

What special side-effects do oral steroids cause in children?

In children long-term steroids will stop growth, but so does chronic asthma. If minimal doses, just enough to control the asthma, are carefully used the benefits outweigh the side-effects of steroid and rapid growth is the result. However, since the advent of inhaled steroid (Becotide) it has become very uncommon for children to require continuous oral steroid therapy, except when dangerous attacks make this treatment unavoidable. Also short courses of oral steroid in high dosage *do not* suppress growth and if given at the right time will abort the majority of attacks, as described elsewhere. Children are subject to all the other side-effects listed, but in low doses serious problems are very rare indeed.

Can steroids by mouth or by inhalation cause abnormalities in the unborn child?

There is no evidence that pregnant women taking oral steroids in the doses usual for asthma have a greater number of abnormal babies.

To the author's personal knowledge over twenty-five perfect babies have been produced by women taking beclomethasone dipropionate for asthma (Becotide) or rhinitis (Beconase) constantly for up to 13 years on end.

The fear of effects on the foetus from beclomethasone or other steroids has reached ludicrous proportions among ill-informed doctors. For example, a woman was advised by two doctors to have a termination of her 8 week pregnancy because she was taking Beconase for rhinitis. No consultant opinion was obtained before advising abortion.

What are the Drugs used for the various types of Allergy Reaction?

ALLERGIC ASTHMA

Drug	Formulation	Effectiveness	Side-effects
Bronchodilators: Ventolin, Bricanyl, Atrovent, Medihalers and many others	Injection, gas aerosols wet aerosols, powder inhalers, tablets	Usually quick relief if responsive	Uncommon even in excess except tremor with tablets
Aminophylline: Aminophylline SR, many types	Injection, tablets, slow-release tablets, suppositories	In UK mainly background therapy only. Usually active only when near tolerance level	Nausea, vomiting. Can have toxic effects on injection if already on tablets
Reaction Blockers: Intal	Powder inhaler, gas aerosol, nebullized solution in infants	Variable. Best in children and young people. Regular use essential	None significant
Local Steroids: Becotide, Bextasol Pulmicort	Gas aerosol or powder inhaler	Very effective, if used properly and regularly in correct dosage at all ages	Occasional thrush or hoarseness

Oral Steroids

Prednisolone, prednisone, Prednesol, Betnesol, etc.	Injection, tablets, depot injections	Soluble or injected work fastest. Very effective	Wide ranging (see text)

ALLERGIC RHINITIS OR POLYPS

Drug	Formulation	Effectiveness	Side-effects
Antihistamines Literally hundreds of compounds available. Commonest Piriton, Benadryl, Optimine, Daneral, Antistin, Tavegil, Triludan, Hismanal	Tablets, drops, sprays	Variable. Often effective dose not tolerated	Drowsiness can be serious problem
Decongestants Numerous preparations. Antistin-Privine, Iliadin, Otrivine etc.	Sprays, drops	Very effective for short-term use. Variable results	None in short-term. Can damage lining of nose if used in excess
Reaction Blockers Intal as Rynacrom or Lomusol preparations	Spray or powder	Moderate. Suitable for long-term use	None

Drug	Formulation	Effectiveness	Side-effects
Local Steroids Beconase (Beclomethasone), Syntaris (flunisolide)	Aerosols, watery suspensions, liquid sprays	Very effective if used regularly long-term	Occasional slight nose bleeds. No general side-effects
Systemic steroids Oral tablets, delayed-release injections (Kenalog, Depo-Medrone)	Tablets, injection	Dramatically effective short-term	Steroid side-effects only if used long-term

URTICARIA

Drug	Formulation	Effectiveness	Side-effects
Antihistamines All sorts	Tablets, creams, etc.	Variable	Drowsiness
Local steroids	Creams and ointments	Variable, effective short-term	
Oral steroids	Tablets	Very effective short-term	Steroid side-effects if used long-term
Nalcrom (Intal) Orally to block foods	Capsules	Occasional dramatic success	None

ECZEMA

Drug	Formulation	Effectiveness	Side-effects
Oral steroids For treating acute situations only	Tablets	Very effective	None in short-term use
Local steroids Usually used for long periods	Creams, ointments, sprays	Variable	Can cause skin atrophy and general steroid effects *in excess*
Anti-itch Anti-histamines, tranquillizers, sedatives, emollients, etc. Calamine, oilatum baths, various soothing preparations	Tablets, creams	Variable	Mainly drowsiness

ULCERATIVE COLITIS

Drug	Formulation	Effectiveness	Side-effects
Oral steroids When necessary in acute phase	Tablets	Very effective	Usual side-effects if used long-term

	Tablets	Helpful as maintenance	Is a sulpha drug, sometimes causes side-effects
Salazopyrin	Tablets	Helpful as maintenance	Is a sulpha drug, sometimes causes side-effects
Local steroids Beclomethasone, Predsol enema, etc.	Enemas, suppositories, foams	Very effective	None significant

CONJUNCTIVITIS

Drug	Formulation	Effectiveness	Side-effects
Intal (as Opticrom)	Drops	Variable	Irritation
Anti-histamines – many types;		Variable	Irritation
many steroids – preparations (Do not keep partly used drops beyond expiry date)	Drops	Effective	May cause increased pressure in eye if used for long periods. Use only on medical advice

EMERGENCIES
(e.g. severe asthma, anaphylactic shock, angio-oedema, acute urticaria)

Drug	Formulation	Effectiveness	Side-effects
Adrenaline	Injection	Dramatic relief	Palpitations, fear, etc
Anti-histamine	Injection	Slower effect	Drowsiness
Steroids	Injection	Takes some hours to work	None in short-term use
Bronchodilators (salbutamol, terbutaline)	Injection or wet aerosol using compressed air or oxygen	Rapid relief if effective	Shaking, fast pulse
Aminophylline	Injection	Rapid relief	Can be toxic. Can be dangerous if tablets also being taken

14 How steroids and other drugs are used for asthma and allergy

The steroid compounds used as drugs resemble the natural hormones closely, and can replace these hormones when the adrenal gland has failed. Their main usefulness, however, lies in their ability to suppress allergic reactions, immune reactions, and inflammation anywhere in the body when necessary. Alteration of the structure of the steroid molecule can intensify the anti-allergic and anti-inflammatory actions, while unwanted effects are minimized as far as possible.

The dosages given depend on the effects required. For example, *very* high dosages for long periods are needed to suppress rejection of transplanted hearts or kidneys, but the dose to suppress rejection also suppresses immunity and opens the door to infection. Moderately high doses are necessary for effective suppression of severe auto-immune reactions, where the body is reacting violently against itself and committing a kind of immunological suicide.

Allergic diseases of all types constitute one of the commonest indications for the use of steroids, and a rapid and dramatic improvement usually points to an allergic causation. In the past, relapse of allergic symptoms swiftly followed by stopping oral steroids, but now local ('topical') application can frequently take over and maintain control. Obviously a continuing reaction affecting the kidney or the blood vessels still has to be treated with oral steroids, because access can only be gained through the circulation.

Many allergic problems are neither life-threatening, nor otherwise serious, and may be no more than a minor nuisance. Hence, to use oral steroids for treatment of minor allergies, *except* as a temporary measure to gain control, is quite unjustified. Anti-histamine drugs are usually more suitable, but may either produce unacceptable side-effects or be of limited effectiveness.

Obviously what is needed is a high local concentration of an active steroid, to suppress the allergic reaction, using a steroid which is not absorbed into the circulation so that it causes the usual side-effects, or the use of a steroid which is broken down to an inactive steroid in the liver and does not cause side-effects.

The objective of the drug manufacturer must, therefore, be a steroid drug which will produce the desired effects without the side-effects. How this has been accomplished will be described later in this chapter.

How should oral steroids be used to control allergic problems?

The indications for oral steroid therapy are many, but in my opinion a major usage is as a crutch to bring a situation under control. For example, about half the asthmatics referred for a consultant opinion need a clean-out with oral steroids before control with inhaled steroid (Becotide) can be effective, and the same is true in many cases of severe rhinitis or polyps. The principle of a short introductory course of oral steroid, followed by local steroid for maintenance, is only gaining ground very slowly.

Oral steroids for flare-ups of chronic asthma should be started when it is clear that the situation is deteriorating, as recognized much more easily by using a peak flow meter. Early treatment means rapid recovery, fewer steroid tablets in total, less adrenal suppression, and no danger (Table 14.1).

In eczema steroids are not used orally as a rule unless the situation has become serious, as when there is generalized infected eczema. Again, occasional short courses, or alternate-day steroids, will give great relief and cause no harm, along with antibiotics to control infection. The period of relief can be used for skin test, dietary experiments and general investigations directed at finding a cause for the problem.

Should oral steroids be given for seasonal asthma?

Seasonal asthma can be very severe, to the extent that deaths always increase at the peak of the pollen season. Pollen-sensitive

Table 14.1 Instructions for the use of steroid tablets in an acute attack of asthma

---

If you or your child has a severe attack, first try three puffs of a Ventolin or other bronchodilator inhaler. If no relief from inhalers, either telephone your doctor or proceed as detailed below. *Do not delay*, as early treatment is very important.

1. Take four steroid tablets. Nearly all types of steroid tablet are of equal strength and dosage. Betnesol should be dissolved in water and is much easier for children to take.

2. If no better in an hour, take two more then call the doctor.

3. If obviously improving, take another two tablets in 2 hours (total in a day up to ten).

4. Even if you have definitely improved by next morning, you should go to your doctor's surgery for advice on dosage or further treatment.

Notes on dosage
If you are always or often taking steroids, taper off dosage by taking 8-7-6-5-4-3-2-1-0 tablets per day. If you are coughing up yellow or green sputum you may need antibiotics as well.

If you very seldom take steroids, and you recover very rapidly the tablets can be safely and abruptly stopped, or tapered off quickly, as 4-2-0 per day.

This treatment is not dangerous – but acute asthma can be!

---

people may not realize how dangerous it can be to ignore the asthma and expose themselves to a high concentration of pollen by outdoor activities.

Unfortunately some doctors still fear steroids, not asthma, and do not give oral steroids to cases of severe seasonal asthma, or give quite inadequate doses.

How can a patient with asthma 'get off' oral steroids?

Steroid-dependent patients must not try to stop steroid treatment without the guidance of family doctor or consultant. The remarks made here are intended purely to increase awareness and to warn of the difficulties and the dangers which may be encountered. It may not be possible to be weaned off steroids unless an intensive search for causative factors which could be removed or avoided has been carried out.

Oral steroids must be stopped slowly if the drugs have been taken for a long time, because the middle zone of the adrenal, where the cortisol is produced, can only resume production slowly. The effect of taking the tablets daily is to keep the level of steroids in the blood above the normal level, thus suppressing the production of ACTH by the pituitary. As a result the adrenal is never stimulated, and may eventually atrophy from disuse. Taking the total daily dose of steroid at 8am has been shown to have less suppressive effect on the adrenals, and may be advised.

While attempting to withdraw steroids it is essential that full use is made of all alternative treatments, such as Becotide, Intal, bronchodilators and aminophylline. The objective is to keep the daily dose of oral steroid at the lowest level compatible with effective control of the disease, best achieved by the use of a peak flow meter to monitor the asthma several times a day.

Once the dose has been reduced to 10mg of prednisolone, or an equivalent dose of another steroid preparation, while using every alternative treatment, the scene is set for an attempt to get off steroids completely, but this must never be done quickly. For example, the dose can be reduced to 7.5mg for a week or two, and if all is well it can be reduced further to 5mg for a week or two, but it is below this level that problems are usually encountered. This is the point at which 1mg tablets of prednisolone may be used for even more gradual reduction of dosage at the rate of 1mg per week, fortnight, or even more slowly. In the presence of definite adrenal suppression it is usual to expect withdrawal symptoms at the level of 3 or 4mg per day, a warning to go slowly and make sure that all other treatments are effective. If control is being lost the situation will need to be reassessed. If there has been significant adrenal suppression, time must be allowed for recovery to take place, and also for the pituitary to start to produce ACTH again, which will, in turn, stimulate the adrenal. ACTH injections can be given at this point, to try to stimulate the adrenal, but the result is often disappointing. Also ACTH by injection will prevent the pituitary making its own ACTH again. It is, incidentally, important to give a small test dose first to make sure that the patient is not allergic to synthetic ACTH or to pork ACTH if derived from pig pituitaries.

The age of the patient and the length of time steroids have been taken must have an influence on the outcome of an attempt to get off steroids. Below 3mg the withdrawal symptoms can be very troublesome, and both doctor and patient may have a difficult time. At one extreme are those who are fanatical about getting off, and at the other are those who give up too easily. Recent experience with patients who have been on steroids for up to 25 years has suggested that if the withdrawal symptoms are very troublesome it may be best to make a sensible compromise by continuing on a dose of 3–5mg a day. This dose is really a form of replacement therapy for the cortisol which the adrenal is no longer capable of producing.

Many patients finally break free after varying periods, using all available alternative treatments, but control must be good and the asthma stable. If frequent acute attacks still occur, requiring high doses of steroids, the pituitary and adrenal will again be suppressed, and the process has to be started all over again. Much patience and perseverance is necessary from everyone involved.

The continued presence of a pet, or intense sensitivity to an allergen which is difficult to avoid, such as dust mite, may cause great difficulty in weaning a patient off steroids. This is a situation where pets must be banished, if specialist treatment cannot be found. The least that can be done is to review all the known or possible allergic factors, but because of prevailing lack of knowledge of the importance of allergic factors it is probable that few patients in this situation get the best treatment.

An alternative approach, which is more common in the USA, is to give the steroid tablets alternate mornings. Less adrenal suppression is caused but in the author's experience this method is often disappointing.

When is it reasonable to accept oral steroids indefinitely?

Many patients and their doctors seem afflicted with 'steroid phobia', fearing the possible side-effects of steroids more than the asthma. It is not realized that high doses of oral steroids for up to 3 weeks, will not cause side-effects unless the patient has an active peptic ulcer. Low doses for a long time *do* eventually cause all the side-effects, however low the dose. What is worse, low doses often do nothing to help the asthma either, so that all that is being accomplished is to establish dependence on a drug which is insidiously destroying bone, skin, and tendons.

When there is no clue to the cause and the asthmatic state is severe, it is easy to become trapped into steroid dependency, but many patients would prefer to live reasonably with steroids than miserably without them. Fortunately steroid dependence is very much less common than before the introduction of inhaled corticosteroids such as Becotide and Pulmicort.

With steroid therapy, as in any other treatment for asthma, the dosage must be suitably adjusted so that it is doing the maximum good with the minimum side-effects. This may necessitate short bursts of high-dosage treatment at intervals, preferably monitored by a peak flow meter, otherwise more harm than good may be done.

Many patients are so accustomed to their chronic asthma that familiarity breeds contempt – they are often far worse than they feel, and may lapse into a dangerous state in which sudden death can, and does, occur.

What precautions must be taken by steroid-dependent patients?

Steroid-dependent patients must carry a steroid card or wear a Medic-Alert bracelet (*see* Chapter 7) in order to warn any doctor that they can be at serious risk if extra steroids are not given in the event of surgery, accident or other severe stress. This is why there is always a question about steroids on the form to be filled in before a surgical operation (there is no need to worry as long as extra steroids are given before surgery). It is essential to carry the steroid card *always*. Irreversible shock could ensue if nobody knew you needed extra steroids. In fact, there are many other drugs in common use today which can cause similar problems unless some indication that they are being taken is carried on the person, yet many patients are blissfully unaware of these avoidable dangers. Ask your doctor if you are worried.

The above comments apply to all patients on long-term oral steroids, but patients who have had short courses in high dosage, or who have had a depot steroid injection for summer hay fever

(Kenalog, Depo-Medrone, and so on) may have a slightly decreased response to severe stress for about 6 weeks. This is not serious, but it will do no harm to have some indications of this on a card in the wallet or handbag, especially if several depot injections have been given.

When a patient who has been taking oral steroids for a long time has been successfully weaned off the drug, usually on to Becotide, the reserve capacity of the adrenal to cope with stress may be impaired for up to 2 years – so again some indication of this should be carried on the person.

Steroid cards are easily lost or mislaid, and sometimes doctors forget to issue them. It is safest to become a member of the Medic-Alert Foundation, and wear a bracelet or necklet on which is engraved any essential information of this sort.

What is Becotide?

In July 1970 I was asked to try out a new way of treating asthma by using an aerosol of a new steroid called beclomethasone dipropionate. By selecting only well-researched cases of allergic asthma for the trial, the new treatment was soon found very effective, yet without the side-effects usually associated with oral steroids.

Adverse reports from previous trials in Edinburgh had convinced the makers, Allen & Hanbury, that the drug was useless, but these new results persuaded them to continue trials. Soon there was enough data for me to present my conclusions to an international conference in France in 1971, and to publish in the British Medical Journal in 1972, demonstrating that this was a real advance in the treatment of asthma, especially in children and young adults.

The treatment is now used throughout the world, known in this country by the trade name of 'Becotide'. Thus, the most important advance in the drug treatment of asthma in the last 25 years was nearly discarded. Personally, I am proud to have rescued this drug by demonstrating its effectiveness, indirectly helping millions of asthma sufferers all over the world.

Why is Becotide such an important development in treatment?

Becotide has made a very significant contribution to the suppressive treatment of asthma by providing an alternative to oral steroids, without long-term side-effects. Management methods are dealt with elsewhere, so the patient will know how to make the best of Becotide. This drug has given a new life to a great many patients, particularly children, some of whom become champion athletes.

Ten years ago I had hundreds of asthma cases where oral steroids were essential to maintain them in reasonable health, but using Becotide this treatment is seldom required today. This demonstrates the tremendous improvement this drug has made in the treatment of chronic asthma. Today it is only in the most severe type of case that continuous treatment with steroid tablets is necessary.

Why is Becotide effective without causing steroid side-effects?

This steroid compound, beclomethasone dipropionate, had been used for many years under the name Propaderm for the treatment of eczema because it is so surface active. It can be used liberally because beclomethasone dipropionate has intense anti-allergic and anti-inflammatory effects on the skin or on the lining of the respiratory system, but if absorbed the steroid is broken down in the liver into another compound which is quite inactive. The intense local effect without side-effects, is exactly what is required for the treatment of respiratory allergy. The dose required is very small indeed, inhaled as tiny particles from an aerosol or a powder inhaler. In fact, only 10 per cent of the drug reaches the lining of the bronchial tubes.

It had always been obvious that if steroids could be administered directly to the bronchi, where the drug is really required, then it might be possible to avoid generalized side-effects. Also, because the tiny particles are almost insoluble in water they exert a prolonged local effect on the lining of the bronchus or the nose, which becomes less irritable, and the allergic reactions are suppressed.

What is the correct dosage of Becotide?

Each puff of aerosol delivers 50 micrograms (mcg). The most practical dosage is three puffs three times a day, because this is more convenient and less liable to be forgotten than the usual dosage of two puffs four times a day. For more difficult cases three puffs four times a day can be given, or the special strong aerosol which gives 250mcg per puff can be used ('Becloforte'). Once the asthma has been properly controlled two or three puffs twice a day is often adequate, but all depends on the severity of the problem.

The Becotide Rotahaler uses capsules containing 100 or 200mcg of Becotide mixed with lactose powder. It is usual to use one 200mcg Rotacap of Becotide night and morning, but the dose can be increased as required. The full dose of Becotide is equivalent to 10mg of prednisolone per day at the most, or other equivalent steroid tablets. Thus, patients who depend on a high dose of oral steroids are the least likely to be successfully transferred to Becotide alone. It is important to emphasize that there is no need to reduce or stop Becotide treatment prematurely, because although it is a steroid it does *not* have long-term side-effects even when used daily for more than 13 years.

The latest delivery system is the 'Becodisk', giving doses of 100 or 200 micrograms. This system is by far the easiest to use and results show it is the most effective.

Should Becotide have an immediate effect?

No – It is not a bronchodilator. Badly informed patients often give up using Becotide because they do not feel better at once when given this 'wonder drug'. It takes at least a week to achieve control and regular daily dosage is essential.

Does transfer to Becotide have any indirect side-effects in steroid-dependent asthmatic patients?

Oral steroids suppress allergic symptoms in any part of the body, because the drug is distributed everywhere. This fact can produce surprising 'side-effects' when a steroid-dependent case is transferred to Becotide, which has strictly local effects only.

For example, many patients complain that although their asthma is often better controlled than before, they have begun to have very troublesome symptoms of allergic rhinitis, or a recurrence of nasal polyps, or of eczema which they have not seen for years.

The reason is that allergic problems in other body systems had been suppressed by the circulating steroid, but because Becotide is strictly a local treatment the unrecognized hidden allergies become obvious. In fact, it was the unmasking effects of steroid withdrawal which directed more attention to the nose, so that Becotide was used in Derby for treating the nose as well as the chest from the first few months of the initial Becotide trials in 1970.

Why does using Becotide for years not damage the bronchi?

For a long time many doctors were afraid that continuous inhalation of Becotide might lead to degenerative changes in the lining of the bronchi, mouth or nose, similar to those observed in the skin after using steroid ointments for many years. However, many investigators from many countries have actually taken biopsies from the bronchus and shown that no adverse changes are taking place, even after long-term use. (A biopsy is a tiny piece of tissue removed for microscopic examination.) Some patients in Derby who have been taking Becotide nasally for 14 years have had repeated biopsies of the lining of the nose and no changes whatsoever have been found. The reason for the lack of side-effects may be that our bronchial tubes and nose are not lined with skin, but with a very active layer of cells which are continually dying off and being replaced. However, it is remarkable that no damage occurs, and it seems reasonable to assume that it never will because Becotide has been used so widely for so many years that this complication would certainly have been reported. The same considerations apply to the use of similar preparations in the nose for nasal allergies.

How can a patient make the best of Becotide?

Treatment with Becotide may be recommended when asthma is diagnosed for the first time, or because Intal has proved ineffective, or in an attempt to transfer to Becotide in place of oral steroids (Figures 14.1 and 14.2).

In every case the primary problem is that if the drug is not properly inhaled it will have no effect. This is because the particles of Becotide have a predominantly surface-active effect on the inside of the bronchial tubes, and to exert this effect it has to get there. Even when properly inhaled only 10 per cent of the drug particles reach the bronchial tree. The remainder either stays in the mouth or throat, or is swallowed, so it is sound practice to drink something just after use to get rid of the surplus.

The technique of inhalation is therefore of vital importance. The approach I find most effective is to show patients how to exhale as far as they can to empty the lungs, usually until they hear themselves wheezing. The inhaler is then placed between the teeth (not just the lips), to make sure that there is a clear airway from the inhaler right back to the throat. The patient then fires the aerosol and inhales *simultaneously*. Effective inhalation gives a slightly cold sensation in the chest. This performance must be repeated for *each* inhalation, and it should be carried out with great care because Becotide simply *will not work* unless it reaches the target.

These remarks apply equally to bronchodilator aerosols, though these also work quite well when used improperly because the drug is absorbed from the mouth into the bloodstream. As a result a Ventolin aerosol can be effective immediately when used in a way which would render a Becotide aerosol completely useless.

Unless time and trouble are taken in making certain that the patient is using the inhaler correctly results are often poor. Ideally the usage of the aerosol should be checked every time the patient attends surgery or hospital out-patients.

It must also be emphasized that this drug must be taken on a regular daily basis, otherwise the asthma will gradually get out of control again. Many patients, especially children, feel so much better that they begin to forget, become careless and then

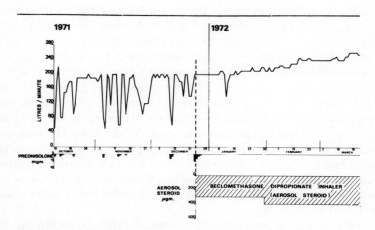

Becotide brought this 10-year-old child under control. She is
now twenty-four and married, but still has to take a small dose
of Becotide.

Figure 14.1   Becotide used to control chronic childhood asthma.

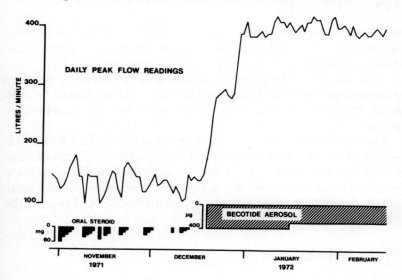

This man aged 50 had had very unstable asthma with frequent need
for high doses of oral steroids. Becotide was dramatically
successful in controlling the situation, and does so to this day.

Figure 14.2   Becotide used to control late onset asthma.

wonder why they are in trouble again. Slow steps in the reduction of the dose are ideal, to find out what dose the patient actually needs. Stopping the treatment prematurely is completely counter-productive, and sudden reduction of dosage is also unwise. Care must be taken always to have an adequate supply when away from home.

In recent years the Rotahaler, using capsules (Rotacaps) containing 100 or 200mcg of Becotide mixed with lactose powder, was invented because some people never learn to cope with using an aerosol. The Rotahaler is ideal for the very old and the very young. Once again complete exhalation is the first step, followed by full inspiration from the Rotahaler. Never blow out through the Rotahaler because this will make the powder damp so that it will not fly.

The 'Becodisk' system, also available for Ventolin as the 'Ventodisk', as already mentioned, is the best delivery system developed so far.

What is Intal?

Intal (sodium cromoglycate) is a unique preventative drug which can be used by inhalation into the nose or bronchi, as eyedrops or orally.

This drug has the property of blocking the reaction between allergen and mast cell (Chapter 1). Thus, this drug must be used *before* exposure, or on a *regular* daily basis, to exert a protective effect.

Intal for asthma does not have an immediate effect unless it is of the type called Intal Compound, which includes in the capsule a dose of isoprenaline to act as a bronchodilator. Many specialists, including myself, do not approve of this double formulation, which can lead to patients taking repeated doses of Intal for the bronchodilator effect alone.

How is Intal used?

For asthma dry lactose powder containing Intal is given using a special inhaler. The usual dose is one capsule three or four times daily, and for chronic asthma regular use is essential. An aerosol inhaler is now available for those who prefer it.

For very small children unable to use an inhaler an Intal

solution can be administered in the form of a nebulized mist, using an air compressor.

Allergic conjunctivitis can be treated with Intal eye drops, allergic rhinitis by Intal powder or spray, and food allergies sometimes benefit from large doses orally.

It is not uncommon for allergic patients to react in the nose or in the chest to short-term encounters with animals when visiting relatives or friends. In such cases Intal is most useful when taken shortly before the visit.

How effective is Intal?

Used regularly, and usually along with bronchodilators, it is more beneficial for children than adults. The main indication for use is chronic asthma. It is of no value in the treatment of an established asthma attack.

Effectiveness varies somewhat, and relief may wane after some years of use. Reassessment at intervals with peak flow or other lung function measurement is important in children. In older asthmatics benefit is much less common. Used nasally for hay fever and for perennial rhinitis, the milder cases respond best, and the effects are not dramatic. Frequent use is essential.

Used as eye drops for conjunctivitis, the effects vary, and patients often complain of stinging and irritation. This is due to the preservatives, stabilizers and anti-bacterial substances which are essential in eye drops.

Intal for food allergy or suspected food allergy is dealt with in the food section. Results vary a great deal, but sometimes dramatic relief of gut symptoms occurs.

What are the side-effects of Intal?

The short answer is none at all, except in very rare cases of allergy to the drug itself. Occasionally excessive use of Intal Compound can cause side-effects from the effects of the isoprenaline.

In children the cessation of acute attacks gives great reassurance to the family, who are most relieved to be rid of these frightening episodes. However, regular checks on the peak flow rate may reveal a result well below normal. Because the benefits of Intal may be more subjective than objective, a false sense of security may exist unless regular checks on the peak flow rate are made.

What are bronchodilators?

These drugs are given as tablets, syrups, suppositories, aerosols or powders (or injections in an emergency) to relieve bronchial spasm of any cause. There are two types – some for short-term emergency treatment and other for long-term control. Here I shall only deal with the long-term bronchodilators as emergency treatment is dealt with at the end of this chapter.

How do bronchodilator drugs work?

The bronchial tubes have muscles wrapped around them right down to quite small branches, and these can act as a protective mechanism by constricting and narrowing the bronchi to prevent the entry of, for example, an irritant gas. Though we are unaware of it, they are controlled by the involuntary nervous system by means of special receptors (i.e. sensors) near the muscle. The lining of the bronchi is provided with tiny sensors which respond to irritation or cold, and are also triggered off by the mediators released by an allergic reaction. Thus, many sorts of stimuli can cause these muscles to contract, thereby narrowing the bronchi and causing bronchospasm, wheezing and obstruction to the passage of air.

Bronchodilators work by stimulating other receptors which relax the muscles and thus increase air flow. Research has shown that there are at least two types of receptor in the lining of the bronchi, named beta 1 and beta 2. The importance of this is that the heart also has beta 1 receptors, so drugs which act on beta 1 in the bronchi will also affect the heart. Thus, drugs such as Ventolin (salbutamol), which act selectively on beta 2 receptors alone, will relieve the asthma without upsetting the heart. The drug reaches these receptors either directly by aerosol, or indirectly through the bloodstream.

How effective are modern bronchodilators?

Doctors try to select from the large range available those drugs which seem to help their patients most. As detailed elsewhere, however, it is impossible to estimate how effective a drug is unless measurements of the airway before and after use are carried out. The simplest way to do this is by using a peak flow meter, which will also show how much below normal the patient may be before using a bronchodilator. Some asthmatics, especially the young ones, are very responsive to bronchodilator aerosols, so that the reading on a peak flow meter will reach nearly normal or even normal levels after a short time. Obviously such responses cannot be expected in older people, so there is a great deal of variation in reversibility of the asthma, which does not depend simply on the muscles of the bronchi, but on many other factors as well.

If bronchodilator aerosols have become ineffective in spite of taking many puffs it is time to seek informed medical advice. This may be the point at which steroids are urgently required to prevent a serious situation arising, and is always a danger signal.

What are the side-effects of bronchodilators?

The earlier bronchodilators such as ephedrine, adrenaline, isoprenaline and similar drugs affected other types of receptors as well as the beta 2 receptors. As a result they affected the heart, making it go faster, and sometimes could also act as a stimulant and keep the patient awake. Some aerosols contained large doses of isoprenaline, and were suspected as one cause of the abrupt increase in the death rate from asthma about 16 years ago, but not proved.

Today's selective beta 2 bronchodilators are, therefore, a major advance in treatment, but it is relevant to mention that when salbutamol (Ventolin) is taken by mouth, or in large dose by aerosol, it has to go round the whole circulation to reach the target. The ordinary muscles also have beta 2 receptors, so this is why tremor may occur. In fact some patients complain that they can hardly sign their name and are anxious lest it should be thought that they have gone senile or alcoholic. This is one of the reasons for the preference for inhalation of drugs, which thus go direct to the target without upsetting the rest of the body, but in children or those who cannot inhale properly oral preparations may be essential.

Drugs called beta-blockers are now widely used for high blood pressure and other cardiac problems, but can cause alarming attacks of asthma as they exert the opposite *effect to beta-stimulants.* Some drugs are worse than others in this regard, and have to be selected with care in asthmatics who also have cardiac problems. Sometimes beta-blockers will produce an asthma attack when the presence of latent asthma had not been recognized previously, so it is important to stop and go back to your doctor if treatment makes you worse.

When should a nebulizer be used?

Home nebulizers resemble a scent spray, and create a fine mist of bronchodilator solution which is inhaled by the patient. Nebulizers operate on compressed air, supplied by a little compressor, or by a foot-pump worked by a willing relative. The most advanced type is ultrasonic, and the most expensive. The usual National Health Service oxygen cylinder does not supply enough pressure to work a nebulizer properly, because of the design of the control valve.

Nebulizers can be a great help in very young children who cannot use any inhaler or aerosol properly, and the medication used can be either a bronchodilator such as Ventolin or Bricanyl, or a liquid form of Intal, which has proved very useful in severe asthma in infants.

Recently it has been shown that a mixture of Ventolin and Atrovent may be more effective than either separately, and new and much longer acting bronchodilators such as salmeterol should be available soon, as clinical trials are very encouraging. Inhalation of nebulized Becotide has now been found to be very helpful in treating wheezy babies. This is important, because Ventolin is not helpful below 15 months of age.

Children subject to severe sudden attacks of asthma can benefit from a home nebulizer for emergency treatment as it will provide relief just as quickly as an injection. In fact, many children who get an inhalation from a nebulizer in the casualty department do not need to be admitted to hospital. Obviously if a nebulizer is available at home an asthma attack will be much less upsetting for everyone concerned.

Larger doses of bronchodilators can be given with a nebulizer, and the water or saline which is simultaneously inhaled prevents the bronchi from drying out, or the sputum from becoming too sticky. Severe cases of asthma or chronic bronchitis can benefit

greatly from the use of an efficient nebulizer when the usual
aerosols are ineffective.

However, frequent sudden attacks mean poor control, and
that the treatment should be reviewed. Increased use of bronchodilator aerosols or nebulizers is always a danger signal,
suggesting that medical advice should be sought without delay.
If relief is not obtained from a nebulizer the situation is probably serious.

What is aminophylline, and how useful a drug is it?

Aminophylline is one of the oldest drugs used as a bronchodilator, and it is usually given by mouth. Nausea or sickness was a
common side-effect which limited its usefulness, but in recent
years slow-release tablets have been developed which do not
cause this problem, and are very widely prescribed (Neulin SA,
Slo-Phyllin, Aminophylline SR, Theocontin Continus, and so
on).

This drug is not fully effective unless the amount in the blood
is just below that which would cause toxic side-effects. Blood
tests help to establish the right dosage to achieve this level, but
there are few facilities for these tests to be done in this country. It
is quite likely that many patients are underdosed and derive no
benefit, while others may have too high a level.

Suppositories given at bedtime are quite often used, and can
be useful in preventing night attacks. Syrups are often given to
children but may not be very effective.

Can aminophylline have any serious side-effects?

Intravenous injections of aminophylline have been a routine
emergency treatment for acute asthma for many years. This
injection may be given by the family doctor, by the emergency
doctor, or in the casualty department of a hospital.

Slow-release preparations in common use may sometimes give
levels of aminophylline in the blood which are fairly high. When
a large injection is given on top the results can be very serious
including cardiac arrest.

Patients taking this drug should, therefore, carry a card or

bracelet to warn doctors that they are taking slow-release aminophylline and should not receive large doses intravenously.

What about the miscellaneous other bronchodilator tablets, syrups, and so on?

Under this heading is a selection of mixtures of aminophylline,
ephedrine and other bronchodilators. Ephedrine can act as a
general stimulant but can also cause difficulties with passing
water in old men.

Many of these miscellaneous preparations are not particularly
effective nor do they produce much in the way of side-effects. For
this reason many such mixtures are available from chemists
without prescription.

What is the place of bronchodilators in asthma treatment?

Bronchodilators are all that is required to treat mild or occasional asthma. Inhaled bronchodilators, aerosols or powder usually
give immediate relief which will last for up to 4 hours, depending
on the drug being used.

In moderately severe asthma, or unstable asthma, regular use
may be required, but Becotide or Intal will probably also be
necessary because bronchodilators on their own will be insufficient for complete control.

Oral preparations are more of a background bronchodilator
only, while inhaled bronchodilators are usually part of the team
of drugs used in modern therapy for asthma.

In chronic asthma regular usage of bronchodilators is usual,
but as an adjunct to Becotide or oral steroids. The effectiveness
of bronchodilators is poorest when the airway is most seriously
impaired, and improves as oral steroids become fully effective.
*Thus, they tend to fail to help when most needed, and lack of response is a
danger signal.*

15 Specific treatment for allergy by avoidance, specific immunotherapy or desensitization

What is meant by specific and non-specific treatment for allergic problems?

There are three ways to treat most allergic problems, which are as follows:

Suppression

This is attempted by means of drugs which prevent or abolish the symptoms. This approach is quite non-specific, because it is unnecessary to know what causes the symptoms. This treatment may suffice unless control with drugs alone is inadequate, or the drugs are causing side-effects.

Specific avoidance

If the allergen or allergens responsible for the symptoms can be identified accurately then these symptoms will cease to occur if the allergen(s), can be completely avoided. This applies particularly to animals and foods. Complete relief without dependence on drugs can be obtained by avoidance, so this is the ideal treatment, but to achieve it often requires the help of an allergy specialist, who may not always be available.

Specific avoidance is not a 'cure' because contact with the allergen will still trigger off a reaction. Thus indefinite, often lifelong, vigilance is necessary. It is most gratifying to both physician and patient to effect complete relief without drugs by means of specific avoidance, but suppression with drugs is the usual approach today.

SPECIFIC DESENSITIZATION OR 'IMMUNOTHERAPY'

This treatment is no longer given in Britain, but this section has been retained because the subject is of such fundamental importance to the understanding of allergic disease. Also readers in other countries may find this section very helpful.

This is the only form of treatment for allergies which has any potential for 'cure'. The term 'desensitization' implies complete immunity, while 'hypo-sensitization' means a lesser degree of immunity. Immunotherapy is the term often used today for this treatment. If the patient no longer reacts to severe exposure to the allergen desensitization has been accomplished. The principle of this method of treatment is that giving injections of the known causative allergen in gradually increasing doses will eventually accustom the immune system to the allergen so that a reaction no longer takes place, and the patient no longer has symptoms.

There are other methods of attempting to diminish sensitivity to allergens which are very controversial and not yet accepted. These are the use of allergen extracts given as drops under the tongue, or swallowed in the form of tablets or capsules. Another approach is to attempt to define the dose of allergen which will 'neutralize' the symptoms if taken every day, and a similar method depends on daily self-injection of tiny doses of allergens into the skin. How these methods can achieve a result is quite unknown, but if the results can be validated by modern methods of clinical trial, further scientific research is urgently necessary.

Many hay fever victims have built up considerable immunity to grass pollen by the end of the season, but this will relapse well before the next pollen season. Over the last five years, the author has used daily stimulation of immunity by self-administered drops of strong pollen extract, which are absorbed at once to contact the immune system, so as to retain and enhance the naturally acquired immunity at the end of the season. Results have been very encouraging.

The choice of treatment should always be based on a thorough appraisal of all aspects of the case. In many instances a combination of all available methods of treatment may be necessary, which may cause difficulties in attributing improvement to one method or the other. The objective of treatment should always be to enable the sufferer to live as normal a life as possible, while avoiding the use of drugs with possible long-term harmful side-effects, and using drugs free from such effects to the best advantage.

What is the historical background to the idea that injections of the cause of the allergy might be helpful?

In 1873 Dr Charles Blackley of Manchester proved grass pollen to be the cause of his hay fever by performing nasal challenges and skin tests on himself. He also made the first pollen count, and related it to his own sufferings. The next advance was in 1910, when Noon and Freeman showed that hay fever could be effectively treated by injections of pollen extract. Freeman went on to build up one of the first allergy clinics in the world, where he taught the patients to give themselves a pollen injection every day for 56 days, and how to treat any reactions. As there was no other effective method, patients would willingly undergo such intensive treatment rather than suffer. Today this regime would be considered heroic or dangerous, but the results have probably never been bettered, and the clinic at St Mary's Hospital, London, became world-famous. The 'magic bullet' of the latest drug can never be more effective than complete immunity, which allows a patient to enjoy the summer.

If the cause of the allergic problem is known, what action can be taken?

Avoidance of a known cause, such as a pet or a food, is a very effective policy if it can be properly carried out. It is undoubtedly the safest and most logical type of treatment when it can be practised without excessive disruption of family life, and when the sensitivity is not so extreme that accidental exposure might result in dangerous attacks.

Avoidance is often successful in combination with minimal or intermittent use of drugs such as Intal (sodium cromoglycate or cromolyn) or antihistamines. For example, Intal can be inhaled shortly before visiting a relative who has an animal to which the patient is sensitive. Intal will then block any reaction between the pet and the patient, and unless the sensitivity is extreme this can be very effective, but the drug has to be taken *before* the encounter takes place. In an accidental or unexpected exposure to an animal, bronchodilator aerosols will give immediate relief in the case of asthma, or a decongestant can be used for a nasal reaction.

Complete avoidance may be impossible. In the case of dust mites, for example, an intensive anti-dust campaign can be very disappointing because many patients, particularly children, become so intensely sensitized to the mites that even the tiniest trace of the dust mite and its excreta will be enough to keep the allergy going. Thus, in spite of having the most effective drugs to suppress their asthma, some severely affected patients may never be adequately controlled. It may be possible to reverse their asthma by short-term high doses or oral steroids, but many quickly relapse when the dosage is reduced, and Becotide alone may not give really good control. These are the problem patients where densensitizing injections may be very helpful, but also those who are most likely to have reactions to the injections.

What problems are encountered in attempting to avoid specific animals?

Unfortunately it is common for people sensitive to dogs, cats and horses to have many friends and relatives who also keep these animals. In addition, many people are sensitive to several animals at once, so if the individual is very sensitive avoidance can be extremely difficult.

The amount of affection people lavish on their pets can be a serious problem. Sometimes pets are put before husbands, wives or children. Many patients ask to be desensitized against their animals, but it is usually more practical to find the pet a good home and springclean thoroughly afterwards. Parting with a pet which has become one of the family is hard, but it is a simple, straightforward and effective way of dealing with the allergy. This solution is far better than drugs and their side-effects, or the inconvenience of desensitization. For occasional encounters Intal may be an effective but temporary blocking agent.

When should injections to desensitize against animals be given?

In cases where patients are dependent on animals, such as users of guide dogs or guard dogs, farmers, dog and cat breeders, jockeys and show jumpers, veterinary surgeons and laboratory workers, it is obvious that an attempt to make them immune to the animals should be made.

It is frequent for patients to become sensitized to all the common animals at once and for avoidance to be a practical impossibility because all the friends and relations keep pets. If the patient, often a child, is very sensitive indeed the only practical approach may be giving injections, but this is no longer possible in the UK.

After a pet has been found a new home what action should be taken?

It is essential to have a very thorough springcleaning of the house after the departure of a beloved pet. The following case history illustrates how difficult it can be to eliminate all traces of cat allergen.

A man was aware that he was intensely sensitive to cats, so when he was considering the purchase of a certain house he asked the owners if they had ever had a cat. He was told that they had had a dog but not a cat, and as he was not sensitive to dogs he bought the house. Within weeks he was in hospital with severe asthma. On his return home he questioned the neighbours and discovered that the cat next door had been so friendly with the dog that the animals used to sit together in front of the fire in his house night after night. He had the lounge carpet cleaned but still had symptoms, so he finally burned it, and bought a new one. His symptoms actually persisted until he had redecorated the house from top to bottom.

This extreme case demonstrates how traces of an animal can cause problems to a new owner, so that an allergic subject should always make careful enquiries before buying or renting a house. Indeed, experience suggests that allergic people should not buy old damp houses, because of mites, moulds and traces of pets in them. Renovating old houses, with the inevitable dust exposure, is quite often the beginning of a dust allergy problem.

Sprays containing tannic acid have recently been introduced for denaturing the animal allergens and killing mites.

How effective is avoidance of the home environment by sending children to boarding schools?

In the French Pyrenees, Switzerland, and Germany there are large boarding schools specifically for severely asthmatic children, who have been removed from their home environmental allergens and are living at an altitude where dust mites do not thrive. Similar facilities do not exist in this country, and the few severely asthmatic British children who have been successfully treated in these schools have adapted remarkably quickly to both language and environment. It is possible, with difficulty, to send selected severe asthmatics to these schools, the fees being paid by the National Health Service. Children from Birmingham have been supported by a special fund run by a local Sunday newspaper.

In Britain many local authorities run special schools at great expense for asthmatic and other delicate or disadvantaged children. In my experience these special schools often produce disappointing results, probably because the children do not leave home completely for up to 2 years, as they do in Europe, but come home for holidays and often every weekend, largely due to the schools' psychiatric advisers' concern that the children should not be deprived of parental affection; a view which is ironic when the deprivation of the children of the better-off at public schools is considered!

The idea of sending children away to school originated from the observation that when children were sent to boarding schools their asthma often disappeared, only to return during the holidays. This was regarded as a psychological reaction, with mother especially to blame, but it is more likely that the children were exchanging a house full of dust mites and animals for spartan schools with no carpets, polished linoleum and nowhere for the mites to live (*see* Figure 9.3).

Special schools can be effective if positive treatment, such as desensitization, is undertaken in term-time, with the object of protecting them against the environment to which they must eventually return. It is easy to imagine how an inadequately treated child eventually leaves the special school, only to become an adult chronic asthmatic, unable to earn a living by manual work because of physical disability, and possibly having had an education inadequate for a more skilled occupation.

My attention was drawn to this problem when a 16 year old girl, who had spent 4 years at a local special school, was referred because of her asthma. She was well at school but always ill at home, so she spent most of her holidays in the children's hospital. She was found to be very sensitive to dust mites and grass pollen, was easily desensitized to these allergens, and has since been able to live a normal life.

Albert, who developed severe asthma every weekend when he returned home from the special boarding school, is a good example. He improved dramatically following desensitization against the house-dust mite, and was able to go home for the weekend without developing severe asthma. Some time later the family were rehoused, the adverse effects of the weekend disappeared completely, and he was able to return home and attend the local day school without asthma. Perhaps rehousing would have been the cheapest solution to his asthma problems, as the local authority would have saved thousands of pounds which were spent on keeping him at boarding school (*see* Figure 15.1a and b).

How can pollens and moulds be avoided?

Perennial mould spores such as *Penicillium* and *Aspergillus* are found in old damp houses, cellars, stables and cowsheds, in mouldy hay after a wet summer, and around compost heaps. Obviously these sources can be avoided, but there are always some mould spores both inside and outside. Mould spores are very small indeed, sometimes only 2 microns, and it has been shown that air currents can transport them from the cellar to the attic of a four-storey house in a few minutes. The concentration of spores in the air of a stable, barn or cowshed is extreme, and smaller spores from mouldy hay cause the severe disease of farmer's lung.

Farmers are obviously the most at risk from mould allergy because spores are such a common occupational exposure, and even healthy farmers are well advised to wear a special mask when necessary, especially if operating a combine harvester. Workers who handle stored grain are also exposed to mould spores and, like farmers, to the mites which live in enormous numbers in the grain. There is a certain amount of self-selection amongst these workers – if they cannot tolerate the dust and spores they tend to find a more suitable job.

Damp houses and dusty jobs can be avoided, but for those who are intensely sensitive relief by avoidance may not be so easy to find. In fact, the only time that they may be able to breathe normally may be during a period of hard frost, this being the only time when mould spores are absent from the air. The alternative for the fortunate few is to move from this country to a warm dry climate where moulds in the air are much less common. It is interesting that allergies were almost unknown in the Arab countries until oil money enabled them to drill for water. Parts of the desert now have trees, shrubs, and grass – so now they have pollen and mould allergy too!

What can be done to help severe seasonal allergies?

It is difficult to avoid airborne allergens except by staying indoors, preferably in a room with an air filter, but this advice is seldom practical or essential. Suppressive drugs of the types mentioned elsewhere in this book may give relief which varies from complete to slight, but a good deal of expertise is required to make the best of them. If the results are unsatisfactory it is logical to consider specific desensitization against the allergen, usually grass pollen. In the USA and Canada, ragweed pollen in late summer, is the most troublesome allergen. And sometimes it is impossible to identify the moulds which cause late summer asthma, so suppressive drug treatment is the only remedy. However, drug treatment without side-effects has made great strides in the last decade or so.

Air filters may provide some relief, by filtering out seasonal allergens such as grass pollen and seasonal mould spores. These filters are of many types and can be placed in the central heating system, or operate as a recirculating filter with the window closed, or be installed in the window so as to filter all the air which passes into the room. Experience of filters over the last 25 years has been disappointing unless the patient is strictly confined to the room or house.

Negative-ion generators are being intensively advertised for the allergy patient, but the claims may be exaggerated and are difficult to confirm. The dust particles in the air become negatively charged, and hence fly to the positively charged wall so that marks on the wallpaper may be an unwelcome feature.

All these methods of avoidance are usually doomed to failure because the patient may inhale enough allergen on the way to work to cause symptoms which last most of the day, and then take on another load of allergen on the way home which causes problems at night. Ideally this type of patient should have air filtration in the car as well as in the house and at work because many who work in an air-conditioned environment still suffer from the delayed effects of the pollen taken in on the way to work, or if they go out of the office at lunchtime. Today's motorways have been planted with grass which is not cut so often as it used to be because of financial constraints, and the passage of vehicles disturbs the grass pollen which flies in through the ventilators or the open window of the car. A patient who had to travel 30 miles down a motorway to his office had such severe hay fever that he changed cars from a Ferrari to a fully air-conditioned Rolls Royce. It may be some consolation to the rest of us that this proved an expensive failure, as he still suffered symptoms from the pollen he inhaled before he got into his car.

Avoidance of mould spores and pollen grains can only succeed in a limited way, and no child or active adult can be expected to stay indoors all summer so as to avoid these microscopic hazards. It is clearly desirable to render patients immune so that they no longer react to these allergens, a result which can be achieved in many cases by desensitization, however, this is no longer possible in the UK.

What can be done if the cause of the allergy is known but cannot be avoided?

If the allergic symptoms can be controlled completely by means of drugs which do not cause side-effects the problem is effectively solved. Obviously, the complaint must be diagnosed as being allergic before the correct drugs can be used, a requirement often prevented by the inexplicable reluctance to diagnose asthma in children.

If drug treatment does not give adequate control, as in a case of asthma where attacks are frequent, then an attempt to decrease sensitivity of the patient to a known allergen, such as the ubiquitous dust mite, may be considered. When all the correct drugs used in adequate dosage cannot control the problem, there is no other approach available with any potential for improvement, particularly in severe asthma, where the allergic reaction may be so intense and unrelenting that dependence on oral steroids becomes inevitable.

If the causative allergen is known and the patient can be rendered less sensitive or insensitive to the allergen, complete control is possible, even to the point of reducing or even stopping the medication. This combination of effective suppression with drugs plus specific desensitization is capable of turning a respiratory cripple into a normal happy child or adult, but an intensive approach to the treatment is essential for success. Such a result cannot always be obtained, but the fact that it can be attained at all should be a stimulus to direct effort towards cure rather than relying entirely on suppression with drugs.

What types of allergic disease are most effectively treated by desensitizing injections?

Immediate-type allergy of the respiratory tract due to inhaled allergens is the type of allergy that does best with desensitization, especially in younger patients. This is the type of case where the cause is most easily identified, and where challenge tests before and after treatment can be carried out.

Grass pollens, tree pollens, seasonal and perennial mould

spores and house-dust mite are examples of allergens so difficult to avoid that the attempt to make the patient immune to them is logical treatment. The question of effectiveness will be dealt with elsewhere because it depends so much on the attitude, training and convictions of the doctor concerned.

Allergy to insect stings is also most effectively treated with increasing doses of pure wasp or bee venom. This aspect of allergy has been revolutionized by the availability of pure venom for treatment, and has been shown to be effective. These patients have a very dangerous allergy, because another sting could cause anaphylaxis and death.

How is desensitization carried out?

Desensitization is carried out by injecting increasing amounts of allergenic extract under the skin (subcutaneously). The principle is to introduce just enough allergen into the body to stimulate the immune system to react against the allergen, but without provoking any physical symptoms. The amount of allergen injected increases with each successive dose, and provided that the body's immunity also increases just a little faster than the increase in the dose of allergen, no allergic symptoms will occur. In this way immunity is built up to the extent that exposure to the allergen will cause little or no reaction.

Having reached this ideal state, it is essential, with perennial allergens such as dust mite, to continue for at least 2 years with regular booster injections to keep the immunity at a high level. If the injections are stopped or boosters are not given the result is that any immunity will soon decline and the treatment will have been pointless.

What different types of allergy injection are available?

Extracts of allergens up to about 1950 were always the 'aqueous' or watery type. These are made by soaking (extracting) a weighed amount of the allergen for some hours or days in a saline solution containing a little carbolic to prevent bacterial growth. It is then filtered to remove the spent pollen or other allergen and after checks to ensure sterility and lack of toxicity is ready for use.

Aqueous vaccines are not used so often now, as they need more expertise in dosage adjustment so that the patient's tolerance is not exceeded, but if a sufficiently high dose is reached the stimulus to the immune system seems to give the best results. When an aqueous extract is injected it is immediately distributed throughout the body fluids and is also excreted quickly, so reactions can occur suddenly. Today we seem to be more concerned about possible reactions than was the case 40 or 50 years ago, when many patients, even children, gave themselves daily injections and there were no anti-histamines or steroids to cope with reactions, only adrenaline, which is still the first choice for immediate treatment.

Delayed-release vaccines are usually made by joining the allergen to a relatively insoluble carrier particle, which is quite inert. The idea is that the allergen is not released all at once, but slowly over about a week, after which the next injection, which can be much larger, is given. Immediate reactions are much less likely but delayed relatively mild reactions may occur during the next 24 hours, rarely on the second or third day after. This type of extract is the one most commonly used today, as its advantages outweigh any disadvantages.

This idea of providing a slow release of allergen into the circulation has been adopted with many carrier particles, but attempts are now being made to alter the allergen itself in such a way that it will not cause reactions but will still stimulate immunity. Trials are only in the experimental stages, but are very promising.

How are the dosages of desensitizing vaccines decided?

Because the sensitivity of allergic patients varies from slight to extreme, the makers of desensitizing vaccines provide the doctor with a choice of dosage schedules suitable for mildly sensitive, moderately sensitive and very sensitive patients. The decision as to which schedule to use may be a difficult one, and is arrived at by considering the clinical history, the size and intensity of the skin tests and the results of the RAST if it has been done. The dosage schedules provided by the makers are inevitably a compromise which will not suit everyone, and can be modified by the doctor as necessary.

The dose of the allergen being injected increases each week and the immunity of the patient should increase a little faster than the increase of the dose. If the dose rises faster than the immunity then reactions will be provoked, but if the dose increases too slowly there is inadequate stimulus for immunity to be produced, so it is important to get the dose right.

The problem with the dosage of allergen injections is that no two patients are alike, and the injections themselves are not always standardized. Thus there is a certain amount of guess-work in deciding what dosage the patient will tolerate without problems, so it is sensible to err towards underdosage.

What safety precautions are taken when giving desensitizing injections?

When injections are being given there will always be an emergency tray immediately to hand. This will hold a syringe full of adrenaline already drawn up ready for use, plus other emergency gear for use in case of a severe reaction to an injection. Sudden reactions can happen, but fortunately they are rare, and are nearly always easily stopped by an injection of adrenaline. Do not be worried because your doctor is prepared for trouble – there would be a greater cause for anxiety if he or she were not!

Some types of desensitizing injections, particularly insect venoms and some very potent standardized vaccines from Scandinavia, are only given in hospital. This is because they are so strong that reactions are more likely, and in hospital any reactions can be more efficiently dealt with. They are so much more effective that it is worth the extra trouble. In some centres in Europe rush courses, in hospital, with injections every half hour thus completing the course in a day or two, are being used with great success.

Reactions can be avoided if side-effects experienced by the patient after previous injections are noted, because if no attention is paid to previous mild reactions (which mean that a reduction of dosage is essential) a more serious reaction can occur. A few doctors have the curious idea that to have side-effects is a good sign, because the patient must suffer to achieve a good result!

How effective is desensitization treatment?

This is not an easy question to answer because results depend on so many factors. The allergenic extracts must be as strong and pure as possible, otherwise they will be ineffective. Standardization of extracts is being introduced very slowly, and it is difficult to be certain with the cruder extracts that the material will be the same strength the next time.

The enthusiasm, experience and skill of the allergy specialist is a very important factor in obtaining good results (Figures 15.1a and b; 15.2a and b). This is because he or she can motivate patients, explain what it is hoped to achieve, and encourage them to undergo effective treatment. If the doctor lacks experience or confidence the treatment is liable to be given up too easily, and if the final dose is too low disappointment often follows. Many investigators have shown that the best results are obtained by reaching the highest tolerated dose, so unless a high dose is reached the injections may be ineffective. This point is also discussed in the section below on the reasons for failure of this form of treatment.

Is it possible to desensitize a patient against more than one allergen at the same time?

If there is evidence to suggest that the patient is allergic to more than one allergen it is very tempting to put a mixture of allergens in the vaccine. The result will be that the highest dose which can be given is divided by the number of ingredients in the mixture. As the results depend on reaching the highest possible dose for each allergen this method is self-defeating. Mixtures containing many allergens lead to disappointed patients and disillusioned doctors.

My personal practice for many years was to have a separate vaccine for each allergen to which the patient could be shown to be sensitive. The different vaccines are given on separate days of the week. This can create difficulties, as in one patient where no less than five allergens were found responsible for her summer asthma. Fortunately, however, her son was a nurse, and it was arranged that he should give her a different

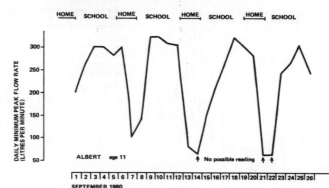

This severe chronic asthmatic child could not be controlled as an out-patient and had very frequent admissions to hospital. He was, therefore, admitted to a special boarding school for delicate children. He had an excellent response to removal from his home environment, but always relapsed in the vacations. When the educational psychologist insisted that the children were allowed home every weekend he began to have severe asthma because of exposure to very poor environmental conditions at home every weekend, as shown on chart.

Figure 15.1(a)   Weekend asthma abolished by desensitization.

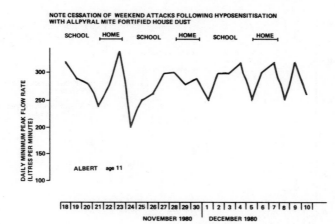

The suggestion that he should stay at school at weekends was unwelcome, so he was immunized against his home environment with a house dust vaccine. The chart shows the lessening of effects of weekends at home.

Figure 15.1(b)   Weekend asthma abolished by desensitization.

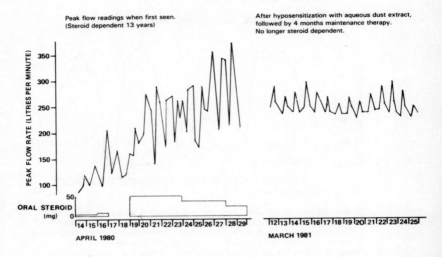

Figure 15.2(a)   Examples of results from desensitization.

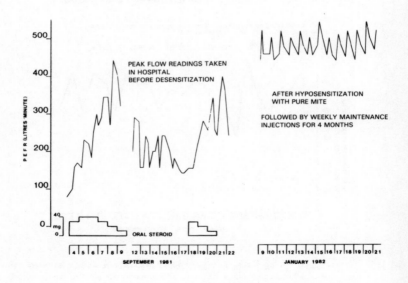

Figure 15.2(b)   Examples of results from desensitization.

allergen injection every day, with an excellent result. If any reaction occurred, it was obvious which allergen was responsible. If really good results can be obtained by such intensive methods, it is worthwhile taking trouble.

How many allergen injections are required to get a good result?

The number of injections, and the time required to obtain a worthwhile result, is determined mainly by the sensitivity of the patient. In a very sensitive person the dose can only be increased very gradually, so that a larger number of injections will be required, because such a person can tolerate only a small increase in dose each time. A mildly sensitive patient can take much larger steps in dosage without reaction, so needs fewer injections.

Dosage is a matter of adjusting the schedule to the patient, so that the immunity developed increases faster than the increase in dosage. On the other hand, if immunity develops more slowly than the dosage increases, the body will react against the allergen injection. Readjustment will give the immune system time to catch up.

The manufacturers of allergy vaccines have made great efforts to reduce the number of injections required to six or to three, partly because this is so attractive to doctors and to patients. Great claims are made, but in areas with a high pollen count the results are very disappointing. In my experience it is usually better to have a larger number of injections, matching the dosage schedule to the patient as far as possible, and to have slow but trouble-free progress with a steady increase in immunity.

Why is desensitization sometimes a failure?

The commonest reason for failure is using mixtures of allergens, which defeat the object of the injections by reducing the maximum attainable dose of each allergen. Also, if a patient is categorized as very sensitive the maximum dose reached may often be too low to bring about any improvement. Manufacturers of allergy-treatment vaccines, especially the aqueous types, may reduce the strength of the vaccine to a quarter of the normal for very sensitive adults, and for children to one eighth. Fear of serious reactions is the basis for these precautions, but cutting down the top dose attainable to such an extent may often result in the injections not being worth giving. Too low a dose is self-defeating, and, as mentioned elsewhere, reduction of the increments in dosage and many more injections, with the object of reaching a high and effective top dose, is the logical approach.

Another cause of failure is stopping the injections at the first sign of a slight reaction, instead of modifying the dose. This may happen when the doctor giving the injections is nervous about giving them – a very understandable attitude. Reactions actually confirm that the bottle contains an allergen to which the patient is sensitive, indicating that readjustment of the dosage so as to stimulate immunity without upsetting the patient should eventually be successful.

How does desensitization treatment work?

Injections of pollen extracts were first shown to protect patients against hay fever in 1910, yet there is still no clear explanation of how this benefit is obtained. Antibodies appear in the serum as a result of the injections which can be shown to combine with the allergens of grass pollen. For this reason they are called blocking antibodies, and it was thought that by combining with the pollen they could prevent it triggering off the mast cells. This idea was discarded when it was found that the amount of antibody produced did not correlate with the clinical results. Even more surprising is the finding that the specific IgE for pollen and for other allergens actually increases as a result of injections, but falls later if they are continued. Again the facts from the laboratory do not fit the facts from the clinic, because there is no clear relationship. Perhaps a more likely explanation, yet to be demonstrated, is that the injections 'educate' the T lymphocytes to suppress the production of specific IgE, or of other unknown substances.

Successful desensitization compels the immunological system of the allergic patient to adapt completely to the allergen, so that exposure will no longer cause an adverse reaction. Thus, the patient becomes a normal, healthy person, because the body has

been 'taught' to cope with these allergens by becoming successfully adapted to them, as normal people do.

How can the patient know when immunity is being acquired as a result of desensitizing injections?

In a perennial problem an improvement may be indicated by a
decrease in the frequency of attacks, no effect from an activity
which would usually cause an attack, less need for medication, a
decrease in symptoms, or an increase in the peak flow rate.
Improvement rarely takes place before the halfway point in the
initial injection course. There are so many variables that the
only really objective way to show that real improvement is
taking place is by challenge testing before and after treatment.

In seasonal allergies the injection course is commenced early
in the year so that it is completed well before the season arrives,
so as not to add insult to injury by injecting the allergen at a time
of the year when it is also being inhaled from the environment.
Again, it is not possible without performing direct nasal or
bronchial challenge tests to find out if a state of immunity has
been achieved, or to predict whether the treatment will be a
success or a failure.

If desensitization is recommended against grass pollen, is it possible to be sure it is worthwhile going to all this trouble?

It is preferable for the diagnosis of pollen sensitivity to be
confirmed by means of a challenge test so that there is no doubt
that the treatment is really necessary. If it is decided to immunize the patient against grass pollen the injections should begin
in January, so that the initial course of weekly injections can be
finished by Easter, because another identical provocation test
will then show definitely if the patient still reacts positively or
has become negative. If negative then a season free from symptoms is to be expected. Frequently the provocation test is still
positive at Easter, in spite of the fact that the full course of
injections has been completed, so booster injections of the top

dose once a week for 5 weeks are given, followed by another challenge test. If negative this time the patient can be assured that any hay fever will not be due to grass pollen, but if still positive there is still time to continue weekly top doses until the first week in June.

Nine out of ten patients who achieve a negative reaction to a challenge test have a completely clear season or only a mild sniffle. Drugs should be unnecessary and the desensitization must be counted as a failure if the patient is dependent on them for relief.

Using this logical way of tailoring the treatment to the requirements of each patient, and monitoring the degree of immunity which is being acquired, makes worthwhile results possible. The patient should be a willing and co-operative partner if the rationale for this treatment is understood.

How long does immunity to an allergen as a result of desensitizing injections last?

In the case of perennial allergens such as the dust mite which are impossible to avoid because they are constantly present in the environment, it is essential to get regular booster injections in order to maintain the hard-won immunity. Booster injections are necessary for at least 2 years, often more, but finally are required only once a month. Absence of symptoms and a decreasing requirement for drug treatment is an indication of lasting immunity, which can be objectively demonstrated by showing that the inhalation of the same dose of allergen which produced an obvious reaction before treatment no longer does so. Challenge tests are carried out at a few special research units in this country, but are not routine elsewhere.

Desensitization against summer allergens such as grass pollen has to be repeated for several years before it will last from year to year. There is no guide to the need for injections in the coming spring except the result of a challenge test, which has usually reverted to positive by November or December. If intensive treatment has resulted in complete immunity, it is usually easier to achieve in the following years, finally becoming unnecessary after a number of years which varies from one person to another.

The use of direct nasal challenge tests to determine if treatment with grass pollen is required in the spring is only carried out at research centres.

What is the potential value of specialized allergy investigation and desensitization treatment?

Several very extensive long-term surveys in England, America and Scandinavia have all shown that if asthmatic children receive the attentions of a skilled allergist during childhood three-quarters of them will have no symptoms as adults, while only a quarter of those who do not receive specialized treatment and advice recover spontaneously. Specialized care implies a really comprehensive investigation of the case, leading to specific avoidance or desensitization where appropriate.

Unfortunately in Britain training in allergy is only just beginning to receive attention, and suppression is usually the only approach available. As a result the majority of the British medical profession is not aware of the value of comprehensive investigations by properly trained allergists, especially in children.

There is also much scepticism regarding desensitizing injections which, if given at all, are often given in a half-hearted manner without the positive approach described here. Consequently, scepticism regarding the effectiveness of this form of treatment is frequently 'confirmed' by poor results. Giving injections for allergy is a controversial topic as the majority of British doctors either consider, or were taught as students, that allergic problems are basically psychosomatic and that the injections are ineffective or dangerous.

The quite incorrect belief that children will grow out of their allergies, at perhaps the age of seven or in their early teens, is still widespread. In America and in Scandinavia, on the other hand, specialized treatment is routine. In Britain three times as many children take their asthma problem into adult life as in these other countries. The toll in human misery, and the expense, must be enormous when it is considered that there are about half a million asthmatic children in Britain, ignoring all other allergic complaints. It is interesting that long-term follow-

If Causative Allergen are positively identified by Skin Test *and* Clinical History, and are unavoidable then injections can be seriously considered. Ideally Bronchial or Nasal Challenge would be positive before treatment but this is not usually available.

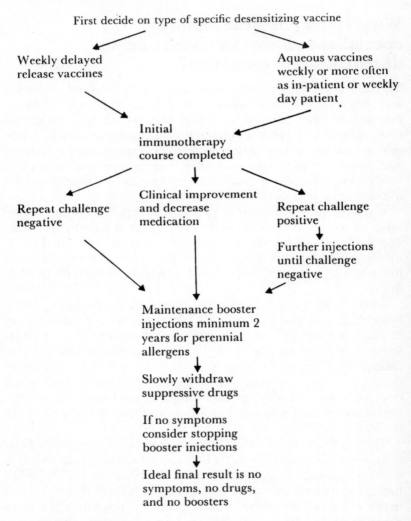

First decide on type of specific desensitizing vaccine

Weekly delayed release vaccines

Aqueous vaccines weekly or more often as in-patient or weekly day patient

Initial immunotherapy course completed

Repeat challenge negative

Clinical improvement and decrease medication

Repeat challenge positive

Further injections until challenge negative

Maintenance booster injections minimum 2 years for perennial allergens

Slowly withdraw suppressive drugs

If no symptoms consider stopping booster injections

Ideal final result is no symptoms, no drugs, and no boosters

Repeat annually for seasonal allergens until seasonal symptoms minor or negligible.

Figure 15.3   The use of desensitization in the pragmatic management of asthma and rhinitis.

up of large numbers of children who had desensitization treatment for their hay fever disclosed that hardly any of them developed asthma due to grass pollen, but many of those who did not get this treatment developed pollen asthma.

Desensitization was more often necessary before the introduction of Becotide, because this was often the only hope of weaning patients off oral steroids. However, where specific desensitization is required, it is more satisfying than just using drugs, as remarkable improvements can be achieved, as illustrated in Figures 15.1 and 2.

Why are desensitizing injections no longer given in Britain?

The Committee on Safety of Medicines, which monitors all treatments for side-effects, issued a directive in October 1986 which stated that desensitizing injections should only be carried out "where full facilities for cardio-respiratory resuscitation are immediately available, and patients should be kept under medical observation for at least two hours after treatment".

As it is most unusual for resuscitation equipment to be available in a family doctor's surgery, and very few patients will wait for two hours after an injection, treatment stopped at once. Neither the author nor any other experienced allergy specialists have ever seen severe reactions so long after the injection, and consider half an hour waiting to be adequate – as recently agreed by an International Committee of the World Health Organization.

Any injected drug can cause fatal anaphylaxis, including local anaesthetics for dentistry or minor surgery. Sudden collapse can, and does, occur in doctor's surgeries, where resuscitation equipment could be life saving. Although desensitizing injections are not by any means the commonest cause of anaphylaxis, very few health centres are equipped for resuscitation, nor are their staff trained in its use. Cost is a major reason for these facilities not being available in the surgery to treat all patients who collapse.

Why were injections banned in 1986?

Eleven patients had died of anaphylaxis from 1980 onwards, five in the eighteen months before the ban. In most cases there were no facilities available for resuscitation, and precautions described here may not have been observed. Enquiry also may not have been made regarding current illness, or previous reactions, before giving the injection. Lack of knowledge and experience of emergency treatment may also have contributed to these disasters, which are less common in countries where allergy is a recognized specialty.

Obviously the committee were right to be concerned, but their action has deprived British patients of this treatment. It seems possible that they regarded desensitization as of doubtful usefulness in spite of many double blind studies, mainly in Scandinavia and USA, which have all shown quite clearly that this treatment is effective, and safe in trained hands.

What have been the long-term effects of the ban on injections?

By February 1989 all three companies who manufactured vaccines for treatment and testing had ceased trading in this country, but still supply materials to Europe. As a result not even skin testing extracts for the diagnosis of allergies can be bought in the UK, except when specially imported for a named patient.

Patients who have been successfully maintained by desensitizing injections for many years may now relapse, and become totally dependent on drugs. There is no option to drug treatment, which is fine as long as the drugs are properly used, and there are no side-effects.

Perhaps the most serious side-effect of the ban is that many doctors, and some patients as well, now consider that investigations to find the cause are not worthwhile because injections are literally banned. It is easier to prescribe drugs than look for the cause, but it is most important to know what to avoid or remove, especially in children repeatedly admitted to hospital.

PART 6

The Management of Allergy

16   Managing asthma

In this chapter the various types of asthma are discussed, with particular reference to the various ways in which the disease may present itself. This is important because these patterns of presentation may fail to be recognized, so that the patient may not receive the correct treatment, as shown in recent surveys of children in the North of England. In this section we are discussing mainly the perennial type of asthma where a long-term plan of treatment is necessary.

What are the main types of asthma?

Acute attacks

An attack of asthma can come on slowly, or with dramatic suddenness, causing great distress and fear of suffocation. The attack may be preceded, especially in children, by sneezing and coughing followed by increasing shortness of breath, wheezing, and the use of all the chest muscles in the struggle to breathe. Shoulders become hunched up and a pronounced stoop may appear due to overinflation. Patients often find they can breathe better sitting up and leaning forward on a table.

Acute attacks tend to occur at night, and have been described as feeling as if the chest has been blown up with a pump and put in an iron clamp because of the difficulty in getting another breath. The pulse is very often fast, and the lips, especially in children, may have a tinge of blue. Really sudden acute attacks are commoner in children and young people and cause great alarm and even panic because there is a dramatic change from comparatively normal breathing to severe distress. Such attacks cause much parental anxiety as they occur without warning, and there may be varying periods of comparative or even complete freedom from asthma between attacks. An acute attack of asthma can sometimes be fatal, a subject dealt with separately. In many cases the acute attacks may slowly cease to occur, only to be replaced by chronic asthma which slowly and insidiously gets worse.

Chronic asthma

Chronic asthma is caused by the continuous presence of a perennial allergen, and is also greatly influenced by the continued irritability of the bronchial tubes so that they constrict easily. The effects of chronic bronchial obstruction depend largely on the activity of the patient. For example, a mild asthmatic may notice a wheeze only when it is provoked by exertion, while a very sedentary person may not notice any disability from chronic asthma until it is so severe that it causes symptoms at rest. Without using a peak flow meter even the most experienced doctors can misjudge the situation completely.

One of the most important features of chronic asthmatics is that their lives are governed by their disability, exertion being subconsciously avoided as far as practicable. Those who say that they are quite well and are having no trouble may easily deceive themselves and others, including their doctor, regarding the severity of their condition.

Asthma triggered by exercise, cold air, laughing and coughing

An asthma attack, sometimes quite severe, is frequently provoked by exercise in children and young adults. This may be the only time an attack occurs, and in some cases quite severe exertion is necessary before an attack can be induced, whilst in others quite slight exertion is enough. It is easy to confuse normal shortness of breath after exercise with asthma so there may be difficulty in convincing the family doctor that the problem is actually asthma. The use of a peak flow meter before and after exercise will show a dramatic drop in the peak flow rate.

Exercise asthma is at least partly accounted for by increased irritability of the bronchi, so that the passage of large amounts of air has a drying or irritating effect and triggers off contraction of the bronchial muscles and wheezing. Cold air alone can cause constriction of the bronchi even without exercise, as in a boy of 12 whose father claimed that he got such severe asthma as a result of walking only a mile home from school that he insisted that a taxi be supplied by the education authority. Some doubt was cast on his claim because severe exercise had no effect, but walking a short distance on a frosty morning caused a dramatic attack, thus confirming his father's statements. Many asthmatic children who cannot run can swim quite well, because the air near the water is humid and moist, so does not trigger off the asthma so easily as does dry air.

An unusual variant of exercise asthma is provoked by laughing or tickling. One patient judged the success of the treatment by her ability to watch a very funny television programme without getting asthma.

Exercise asthma has been intensively investigated and many theories of causation have been advanced, but the only suggestion usually made for treatment is to use a bronchodilator aerosol before exercise, to prevent it. In my experience an allergy, usually to dust mites, is nearly always present, and it has been shown repeatedly that if the patient can be desensitized to dust mite then exercise no longer causes asthma.

Morning dippers

Some people are described as morning dippers because they get severe asthma in the early morning, but when they present themselves at the evening surgery there is no evidence of asthma. One such patient was considered a complete neurotic because she could always blow 600 litres per minute on a peak flow meter at 6pm, a perfectly healthy reading, but when she was given a peak flow meter to take home it was found that she could blow only 60 litres per minute at 6am. This was one of my early cases whose problems emphasized the importance of being able to supply peak flow meters to individual patients to monitor their asthma properly at all times of day or night. Wild swings in peak flow indicate very labile, twitchy bronchi which go into spasm easily (see Figure 16.1). In some cases it is the pointer to an allergen in the bed which may be identified and removed. On the whole, however, it is the rule for all asthmatics to be down in the morning and up at night.

Late-onset asthma

Allergic asthma can develop for the first time at any age, the oldest in my experience being 88 years. The onset of chest symptoms in someone who has never had any chest trouble before should lead to a suspicion of asthma rather than bronchitis. It is quite common for people between the ages of 40 and 60 to develop asthma for the first time, usually following a chest infection, after which the wheezing persists. It is therefore very easy to assume that the patient has chronic bronchitis, especially as airway restriction can be severe, and tends to be continuous rather than fluctuating. Allergic rhinitis and sometimes polyps are often associated, skin tests are always negative, and a cause can seldom be identified. This type of asthma is therefore in a class by itself, quite distinct from the common asthma in younger people where skin tests are positive for common allergens, and the airways vary from day to day, as is easily shown by using a peak flow meter.

Unusual presentations of allergic asthma

Asthma can present in unusual ways which may not be recognized, even by chest specialists. For example, a persistent cough at night or even all day may be due to allergic asthma. This cough will resist all kinds of medication and sometimes the patient, usually a child, may even cough in their sleep. In the end the patient gets accustomed to it while everyone else in the house becomes thoroughly irritated by it.

Coughing can also bring on asthma because of the effort, thus causing curious episodes where the patient can fall unconscious after a bout of coughing. This is known as cough syncope, and these attacks can often be misdiagnosed or disbelieved. A boy of 12 seen recently had caused much anxiety because his parents were awakened by his cough in the night followed by a loud thump. They found him unconscious and blue in the face on the floor night after night, but fortunately he soon recovered. The family doctor could not believe this and refused to come and see him in the night when these curious attacks were happening – this boy may well have been in serious danger each night.

What is the importance of accurate assessment of the severity of the asthma?

After the diagnosis has been made, the first essential is to assess the severity of the asthma so that the most appropriate drugs can be prescribed. Assessment is very important because under-assessment leading to under-treatment is so common.

Many asthmatics have only occasional wheeze, or wheeze with colds only or have seasonal asthma only. These cases are usually easily controlled with bronchodilators alone.

Mild chronic asthma, perhaps with a superimposed summer asthma or hay fever, may pose a greater problem, but the effects depend to a large extent on whether the individual affected is physically active. A sedentary person may not notice or bother about a persistent mild wheeze, so athletic patients are often the first to come for treatment.

The next stage could be the moderately severe chronic asthmatic, with constant wheeze, worst at night and in the morning, with attacks which are occasional but sometimes severe. This may progress insidiously with victims unconsciously restricting their activities to avoid shortness of breath, so that the airway obstruction can become severe without either patient or doctor being aware of the true situation.

A pattern of acute frightening attacks, usually in children, may cease, to everyone's relief, but it may not be realized that the victim avoids all activity and is now a severe chronic asthmatic. The doctor should therefore adjust the treatment according to what is necessary or desirable, but many doctors are unaware of the fact that it is almost impossible to judge the severity of asthma accurately by physical examination.

For example, a patient was delighted because treatment for his severe summer asthma with pollen injections had been a complete success. I was amazed to find that his peak flow readings in the winter were so low as to indicate very severe asthma, yet he had no complaints at all. The reason was that he never exerted himself in the slightest, his daily routine being to get up, have breakfast, drive to work, sit in his office, drive home, sit looking at TV, and then go to bed again. It was only in the summer that his asthma bothered him by encroaching on his very last respiratory reserves.

Two severely asthmatic ladies also illustrate this kind of situation because when they were asked to keep a symptoms chart they both recorded that they had no asthma at all. I knew that they both had very severe chronic asthma, so I asked them when they thought that their asthma was bad enough to record. Both patients, years apart, gave exactly the same answer, which was 'I know I have asthma when I am so breathless that my husband has to carry me to the loo'. Yet they rarely consulted their doctors!

How can the severity of asthma be accurately assessed?

Although the bronchi may be partly obstructed so that the supply of air is restricted, it is only when very little air can get through that the victim becomes obviously short of breath and distressed at rest. This is because, like all other vital organs, the lungs have very large reserves. Subjective impressions regarding the severity of the asthma can be very misleading, so it is essential to have some kind of objective measurement. The simplest and most practical method is a portable peak flow meter, which can be used anywhere as often as necessary, and is available from the makers or the Asthma Society.

The use of this device has already been covered in Chapter 9 along with normal values, for age, height and sex so that the performance of the patient can be compared with what it should be.

Patients may also fill in specialized graph sheets showing the readings on rising, at lunchtime, teatime, bedtime and in the night if awake. This gives a graphic picture of the severity of the asthma and of its variations at different times of the day. The treatment taken must also be recorded, as without this information the graph is meaningless. It is often possible to adjust treatment for maximum effect by having the patient telephone the readings every week.

In asthma the results of all lung-function tests can vary from day to day or even from hour to hour, so a single visit to the respiratory-function laboratory at the hospital may give a false impression. One patient had to take so many puffs at her Ventolin inhaler to enable her to get to the laboratory that she got deceptively normal results – but nobody asked her if she had taken any treatment that morning! Elaborate lung-function tests are not really essential in asthma, but are very helpful in cases of alveolitis, or chronic bronchitis, where information on oxygen transfer to the blood and accurate assessment of all aspects of lung function is required.

Family doctors should have a peak flow meter in the surgery, and another in their bag. A doctor who does not have one at all, as is still common, is not equipped to assess the severity of asthma in any patient. No doctor would practise without a stethoscope or a means of measuring blood pressure, and in my opinion a peak flow meter is more essential. Patients can promote measurement instead of guessing by asking if they can have a peak flow meter test at their doctor's surgery.

What are the other uses of the peak flow meter?

In hospital, because very frequent visits to the lung-function laboratory are not possible, the peak flow meter can be used on the ward several times a day, and the results charted just like temperature and pulse rate. Charting progress in this way is not only a very helpful monitor of the effects of treatment, but may

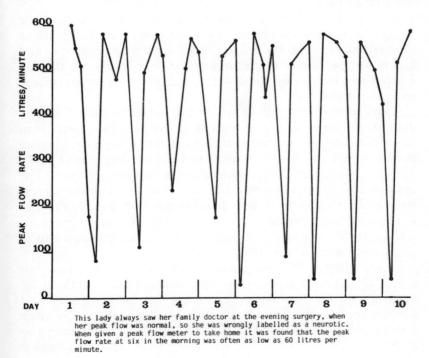

This lady always saw her family doctor at the evening surgery, when her peak flow was normal, so she was wrongly labelled as a neurotic. When given a peak flow meter to take home it was found that the peak flow rate at six in the morning was often as low as 60 litres per minute.

Figure 16.1   A remarkable example of daily variation in peak flow rate.

prevent patients being sent home before they are ready, as may easily occur if their subjective assessment of their own recovery is accepted.

The peak flow meter can be used for diagnosis in many ways. For example, in seasonal asthma, especially when skin tests are unhelpful, monitoring through the season will show if any relationship exists between the pollen or the mould-spore counts, if available in the area. When the patient is affected by a certain pollen or mould spore, the peak flow goes down as the number of pollen grains or mould spores goes up. (Figures 5.4 and 5.5 show examples of this.)

When allergy to foods is suspected the readings before and at frequent intervals after taking a suspect food will establish whether the food is involved. One patient used this method so cleverly that his average peak flow rate increased from 120 to 500 litres/minute, as many common foods were identified and eliminated in turn.

Monitoring can also give good evidence of the effects of the environment, or of avoidance of suspect causes, or of alterations in environment. Figures 4.2 and 4.3 illustrate these points, and Figure 16.2(a) shows the improvement on a holiday in the sun where there were clean, tiled floors, and also the prompt relapse on return home.

Apart from investigations which can easily be carried out by the patient, the most important role of the peak flow meter is in monitoring the effects of drug treatment and as an early warning system which enables the patient to keep one step ahead of the asthma situation and take appropriate action in good time. The approach to treatment described in this book would be almost impossible without peak flow monitoring, and this regime was worked out as a result of the availability of many meters for clinical trials. A meter is indispensable for the management of any serious asthma problem.

In my opinion this instrument, used as described, has provided the greatest advance in the management of asthma for many years. Unfortunately it has not yet been used to best advantage, but this is not the fault of those who suffer from asthma. The mini-meter has substituted facts for guesswork or impressions, and I wholeheartedly agree with those who think it should be prescribable on the National Health Service.

Does having their own meter make patients neurotic about themselves?

Patients in possession of their own peak flow meters do not become neurotics, because the more information patients have the less anxious they become, and consequently the less trouble they are to their doctors! A chronic asthmatic or his or her doctor without any means of measuring the asthma are in total ignorance of the true situation, but a peak flow meter will shed a welcome ray of light on the real state of affairs. Patients who possess a peak flow meter also have an advance warning system which tells them when to seek advice, and when to take emergency treatment.

Is there any way in which the severity of asthma can be accurately assessed without instruments?

There is a technique I have found helpful over many years, which can be used by anybody and should be more widely known. Another person places one hand in the middle of the back of the asthmatic patient, and the other in the middle of the chest, and applies steady pressure while the patient breathes out through the open mouth. It soon becomes obvious if the patient has considerable air-trapping and wheezing. Continued pressure can be applied slowly in this way until the trapped air is squeezed out as far as possible, and the next inhalation will bring in at least one lungful of relatively fresh air. The person applying the pressure can also feel how the chest has tended to assume a spherical shape, and, in the older patient, how stiff the chest has become. This is because the chest has been in this blown-up state for so many years that it has become fixed in the fully inflated position. This simple manoeuvre, which anyone can perform, demonstrates roughly the severity of the asthma, and also the amount of overinflation and wheezing.

When a doctor listens with his stethoscope to an overinflated chest he or she may not hear any wheezing. Thus a false sense of security can be induced in doctor, patient and relatives unless it is realized that nothing is heard because there is not enough air moving to produce a wheeze! A silent chest is a very dangerous chest urgently needing emergency treatment. I obtain more information from squeezing my patients' chests than by listening to them with a stethoscope, but this method of examination is seldom taught and not widely known.

What are the general principles in the management of asthma?

Now that the various treatments available have been described, it is time to discuss how these remedies can be applied most effectively to the daily management of the allergic patient.

The management section is one of the most important parts of this book, because the treatments available today are so often underused, misused, or even not used at all, especially in asthma. Drugs may have to be taken indefinitely, even for life, so it is important to know about side-effects, and how drugs should be taken for maximum benefit.

This book offers the author the opportunity to discuss openly his views on the effective use of the drugs already available for the control of all types of asthma. It must, however, be emphasized that the methods described may not suit every asthmatic, that treatment must always be under medical supervision, and that many of the subjects discussed may be the subject of much medical controversy and disagreement. The methods of treatment described are practical and pragmatic, usually work and are now being used more frequently. Always make a point of discussing your treatment in detail with your doctor, who should be able to advise you.

The first essential after diagnosis is accurate assessment, so that adequate treatment can be prescribed which will reverse the obstruction as completely as possible. Methods of management can then be tailored to the needs of the patient. The case requiring only an occasional puff of bronchodilator needs no further discussion, but asthma which has become a threat to education or employment is a more serious matter requiring more aggressive treatment.

My personal preference is to treat intensively and effectively at the outset, then readjust treatment for maintenance. This unusual approach gives dramatic and rapid improvement to the maximum possible extent. Full control of symptoms is rapidly achieved, confidence is established, future co-operation assured, and patients begin to learn how to control their own problems effectively.

Should asthmatics understand and control their own treatment to a greater extent?

Chronic asthma in Britain presents an enormous problem, which cannot be dealt with adequately unless patients are trained to look after their own problems as far as possible. Unfortunately, education of patients in self-management and knowing when to summon medical help is still neglected, and patients often complain that they seem unable to obtain informed advice from their family medical adviser. Perhaps this is unfair, as doctors may feel out of their depth in the subject and may avoid committing themselves, or their difficulties may be the result of incorrect teaching when students. The possible role of the family doctor in the management of asthma and other allergic problems is of great importance, and is dealt with separately.

Every severe attack, especially if it has caused a hospital admission, should be regarded as a failure of control which could probably have been avoided. There are good precedents for this approach in other diseases. Diabetics test their own urine, control their own diet, and may alter the self-injected dose of a potentially lethal drug, insulin, but the allergic patient is very often poorly informed and confused regarding how to control the condition adequately with drugs.

The objective should be to maintain the patient in a state as near normal as possible, without undue side-effects from the treatment, and without deterioration. In asthmatics where 100 per cent reversibility is attainable, that is the objective. In those less responsive to treatment the maximum percentage of normal peak flow reached as a result of treatment should be the target.

When symptoms have been effectively controlled the next important target should be the identification of the causative allergen followed by its avoidance, or when unavoidable, by desensitization. Finally, drugs may be phased out and the patient remain well without them.

The general principles of management outlined here are mainly directed at preventing the development of acute problems by timely and effective treatment or common sense avoidance. In a book for the lay public it may seem out of place to make so many positive suggestions regarding the management of allergic disease, but it is necessary for this information to be made public because of the difficulty in obtaining informed advice elsewhere.

Why is asthma so often under-treated?

It is very common for chronic asthmatic patients to be inadequately treated. Frequently a trial of oral steroids in heavy dosage for long enough to assess potential reversibility has not been made because of unfounded fears of steroid side-effects. In other cases Becotide has not been used because it is a steroid, although it does not cause typical steroid side-effects. Perhaps the commonest cause of under-treatment is reliance on the subjective statements of patients who are often quite happy with a very low level of airway. Also, when the airway obstruction has been reversed as far as possible and the situation stabilized with inhaled steroids and bronchodilators, further investigations may often be considered unnecessary. However, all that has been accomplished by this point is effective suppression with drugs, which is only really satisfactory if there are no side-effects, the drugs continue to be effective, and there are no frequent crises.

How much improvement can be obtained in chronic asthma by using drugs available today?

It is often possible to clear asthma completely by using oral steroids in a dosage appropriate to the severity of the asthma until no further improvement is obtained. This is easiest to achieve in children and young adults, as they are less likely to have any permanent damage.

It is always preferable to monitor this clearing of the airways with a peak flow meter, as this instrument shows how much improvement is taking place day by day. When further improvement has ceased to occur these maximum readings will also indicate the optimum reversal of the asthma.

The chart giving normal peak flow rates according to age, height and sex can now be consulted – the predicted normal may be regarded as the ideal. The highest peak flow readings obtained will now indicate how reversible the individual case may be, and what percentage of the predicted normal is attainable.

Allergic asthma is reversible to a variable extent, but chronic bronchitis is not. The degree of reversibility reflects how much of the airway obstruction is the result of chronic bronchitis. Every grade of response from none at all to complete reversal may be seen, and the response is quite unpredictable.

An example of a good response in an asthmatic is given in Figures 16.2(a) and (b) which shows that when maximum reversal has been achieved the oral steroid is reduced quite rapidly and inhaled steroid (Becotide) is phased in at a level of 15mg of prednisolone (three tablets). The oral steroid is then tapered off slowly at a rate which depends on the individual case.

To illustrate the importance of clearing the bronchi, let us look at the cases of two sisters, aged 26 and 27, who had been on a small dose of steroid tablets for 13 years as prescribed by their elderly family doctor who had since retired. Both exhibited all the obvious steroid side-effects such as moon face, obesity and even bruising, but the most striking feature was that they were actually deriving no benefit at all from the single daily tablet, though it was causing all the side-effects. This was confirmed by the peak flow readings which were below 150 litres/minute in both cases. The predicted peak flow rate was 500 litres/minute, so they were only 30 per cent of normal. In spite of this very low reading, they had no complaints at all because they instinctively avoided exertion, and thus never even felt breathless.

The first step in both cases was to increase their dose to eight tablets per day (40mg of prednisolone) under peak flow meter monitor. Within a week both women could blow nearly 500 litres/minute, confirming that they were completely reversible with no permanent damage. Obviously their bronchial tubes had been clogged with thick sputum obstructing the passage of air. When this sputum had disappeared it was possible for Becotide to operate effectively on the lining of the bronchi. It was notable that Becotide had been tried before and dismissed as useless, because it did not work immediately.

It was now possible to cut the steroids down rapidly, but in both cases it took nearly a year to withdraw oral steroids completely because they had suffered considerable adrenal suppression over the preceding 13 years. Nevertheless they both came back to normal levels, their asthma is still perfectly controlled, and there are no side-effects. These two patients are particularly memorable because they had been given the steroid

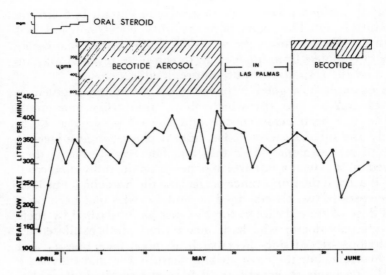

This is a good example of how to gain control with oral steroids and to retain it with Becotide. Note that she was able to stop treatment in the Canaries with only a slight drop in the peak flow rate, but relapsed promptly on return home due to environmental allergens.

Figure 16.2(a)   The results of pragmatic treatment of chronic asthma.

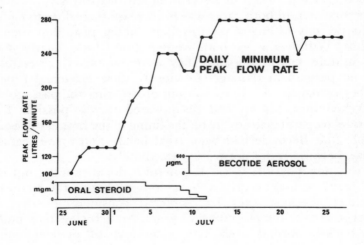

Figure 16.2(b)   The results of pragmatic treatment of chronic asthma.

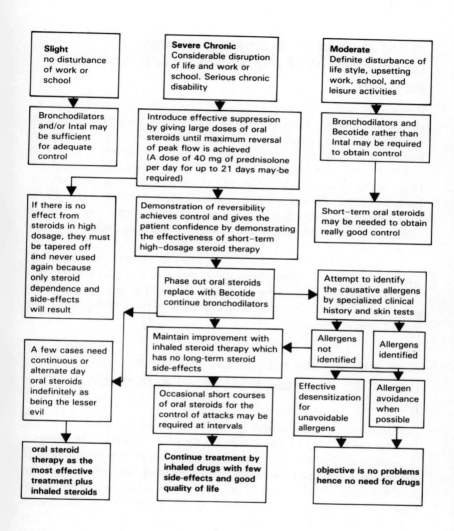

Figure 16.3 The pragmatic management of chronic allergic asthma at all ages.

tablets for so many years without consideration of long-term side-effects.

What should be the next step once stable control of the asthma has been attained?

From the point of view of allergy diagnosis and investigation, this is the point where intensive investigation to find the cause can begin. For example, bronchial provocation tests can now be performed if the peak flow is high enough for safety.

Long-term and tedious, but potentially helpful investigations require the close co-operation of doctor and patient, who should both have the identification of the causative factors in the illness as a primary aim. Identification of specific causes may lead to effective avoidance, or specific desensitization, with the final target of being able to do without drugs.

To attain these objectives patients often have to help their medical adviser to help them by giving the closest co-operation and compliance with recommendations for treatment and avoidance, and by keeping meticulous records of peak flow, drugs and symptoms.

Are antibiotics either necessary or useful in the treatment of an asthmatic attack?

Antibiotics are very often given to asthmatics when they are having an attack, often without any other effective treatment. Actually antibiotics are usually unnecessary in an asthmatic attack, and the use of antibiotics is frequently merely a habit, or an 'insurance policy' in case the patient has a severe chest infection. This practice is particularly common in childhood asthma, when the ideal treatment might be a few steroid tablets which would have a dramatic effect in a matter of hours. Unless there is positive evidence of infection such as fever, sweating, cough, infected sputum, inflamed tonsils or obvious evidence of illness, antibiotics are seldom genuinely required for the treatment of acute asthma. This view has been confirmed recently by a well-conducted clinical trial. Chronic sinus infection however, may make asthma more difficult to control. Antibiotics may be required for several weeks, along with steroids, in this sort of case.

Antibiotics may cause unwanted side-effects in the patient, such as thrush and diarrhoea, and, even worse, infections at large in the community may become resistant to useful antibiotics. The human gut, especially the colon, is inhabited by very large numbers of bacteria nearly all of which are harmless. When antibiotics are given, both good and bad bacteria are killed off, and organisms such as the thrush fungus, which are not affected by the common antibiotics, get the opportunity to become dominant. The ecological balance of bacteria in the normal human bowel is disturbed, and some deficiency of vitamins which are made by these organisms may ensue, creating what is known as 'the Candida Syndrome'.

Can an asthma sufferer safely cope with an asthma attack without seeking medical advice?

Over the years I have found it essential to educate patients in how to handle their own asthma in order to avoid the development of severe attacks. Difficulties in achieving this aim are the result to a large extent of the fact that many doctors are extremely nervous of the side-effects of steroids. As a result oral steroids are not given at the right time, or, if given, the dosage is insufficient. Also it is impossible to ensure that all the partners in a large general practice are aware of the best approach. A copy of the consultant's suggestions for the treatment of the case is unlikely to be available in the night, or when a deputizing service is on call – and doctor and patient have never set eyes on one another before.

In my opinion it is essential for patients to hold their own supply of oral steroids and bronchodilators, and sometimes even syringes and injectable bronchodilators. All severe asthmatics should have their own peak flow meter to use as an early warning system.

Printed instructions on emergency treatment should be given out so that the patient has firm guidelines as to what drugs to take and when to summon help or get to the hospital casualty department.

If the patient is really distressed it is better to play safe and arrange direct admission to hospital without waiting for further advice. Even experts find it difficult to judge how the patient will fare within the next half hour. The risk to life is from severe asthma plugging the bronchi and causing acute lack of oxygen, but there is no risk in giving a large dose of steroid. Using the soluble type of steroid in children I have frequently seen an improvement within half an hour, but it is usually thought that 4–6 hours is required. The best approach is to give a large dose of steroids first and then to send for medical help. In a severe case it is *totally* unreasonable, especially in bad weather, for the patient to have to go to the surgery.

What are the danger signals in chronic asthma?

The reserve capacity of the vital organs such as heart and lung is very large. Unless the patient is physically active the requirements for air may be utilized only to the minimum extent, by means of masterly inactivity. Patients are often unaware that they are existing just above the insufficiency level. If they go below this critical level an emergency situation may arise quite rapidly from which rescue may be difficult.

People who suffer from chronic asthma often become so well adjusted that they are quite unaware of how bad the asthma really is, and may refuse to believe this unless they are monitored with the peak flow meter.

The next couple of pages are devoted to describing the danger signals which, if recognized in good time, should lead to effective treatment and saving of life.

Table 16.1 may seem unnecessarily alarmist, but most serious or fatal attacks of asthma can be avoided if the danger signals are recognized in good time by the patient, relatives or family doctor.

What are the common triggers for an attack of asthma?

Seasonal attacks caused by pollen or mould spores may follow a day in the country, or camping in long grass, or working in the

Table 16.1 Stages in the development of a serious attack of asthma

Characteristics	Action
Decreasing physical capability, such as unusual breathlessness when going upstairs, walking a short distance or doing light housework, etc. Increasing need for bronchodilators or other medication.	Increase treatment and/or seek advice.
Confined to bed or chair but able to get up with moderate difficulty. If a peak flow meter is available a marked drop from the usual range will be observed.	Medical help and advice essential.
Confined to bed or chair: chest overinflated; sufferer struggling for air with rapid, shallow breaths at 30/minute or more in adults (breathing rates in children vary with age). Pulse rate over 110/minute in adults and 120/minute in children. No audible wheeze is a bad sign and may mean that not enough air is moving to make any noise.	Hospital necessary without delay. Oxygen and nebulizer if available. Do not be reassured if no wheeze heard.
Totally confined to bed or chair. Unable to speak or move; perhaps becoming blue in the face – indicates a potentially fatal outcome and the need for immediate emergency measures. Children tend to get blue more quickly and easily than adults but it is a sign that the attack is really severe and that no risks should be taken.	Instant emergency action essential or it may be too late! Oxygen and nebulizer if available.

garden or on the farm. Exposure to animals or excessive house dust is also a common trigger factor.

Infections, by either bacteria or viruses, often trigger an attack because of increased production of sputum and swelling of the lining of the bronchial tubes. Antibiotics are seldom necessary unless the patient is obviously ill as well as breathless and wheezy. Virus infections in childhood are a very common cause.

Medicines, especially those containing aspirin or dyes, may trigger an attack. Drugs are not a common cause, but an attack can be triggered off by the drugs commonly used for hypertension or heart trouble known as beta-blockers.

Constant exposure to an allergen such as dust mite increases the irritability of the bronchial tubes so that they tend to constrict easily. An acute attack can be brought on by sudden increase in the amount of allergen inhaled, or by exposure to irritating gases or fumes.

Irritation from tobacco smoke, fumes from bleach used or spilt in the house, excess exhaust fumes, and sulphur dioxide used as a preservative in soft drinks, can all set off a spasm in a chronic asthmatic. Emotion can sometimes be a trigger, but only rarely.

Is it easy to tell if an attack of asthma is becoming dangerous?

Many people wrongly believe that only sudden attacks are dangerous. It is surprising but true that many asthmatics become so accustomed to their condition that they fail to recognize when an attack is serious. As a result medical help is often not sought until the situation has got out of control. This statement is reinforced by a recent survey of 90 deaths from asthma in which it was concluded that 77 might have been avoidable with timely and correct treatment. It is also significant that in 67 cases the severity of their attack was totally misjudged by the patient or the relatives, and in 25 out of 36 cases seen by the family doctor the condition was not considered to be serious.

Chronic asthmatics should observe the usual state of their disease so that the warning signals of a potentially dangerous deterioration can be recognized and treated in good time. The rest of the family should also be on the alert, as a really chronic asthmatic patient frequently minimizes the complaint to a remarkable extent, and will resist any suggestion of sending for medical help. To possess a peak flow meter is a great help because it will provide a means of measuring the severity of the attack objectively.

Can seasonal asthma be serious?

It is at the high peaks of the pollen count that those who get asthma as well as hay fever begin to be seriously affected. It is important to realize that if the pollen count is high then sufferers can expect serious asthmatic problems, and that if they continue to be exposed to pollen they may become seriously ill. Pollen asthmatics are very foolish to play golf or walk in the long grass, or to assist in hay-making.

Patients may not realize that a rapidly increasing pollen count may be a serious danger, and may not send for a doctor until too late. Particularly with children, the situation may worsen very rapidly, and it is important to keep one jump ahead of the asthma. In such a situation it is safer to dial 999 or go to the nearest hospital accident and emergency department rather than wait for a doctor to call.

Because of fear of steroid side-effects patients with seasonal allergies are often deprived of the benefits of this treatment. I have frequently seen patients who spend 6 weeks in bed with asthma every summer because they have been told that they have to 'put up with their asthma' because steroid treatment is dangerous.

I hope that this is a rare occurrence today, because there is no reason why a patient with severe seasonal asthma cannot be treated with oral or inhaled steroids (Becotide), because the season is self-limiting. The number of deaths from asthma always rises abruptly at the peak of the pollen season, indicating quite clearly either lack of judgment by doctors or lack of realization by the patients of how seriously they were being affected.

It is totally unnecessary for any patient to be seriously ill from seasonal pollen asthma if the condition is recognized and treated with modern drugs in good time.

Why is the death rate from asthma not falling?

Deaths from asthma now exceeds 2,000 per year in England and Wales, despite the development of effective and safe drugs.

In my opinion there are four main influences: the patient, his or her family doctor, the hospital services, and the intensity and severity of the onslaught of the attack. Frequently the patient is partly to blame. He or she may have decided that the doctors cannot or will not help, medical advice is not sought in time, treatments are not taken as directed, or improperly taken, and the condition may be much worse than the patient realizes or will admit. Doctors can also fail to recognize when an asthma problem is severe, or fear the possible side-effects of steroids more than the asthma, as half the deaths happen unexpectedly at home or on the way to hospital. It is true that an overwhelming sudden attack can kill before anything can be done, but this is rare.

Surveys of deaths from asthma during the last 20 years have invariably revealed that the majority of patients have been in serious trouble for days, or weeks, before the crisis occurred which prompted their admission to hospital. Many of those who died had not had steroids at all, and a minority had not even consulted their doctors because they were so accustomed to their condition that they did not think anything more could be done to help them.

What can a specialist offer the chronic asthmatic?

The main purpose of the consultation should be to assess the situation accurately and to advise on management so that the best possible results without undue side-effects can be obtained from treatment. This involves the identification of any environmental factors and skilled interrogation on many aspects of the case, as well as general examination, skin tests, blood tests and lung-function tests.

The type of case referred for advice will often already have been treated with a variety of drugs over the years and may be dependent on low-dosage oral steroids producing side-effects but no relief. Management techniques will vary according to the severity of the asthma or other problems. Obviously slight cases are seldom referred for consultation, but the severity of the problems may be underestimated. Specialist advice should be sought if the asthma is becoming more difficult to control, treatments less and less effective, and life more restricted. Steroid dependence suggests specialist help before it becomes permanent.

As for the chronic asthmatic who has become dependent on steroids, the average general practitioner will not have many patients of this type, and hence is unlikely to have much experience of managing these problems. A physician specializing in chest diseases, or even better with an interest in allergy, will see many similar cases, and therefore should be able to give suitably expert help and advice.

Specialized attention is usually necessary for these problems, and there should be no difficulty in obtaining referral to the appropriate specialist from the general practitioner.

Unfortunately, since desensitizing injections were stopped many doctors assume that investigations to find the cause are pointless. Nothing could be further from the truth, as drug treatment can be much more effective, or even ceased, if a removable cause can be found.

How could the family doctor play a more prominent part in the management of allergic diseases?

Allergic problems are distressingly common, but very few doctors have had any instruction in their effective management as medical students. Many good and sympathetic doctors may feel inadequate and defensive when asked to cope with the curious and unpredictable phenomena of allergy, and all they can do is to suppress symptoms blindly with drugs.

Patients may sense a lack of confidence, perhaps even hostility, from their doctor, which they may have unwittingly provoked themselves in many ways. This sort of 'them and us' situation is mutually defeating, and it is more profitable to speculate on how the doctor/patient relationship could be improved.

Ideally the family doctor should know everybody on his or her practice list, and have a lifelong personal relationship with each family. The doctor's supervisory and advisory role might start with the diagnosis of pregnancy, followed by advice on maternal diets in pregnancy. If allergy is prominent in the family history, avoidance of excess milk or eggs in the diet before and after birth should be advised.

Pregnant asthmatics should pay special attention not only to diet but to the adequate control of the asthma. When necessary, Becotide is the best method of control, there being no risk to the foetus. It is important that the asthma be as well controlled as possible because the foetus depends on oxygen from the mother.

The doctor should be aware of the possibility of milk allergy in infancy causing feeding problems, eczema and failure to thrive.

Milk-free alternative feeds can be tried without difficulty as special foods are prescribable through the National Health Service. Breast feeding, avoidance of early weaning, and perhaps avoidance of foods which tend to cause allergy in babies from allergic mothers, might help prevent the development of serious allergies in childhood.

In childhood, rhinitis, hay fever, eczema, asthma and glue ears can be observed in the early stages. The family doctor could play a major part in prevention by advising against animals in the home and classroom, and against horse riding, in susceptible families. A knowledge of the various guises of allergy in childhood could make the work of the family doctor much more interesting and rewarding. Awareness of the 'stigmata' of allergy such as the shiners, the crease, and the 'salute' will point out the allergic children who will require extra attention.

There can be no doubt that an overanxious parent can easily irritate the most easy-going doctor, but the introduction of effective treatment and informed advice can soon remove parental anxiety. It would be ideal if family doctors were able to manage allergic patients effectively, especially as they can provide long-term supervision.

Thus, in conjunction with the health visitor, the practice nurse, the midwife and the community dietician, the family doctor could act as the leader of a team which would have as one objective the prevention, recognition and early treatment of allergic disease in children. Continual supervision and effective management of patients throughout their lives could be rewarding and satisfying for the medical professionals. Some patients might even be followed from conception to the crematorium, as allergy can be a life sentence!

Perhaps this concept of the ideal doctor/patient relationship is just a dream, but family doctors could look after most allergy problems effectively if the training was available. Asthma is so common that effective management in general practice is probably the only way to deal with the problem adequately.

What is the relationship between the family doctor and the hospital or chest clinic?

Many sufferers from asthma and other allergic diseases believe, quite incorrectly, that attendance at a National Health Service out-patient clinic means that the clinic is in charge of their treatment. This belief is fostered by some family doctors who refuse to alter treatment because the patient is 'under the clinic'. This is quite wrong and illogical, as the family doctor is on the spot and can treat as necessary, refer to the clinic urgently or even request a home visit by the consultant, under the National Health Service.

Confusion can arise when management is shared between hospital and family doctor because of poor communication, and sometimes contradictory opinions. This is particularly important in relation to the common conviction amongst family doctors that oral steroids are dangerous and only to be used as a last resort. When patients are given a contrary impression by the hospital or clinic they do not know who to believe. (They should accept the hospital opinion.)

In my view consultant and family doctor could form a very useful partnership for the benefit of the allergic patient, but for this to happen, it requires much more communication and personal liaison than is usually achieved. The out-patient clinic should not need to play a major part in management if the family doctor and patient work together in harmony.

Ideally, asthma and other chronic allergic problems should be managed by the family doctor, who should be in the ideal position to control management, is more accessible in an acute situation, and can provide greater continuity of care, follow-up and assessment of progress over a lifetime. Unfortunately, a hospital out-patient clinic sometimes provides a succession of junior doctors with little experience of asthma. Large group practices, which may mean that a patient sees a different doctor at each visit, may also fail to provide the continuity which is so important to foster confidence and co-operation.

What is the correct way to obtain a second opinion without upsetting your doctor?

In Britain family doctors make a contract with the National Health Service to be responsible for the medical care of every patient who joins their practice list, in return for a standard annual fee for each patient. When considered necessary patients can be referred to a consultant at a National Health Service hospital, or for a private consultation if preferred. The consultant will give an opinion, advice and recommendations to the family doctor, and express an opinion directly to the patient, or may leave all explanations to the family doctor. The consultant acts only as adviser to the family doctor, his or her job being to suggest what he or she considers to be the best treatment. The family doctor is quite entitled to disagree with or even ignore this advice, but will seldom do so.

Normally family doctors should be the *first* to suggest referral for further advice, and they will choose a consultant in whom they have confidence and trust from previous experience. An old and wise colleague told me that he knew he had failed if the patient suggested a second opinion before he did! When a patient suggests a consultant who is quite unknown to the family doctor he or she may, reasonably, be reluctant to agree to referral until further enquiries have been made to ensure that the consultant is of good professional repute. Such caution is to be commended, not resented, by patients, as protecting *their* interests.

Doctors in family practice, however, cannot be expected to know where the best opinion in an uncommon speciality can be obtained, and if the clinical problem is not well controlled no obstacles can reasonably be put in the way of obtaining further advice. After all, the family doctor is not bound to take the advice given if he or she does not consider it in the best interests of the patient.

It is always preferable to ask the family doctor for a referral letter. Many patients are reluctant to do this because they think the doctor may be angry or resentful, and refuse referral, or they do not wish to imply they are dissatisfied with their treatment. However, without the indispensable background information which the family doctor should be able to provide regarding previous illnesses and hospital admissions, perhaps together with copies of previous reports, a consultant is at a disadvantage in making the best recommendations for management.

Thus, the proper channel to a consultant is through the family doctor, but much misunderstanding and resentment can arise quite easily. There are many sensible reasons for using the proper approach, but it must also be stated that many family doctors reject requests for referral in a manner which is difficult to justify. To change to another doctor is the best way out of this situation.

In continental Europe or the USA this system of referral by the family doctor is not so clearly defined, and patients may shop around the specialists directly. The family doctors in other countries seldom have defined lists of patients they are responsible for, which makes for a much looser system.

Many patients today are subscribers to a medical insurance scheme such as BUPA or PPP. This may ease the situation regarding referrals to consultants for private consultations. It would seem churlish of a family doctor to refuse a reasonable request for referral from a patient who has been able to provide for private specialist treatment for his family at very considerable expense.

Why should a consultant refuse to accept patients without proper referral from the family doctor?

A consultant, when approached directly by a patient for a consultation, should suggest that the family doctor be asked for a letter of referral, but many patients are most reluctant to do this for fear of rebuff.

In my opinion the best compromise is for the consultant to write to the family doctor asking for a letter of referral and full information about the patient, stating that the patient will not be seen if the family doctor has any objection, and that a full report will be sent to the family doctor. If any consultant accepts a patient without a referral letter the patient should be suspicious of that consultant's standing in the profession.

Some readers may think this is outdated and unnecessary medical etiquette which interferes with their freedom to consult anyone they think may be able to help them. Not so – it is to protect patients against being taken advantage of by certain practitioners who offer treatments which are unproven and may even be harmful.

A patient who visits a consultant who does not insist on proper referral by the family doctor risks a difficult situation if special treatment, especially injections, is suggested. This is yet another reason why the family doctor's co-operation in any recommended treatment should be assured *before* the consultation.

A consultant may see patients from very long distances away.

Obviously it is impossible to take care of a remote patient in an acute episode, especially one requiring hospitalization, so it is essential to have the co-operation and active help of the family doctor who will be on the spot.

The term 'consultant' normally implies a specialist of high standing in Britain, usually holding an appointment as a consultant to a National Health Service hospital. Patients should beware of private clinics where the 'consultant' may be self appointed.

Has 'alternative' medicine anything to offer the allergic patient?

This is a difficult question to answer, because patients do not usually go to practitioners of various alternative techniques unless they have failed to obtain relief or satisfaction from orthodox medicine. Then we hear of the claims for spectacular success, but never the failures. Expensive laboratory tests of hair, blood, sweat (but not yet tears) and cells are carried out by some private laboratories, advertising direct to the public, but these tests have not been adequately validated. Those who make use of them should produce acceptable evidence that they give the correct answers. These comments apply equally to medically qualified practitioners of alternative techniques.

Excessive media publicity has resulted in allergy being blamed for every type of chronic disease which lacks a well-defined cause or cure. The result has been the appearance of increasing numbers of clinics catering for those convinced that their problems are caused by some sort of allergy. Some are run by properly qualified medical practitioners, but many are not.

Fringe medicine also includes acupuncture, hypnosis, homoeopathy, mega-vitamin therapy and many dietary regimes. Clinics advertising direct to the public who do not insist on a referral letter may make remarkable claims, so it is sensible to ask your family doctor's opinion, and if there is any other accepted treatment which has not been tried yet.

What would be a logical approach to a case of chronic asthma?

It is seldom possible to solve the problem at one consultation, so an ideal plan of campaign can be sketched out as follows. This is only an outline plan which will not fit every patient and with which many medical practitioners may not be in full agreement.

First visit

Detailed family history, personal history and history of present illness. Examination of chest and nose and general examination if necessary. Skin testing, perhaps sputum and/or nasal cytology, RAST tests if necessary, simple lung-function test. When necessary arrange for individual peak flow meter, special charts, telephone monitoring. Assess severity and plan treatment to abolish symptoms as soon as possible. When assessment justifies it, high-dose short-term oral steroids, monitored by meter, should be used until situation well controlled.

Second visit (2–4 weeks later)

Response to treatment assessed. Charts inspected. If no response to steroids, taper off and stop. If response has been good Becotide will already have been started, and oral steroids may already have been phased out. Check effective usage of aerosols or inhalers. Note maximum steady peak flow rate which will be future objective of long-term treatment. Case reassessed and any laboratory results discussed. Previously steroid-dependent cases now begin slow withdrawal of drug. It should be evident by now whether the patient's problems are due to inhaled allergens (positive skin tests), or to late-onset asthma with no clues to causation. Local inhaled steroid may also be needed for nasal allergy. By this point a successful case will be fully controlled on bronchodilators plus Becotide, sometimes Intal, with peak flow nearly normal. Printed instructions and a small emergency supply of steroids for early treatment of flare-ups may be given out, if not already available.

Third visit (2–3 months later)

Further reassessment of effectiveness of treatment and recommendations. Patient now much better informed and may often produce useful clues previously not available. Influence of environmental factors such as pets may now be evident. In difficult cases trial diets or nasal or bronchial challenge testing and

RAST tests may be considered if now well controlled. Plan future investigations.

Subsequent visits

Check peak flow and symptoms chart records. Reassess. Check compliance and usage of drugs. Alter dosages if necessary. Consider any fresh clues. Difficulties in long-term control may suggest a further search for environmental factors, or introduction of desensitizing injections, outside the UK, if the cause is known and unavoidable.

Final objective

Identification of cause or causes may lead to avoidance or effective desensitization. May finally be possible to taper off and stop drug treatment without relapse.

What is the value of physiotherapy for asthma and bronchitis?

Large numbers of asthmatic patients used to be referred to the hospital physiotherapy department for breathing exercises, but the efforts of the physiotherapist were seldom rewarded by adequate improvement.

The asthmatic patient can breathe in easily, but has difficulty in breathing out, so the chest becomes over-inflated and tends to assume a spherical shape. In such a situation breathing exercises cannot make much difference and may even increase the air trapping if too vigorous.

In severe bronchitis or with bronchial damage, as in bronchiectasis, there is a lot of nasty sputum to be cleared. Here the physiotherapist can give real help by teaching the correct position to drain off the sputum and in supervising this exercise until carried out efficiently. The major function of the physiotherapist is to teach, and to motivate patients to carry out exercises at home on a regular basis.

What simple exercises can be done at home?

There are two simple exercises which anyone can do for themselves, and which are impossible to overdo – in fact the more the better.

The simplest exercise is to lie face downwards on the floor with the breast bone resting on a fairly rigid pillow, with the weight of the body supported on the fore-arms. When the arms are raised off the floor the body weight is brought to bear on the breastbone, so that the weight of the body itself gradually squeezes out the trapped air. When the patient feels that they must take a breath, they simply put their arms down and push slightly, thus partly supporting the body on the arms to relieve the pressure on the chest, and then inhale some fresh air. This manoeuvre is completely harmless, can be carried out any number of times, and can do nothing but good. It may also tend to remobilize the frozen joints of the ribs and bring back a little movement into the bony cage of the chest.

The second useful exercise depends on the fact that once the chest of the patient becomes fixed, as I have described, breathing air *in* is mainly with the diaphragm, the muscle which divides the chest from the abdomen. When a patient with an immobilized chest wishes to exhale or to cough, he or she exert pressure on the contents of the abdomen, which push in turn against the diaphragm and help to squeeze the lungs, and get rid of the stale air.

Many chronic chest cases cannot cough effectively, and they cannot push out the trapped air or sputum effectively by using these muscles, because they have gone flabby. The simplest way to improve them is for the patient to lie flat on the back and to place on the abdomen a brick or any other weight which will exert a steady downward pressure.

The patient then breathes vigorously out so that the stomach bulges up and pushes up the weight, then relaxes and the weight pushes on the abdomen and helps to expel the trapped air. This exercise is repeated for as long as possible. Many patients find that they can cope with a few pounds at first, but they can gradually work up to even 50 and 60lb. This can be a tremendous help to breathing, coughing and keeping the tubes clear. The nature of the heavy object is unimportant and it can be improvised from almost anything, but the most convenient is 7lb bags of lead shot.

What is bronchiectasis?

This condition can be the result of severe asthma, especially that caused by the mould *Aspergillus*. When the bronchial tubes become very severely damaged the sputum may lie literally in puddles in the chest and can only be got rid of by gravity drainage. The use of frequent doses of antibiotics to try and get rid of it is ineffective and usually results in producing a completely resistant breed of bacteria which is a menace to the patient and to others. If patients can be taught how to keep their chests clear without antibiotics, the chronic infection becomes a nuisance rather than a menace. Asthma is quite often associated with severe bronchial damage, so it is relevant to discuss the treatment here.

Physiotherapy for bronchiectasis is most important because the physiotherapist can give great practical help by teaching patients the positions in which the sputum can be got up most easily. Once they have been taught how to do their postural drainage patients are normally told to do it every day. It is a great nuisance assuming the appropriate position, along with a suitable receptacle for the sputum, twice a day or even more. In fact this is an anti-social exercise even in private, and a mixture of embarrassment and laziness soon sets in after the situation has come under control. If carried out correctly the sputum becomes less and less, so the patients give it up, with the result that the sputum accumulates again and the next event will be a serious infection. The best answer is a sensible compromise, whereby weekly tipping is introduced as soon as the problem is under control. Obviously drainage should be more frequent if the sputum increases and less frequent if there is less. The bronchial damage is permanent and it is only by regularly tipping that it can be kept under control.

17 Managing asthma in children

Surveys of school-children in this country over the years have shown that allergic disease, particularly asthma, but also eczema, seasonal hay fever and perennial rhinitis, have become more and more common. Asthma has been found to be under-diagnosed, or unrecognized, hence under-treated, while eczema is often regarded as not due to allergy, and nasal allergies are also often under-treated. Food allergy as a cause of infant feeding problems may fail to be considered seriously by many paediatricians. 'Growing out of it' has been shown to occur less often than thought, and allergic children often become allergic adults.

This rising tide of allergic disease would be expected to stimulate increasing interest in allergy amongst paediatricians and other consultants to children's units, just as many paediatricians in other countries specialize exclusively in allergic diseases in children. Unfortunately for the children, this has not occurred, in spite of the fact that asthma has become one of the commonest reasons for admitting children to hospital.

If allergic diseases of chest, skin and nose are added together it is found that nearly 20 per cent of children have problems with allergy, and the sheer size of the problem becomes daunting. Guidance in the handling of allergic children is difficult to find, so it is to be hoped that this section will be of some help to parents.

How common is asthma in childhood?

This is not an easy question to answer because surveys carried out in many countries over the last 20 years have not used identical definitions of asthma. Repeated surveys in Birmingham show that asthma is about twice as prevalent as 20 years ago, affecting over 2 per cent, but more recent research has revealed figures up to 11 per cent. This means that there may be as many as half a million schoolchildren with asthma, of whom it has been estimated that 25 per cent are severe and 2.5 per cent very severe.

Of wheezy babies only a few (5 per cent) become asthmatic, but of wheezy toddlers aged from 1 to 3 years 18 per cent develop asthma, and from 3 to 5 years 42 per cent. In fact 80 per cent of asthmatics are said to have commenced their asthma by their fourth birthday, but often the diagnosis has not been made.

Should parents be told when a child has asthma?

A recent survey on Tyneside revealed that over one in ten children were asthmatic, but in only one in eight cases had the parents been told that the child had asthma. The majority of the more severe cases were receiving inadequate treatment. School absenteeism fell *tenfold* in those who were given effective preventive treatment. Another survey in London produced similar results.

These astonishing statistics expose a situation where the avoidance of the word 'asthma' to avoid upsetting the parents had deprived the children of effective treatment from the family doctor. Obviously many doctors still believe that asthma should never be diagnosed, with disastrous effects on many children.

How often is hospital required for asthma in children?

A recent survey in London revealed that in the past few years there had been an increase of more than 100 per cent in the number of children admitted to hospital for asthma. This tendency is also found in the rest of the country and in the rest of the world, so that asthma has become one of the commonest reasons for admission to children's units. It has been suggested that general practitioners could handle most cases at home, but lack the confidence to do so. Increasing difficulties in obtaining a home visit at night has meant that many children are taken direct to the casualty department.

Admission to hospital is a traumatic experience for small children, even when a parent can stay with the child. Screaming at the sight of a white coat and being very 'allergic' to needles points to hospital experience. Effective management with freely available drugs, plus assessment of the allergy situation, will very often prevent admissions to hospital, but adequate instruction of the parents in management is essential.

How often do children 'grow out of' their allergies?

Parents are often confidently assured that their child will grow out of the asthma, eczema or other allergic problems, perhaps at the age of 7 or in the early teens. Unfortunately this is by no means always true. Indeed, the more severe the childhood symptoms and the earlier they begin, the *less* likely it is that they will get better as they get older. Research studies have shown that children with slight allergic problems, which do not affect their activities or schooling to a significant extent, usually do grow out of it by adolescence, but children with severe asthma, eczema or both recover less often, particularly if there is a history of allergy in the family, and the child's problems started in infancy. It is also true that children who do 'grow out of it' may yet develop serious problems in later life. These facts, taken together with the rising incidence of asthma, which now affects at least one child in ten, and the tendency for asthma to be under-diagnosed and under-treated, should lead to anxiety regarding future generations, rather than complacency. For example, chronic asthma inadequately treated often causes a permanent chest deformity with the characteristic posture of the chronic asthmatic.

Must such unfortunate youngsters look forward to a life of semi-invalidism, of being a burden not only to those around them, but to themselves? Can they be helped? Many children can be, provided these changes have not been present for too long. They *are* often reversible, but only with adequate treatment. It is very disturbing to see adolescent patients when it is already too late to help them grow up straight and strong, who are already well on the way to joining the growing band of severe chronic asthmatic adults with both physical and educational handicaps, and poor employment possibilities.

This gloomy outlook should not, however, be accepted as inevitable, as there is good evidence that it can be improved.

Long-term comparative studies of very large groups of asthmatic children carried out in Scandinavia and in the USA have shown that three-quarters recover by adolescence if they have the attention of a skilled allergist, suggesting that children looked after by allergy specialists have a much better chance of being free from asthma when they grow up.

At the moment there is a vogue for publicity relating to recovered asthmatics who are so healthy that they have become leading athletes. Such cases are exceptional and are no guide to the majority. The impression is given to both doctors and patients that the outlook is usually excellent, and that reassurance and drugs are the easy answer. Such sweeping generalizations are unjust, as they ignore the suffering minority who may have a lifelong allergy problem for which they are unlikely to receive specialized help, and whose plight seldom receives publicity. It is not enough to wait for spontaneous improvement which may or may not happen, and reassurance should be given only after accurate assessment of the whole problem, never as routine.

What are the effects of chronic asthma on children?

First of all this depends on whether they are diagnosed as asthmatic and therefore given appropriate modern treatment. A recent survey revealed that only a third of children with obvious chronic asthma had been diagnosed as asthmatic and a quarter of them had serious asthma on exercise without having had any appropriate treatment or advice. Many cases were diagnosed as chronic bronchitis and the children were thus deprived of correct treatment.

It is not usually realized that the phase of acute frightening attacks may merge imperceptibly into chronic asthma. This occurs because everyone concerned is pleased that the frightening attacks no longer happen, but often neither doctor nor parents realize that the child has now become passive, reads a lot, prefers to watch television rather than to play, and takes no part in sports. Such behaviour in a child is unnatural and means that the asthma is becoming insidiously worse. A few children gradually develop chronic airway obstruction, but adapt so well that they are not recognized as asthmatics. They are short of breath on exertion, which they avoid, and many become adult chronic asthmatics.

Chronic asthmatic children wish dearly to be normal and will go to great lengths to avoid undesirable attention because they hate to be different in any way to other children. Sometimes this deceptively calm situation occurs when a drug which stops acute attacks is being used without any assessment of the degree of airway obstruction, by, for example, the use of a peak flow meter. Chronic illness may also cause personality problems, along with lack of stamina and inability to keep up with other children of comparable age or size.

Education is often deficient because of prolonged absences from school, which is doubly unfortunate because with this physical disability the victim may not be able to take up any kind of manual labour, and without education cannot get a skilled job.

Emotional factors can dominate in a few children, and trigger off attacks of asthma. Sometimes the asthma is used to attract attention, and even to manipulate the parents. Effective treatment will usually cut the vicious circle. Very rarely asthma can be used to avoid school, as in the case illustrated in Figure 9.4. It must, however, be emphasized that emotional factors in asthma have been grossly overemphasized in the past and are more commonly the effect than the cause.

With accurate diagnosis, modern drugs, and, ideally, specialized allergy investigations, advice and treatment, the vast majority of asthmatic children are capable of leading normal lives, and it is a tragedy that many do not get the chance.

Can asthma deform the chest?

To the trained eye chronic asthmatic children are obvious even from a distance. They usually have a typical stooping posture, with protruding wing-like shoulder blades and a prominent tummy. Such postural deformities can take many years of adequate treatment to eradicate.

If the asthma persists into adult life the deformed chest will persist, but if the asthma is effectively treated and well controlled the deformity will slowly disappear. If a child with chronic asthma is seen for the first time at the age of 14 or 15 it is probably too late to anticipate much improvement before growth ceases.

What special side-effects do oral steroids cause in children?

In children long-term oral steroids will stop growth, but so does chronic asthma. If minimal doses, just enough to control the asthma, are carefully used the benefits may outweigh the side-effects of steroid in stopping growth, and rapid growth is the converse result. However, since the advent of inhaled steroid (Becotide) it has become very uncommon for children to require continuous oral steroid therapy, except when the risk factor of repeated dangerous attacks makes this treatment an unavoidable choice. Also short courses of oral steroid in high dosage *do not* suppress growth and if given at the right time will abort the majority of attacks, as described elsewhere. Children are subject to all the other side-effects, but in low doses serious problems are very rare indeed.

Do the children of allergic parents develop the same types of allergy as their parents?

Different members of the same family usually react in different ways to different allergens, and there seem to be no rules. For example, the mother may get hay fever in summer, the father asthma all year, and the children colic as infants followed by asthma or eczema. The only instance where the same allergen seems to be frequently involved in several generations is cow's milk, but it may cause different manifestations of allergy in different members of the same family. Allergic reactions to allergens such as pollen or dust mites are so common anyway that it is quite likely that there may be several members of the same family affected by the same allergen, but it is the *tendency* to get sensitized which is inherited.

How does the management of asthma in children differ from that in adults?

Treatment for children does not differ greatly except that the doses of the drugs may be smaller. Oral steroids can be used at any age, and in full dosage for short periods from the age of 5 for asthma, with dramatic effectiveness, but are often withheld for fear of non-existent side-effects. On the other hand long-term oral steroids will stop the child growing, as well as causing all the usual steroid side-effects.

Children respond more rapidly to treatment than adults, and all except the really difficult cases can be completely reversed to normal levels of peak flow rate. Children also get worse more rapidly, as their bronchial tubes are much smaller, more easily blocked and more irritable, and the asthma is much more labile. Children are much easier to treat with effective drugs if care is taken to ensure that inhalers are used correctly and medication taken regularly. Careful and painstaking instruction by a doctor or nurse is often necessary before good results can be obtained using inhaler therapy for asthma, and lack of results is very often due to lack of careful instruction.

Foods are the important allergens in infancy, but inhalants become progressively more important from the toddler stage. Undue or excessive exposure of allergic children or families to pets is asking for trouble sooner or later. This is because even if a pet causes no obvious effects to begin with, this can be the period of sensitization.

Rhinitis, asthma and eczema are very common in childhood. Skin tests can be very informative and helpful in all these conditions from the age of 1 year onwards. Probable causes of allergic problems, such as dust, mites, animals, pollens, and some foods, can be suggested by skin-test reactions even when the history is negative. Surprisingly, many paediatricians and dermatologists believe, quite incorrectly, that skin tests are either dangerous, inadvisable, unreliable, misleading or useless, and that they should not be performed under the age of 6. Parents must be prepared for this negative attitude and should insist on testing.

Being younger, children are much more responsive to the correct treatment. This being so it seems all the more unfortunate that so many children are not diagnosed as asthmatics, and hence denied the benefits of modern therapy. Of those who *are* diagnosed, many are inefficiently treated because of inadequate instruction in the use of the medication, incorrect dosage, or simply not taking the treatment as prescribed.

Can parents safely cope with an asthma attack in their own child?

The short answer is only if the parents have been fully informed regarding how to handle attacks, and have a supply of the correct drugs.

Parents should be given printed instructions so that no confusion can arise in an emergency situation. These instructions should specify the dosages of bronchodilators and steroid tablets which may be necessary for early treatment of a flare-up. For some children it is also necessary to arrange for parents to have bronchodilators which can be injected subcutaneously by syringe if necessary pending medical help, which is often delayed and not always forthcoming. Reasonably intelligent parents can easily be taught how to abort an attack in its early stages and how to manage their child's asthma effectively. It is a great advantage if they have a peak flow meter as an early warning system.

In recent years it has been established that a nebulizer pump using a liquid solution of Ventolin, Bricanyl or a similar modern bronchodilator can be as effective as an injection. Nebulizers are now used in casualty departments for the immediate treatment of children and adults, and if they are available at home, attacks can be dealt with easily without medical help. It must be emphasized that if this treatment is ineffective medical help is necessary without delay, or the child should be taken direct to the hospital.

The instructions for parents faced with an acute attack of asthma which have been used in Derby for many years are given in Table 16.1. They have undoubtedly been effective and helpful, and have stood the test of time.

The smaller bronchial tubes of children are very easily blocked, and therefore inhaled steroid (Becotide) or bronchodilators quickly become ineffective. Oral steroids, which operate via the bloodstream, are rapidly effective and are only needed for a short time before the blockage can be cleared.

Can asthma mix with sport?

The answer to this question is a very loud *yes*, as there are several international sportsmen and women who are or were asthmatics. This is, of course, only possible if the disease is recognized and treated appropriately.

It is most important that asthmatic children are adequately treated so as to be as near normal as possible, and be able to take a full part in sport. If they have to be excused games they are probably being inadequately treated, and graded exercise should ideally be a part of this treatment. If it is permitted to occur, a vicious circle of inactivity will result as the child may be terrified to join in games which might provoke an attack.

In Europe several centres for asthmatic children concentrate on graded exercise to a high degree of fitness, but in this country there is very little interest in physical training for asthmatics. Games where exertion is intermittent are more suitable than cross-country running, for example, and swimming is the easiest and the most suitable exercise for the asthmatic.

18 Managing allergic rhinitis and nasal polyps

What is allergic rhinitis?

The nasal passages form the upper part of the respiratory system, because the function of the nose is to warm and filter the air before it reaches the bronchi. The interior structure of the nose is specially adapted for this task, and hence it bears the brunt of all sorts of airborne allergens and dirt, which are removed before they can enter the lungs.

In view of these facts, it is no surprise that allergic reactions in the lining of the nose are very common, although often mistaken for 'chronic catarrh' or frequent 'colds', which may go as suddenly as they came. In fact, it is likely that untold millions suffer from undiagnosed allergic rhinitis, often associated with allergic asthma and/or eczema, especially in children. It is unfortunate that medical teaching has tended to dissociate the nose from the chest. In fact, chest specialists may often fail to pay attention to the nose, just as nose specialists often ignore the chest – this is an example of excessive specialization.

Allergic reactions in the nose may result in sneezing attacks or varying degrees of blockage when the lining of the nose (the nasal mucosa) swells up and obstructs the passage of air. The nasal mucosa also reacts by producing excess mucus, so that it is described as 'running like a tap'. In some cases these reactions are shared by the sinus cavities, which are situated in the skull above the upper teeth and in the forehead. Most people know that the sinuses can get infected, and cause a great deal of trouble, but it is less often realized that allergy and infection may go hand in hand, and that allergy predisposes to infection.

In a way the nasal mucosa is a mirror of the bronchial mucosa, because it is so common for the nose to react to the same allergens as the bronchi. This is very useful, as the nasal mucosa can often be provoked to produce a reaction which can give a positive identification of the cause of the symptoms, but without causing asthma.

Sneezing, blockage and loss of the sense of smell due to allergic rhinitis are often very troublesome, and make the victim's life a misery. Treatment is sometimes inadequate, because the doctor thinks the complaint is trivial, but patients often complain much more about nasal symptoms than about quite severe asthma. Rhinitis is often a great nuisance, but asthma can be a menace.

Treatment of rhinitis is very easy with the correct approach to management. Apart from attempting to find a removable cause, the pragmatic approach, using a few steroid tablets to open up the nose so that local sprays can operate efficiently, is very effective. Surgical treatment is often carried out to remove the grossly swollen nasal mucosa found in allergic rhinitis, but results are transitory because a chronic allergic reaction cannot be mechanically removed – it will always return unless the case is analysed from the allergic point of view. However, often no attempt is made to find the cause, which could be avoidable.

What drugs are available for treating seasonal rhinitis (hay fever) and perennial rhinitis?

Anti-histamines

Mild seasonal hay fever may be mistaken for a so-called summer cold, and quite often avoidance of excess exposure to grass pollen is adequate treatment. Golf and other outdoor pursuits, however, involve excessive exposure to pollen, so anti-histamine tablets may be required. Many are available over the counter from a chemist, such as Triludan, Allereze or Hismanal, because they are less liable to cause drowsiness.

Drowsiness is the common side-effect of anti-histamines, which can be potentially dangerous when driving, especially with a little alcohol. Pharmaceutical companies are constantly searching for anti-histamines which work without causing side-effects, and some recent new compounds are promising. These drugs may be used as tablets, nasal sprays incorporating decongestants, and as eye drops. The latest are short-acting Semprex, or long-acting Zirtek which you take once a day only.

Decongestants

A great many decongestants are available, often directly from the chemist. The difficulty is that the benefit passes off after a varying time. If overused the effect decreases, necessitating more frequent dosage. Eventually, actual damage to the lining of the nose may occur as a result of abuse of decongestants.

Allergy blocking drugs

Intal for nasal use (Lomusol or Rynacrom) is available to block the reaction between allergen and the sensitized lining of the nose. It is also available to allay eye irritation in the form of eye drops (Opticrom).

Local steroids

Beclomethasone is used for local treatment as an aerosol spray (Beconase), and as a spray of a suspension of the same drug (Beconase Aqueous), and the powder in the Becotide Rotacaps for asthma can also be used as snuff. Flunisolide (Syntaris) has a similar action to beclomethasone and similar effectiveness. Clinical trials have shown that local steroids are more effective than the Intal preparations, and that they do not have any side-effects in long-term use. Newer drugs with more specific local effects, such as Pulmicort, are now available.

Oral steroids

Very severe seasonal hay fever can cause acute misery, and the usual anti-histamines may cause unacceptable side-effects. Though many doctors disagree with using oral steroids for hay fever, they do have a limited place in treatment. Steroid tablets (prednisolone, prednisone, Betnesol, Betnelan, and so on) will give dramatic relief from all the symptoms within hours, but are seldom used for this purpose. Fear of side-effects in short-term use is quite without foundation. A dosage of three, or at the most four, tablets a day is enough, and the dose can be varied rapidly according to symptoms and weather. For example, nothing may be taken on a wet day, but three or four tablets may be required on a sunny, windy day. There is no need for elaborate tapering off of dosages in short-term use. The season for simple pollen hay fever in England is 6 weeks at the most and this treatment may only be required at peaks of the pollen count. There is thus no valid reason for fear of becoming hooked on steroids. Naturally failure to use Beconase regularly for hay fever often results in complete blockage of the nose which can only be cleared by oral or injected steroids. If the patient's season is a long one, as when mould spores as well as grass pollen are involved, over-treatment with oral steroids can occur if strict control is not exercised.

In perennial rhinitis the nasal passages are often blocked by swelling of the lining of the nose, or by nasal polyps, so that little or no air can pass. In this situation nasal spray or aerosol will not be able to gain access to the nasal lining, so the treatment solutions cannot reach the site where they are needed. In this situation oral steroids can also be used, usually in the form of about four tablets a day for five days, and will clear the nose rapidly and dramatically. The tablets are then stopped, and local treatment with Beconase or Syntaris in a dosage of two puffs or squirts in each nostril three times a day can take over with a chance of maintaining control and keeping the nose clear. This short course of oral steroid may be repeated when the nose blocks up again, but not more often than about once in 6 weeks. In the presence of nasal polyps higher dosages of oral steroids for slightly longer periods may be necessary to effect a clearance, and to regain the senses of smell and taste.

The results of this treatment can sometimes produce un-expected handicaps, as in the case of the business tycoon who spent most of his days presiding over board meetings. He had been unable to smell for twenty years, and hence he was under the impression when he passed wind in a meeting there was no unpleasant smell. He suddenly found, to his great embarrass-ment, that this was a longstanding delusion!

A patient with severe allergic nasal problems was advised to have a *few days* on oral steroids to clear his nose, so that local beclomethasone (Beconase), which has no side-effects, could be used effectively for long-term treatment. His doctor refused to prescribe oral steroids, even for a few days, because he was so convinced it was dangerous. The patient's cat then developed asthma, and was promptly treated with a steroid injection by the vet, who said the cat was probably sensitive to the dust mites! The patient, suffering severely with his nose, then wished to consult the vet, because the cat was getting effective treatment while he was not!

What can be done to prevent severe hay fever affecting summer examination results?

If the examination is very important the most sensible and practical treatment is to give steroid tablets. If they are started a few days before the examination all the symptoms will disappear and the student will be totally deprived of any excuse for failure!

Desensitization against grass pollen is undoubtedly the best treatment if it is properly given as described elsewhere. However, this treatment takes much more effort on the part of the patient to achieve immunity (disappointment can occur), and is no longer available in the UK.

What is the role of depot steroids (Depot-Medrone, Kenalog) in the treatment of hay fever?

This form of steroid treatment is an intramuscular injection of steroid compound which is slowly released into the circulation over a period of about 3 weeks. The amount released from the depot quickly rises to a peak and declines slowly.

This is a popular treatment for seasonal hay fever, but is not ideal because the supply of steroid cannot be given intermittently like the tablets. If given too early the effect will have worn off before the end of the season, so that a second injection is required, the effects of which will last longer than the season. Thus, more steroid drugs than are strictly necessary may well be given using this method.

A rare and unusual side-effect is fat atrophy around the site of the injection which leaves a depression which can be unsightly. Depot steroid injections can be used to treat any steroid-responsive problem, but in long-term use the usual side-effects will be encountered. It is a useful alternative method of giving steroids when oral steroid is causing stomach problems.

In perennial rhinitis or nasal polyps depot steroid is also effective, but the dosage of tablets is easier to control. Once an injection has been given there is no way of taking it back.

What are nasal polyps?

Polyps resemble small grapes with a sort of stalk which carries the blood supply. They grow in the nasal passages and cause blockage with loss of sense of taste and smell. Most of them are allergic polyps, the cause is quite unknown, and they can cause misery for many, many years.

Can polyps be removed?

Yes, they can be removed surgically quite easily, but usually tend to recur sooner or later. Surgical removal is not curative, and they may recur many times. Polyps are not malignant growths.

What medical treatment is available for nasal polyps?

Polyps shrink rapidly under the influence of high-dosage oral steroids, responding just like allergic asthma. Once the nasal passages are clear, regular treatment with local steroid (Becotide, Beconase, Syntaris) will often prevent recurrence but never effect a cure.

What causes nasal polyps?

The causes are almost completely unknown. I have found a few where certain foods – instant coffee, wine, yeast, beer, and so on – seem to be causative factors. Polyps are quite often associated with the late-onset 'mystery' type of asthma. Some of these sufferers react violently to aspirin with a serious asthma attack, so they must beware of all headache remedies which contain aspirin.

Why do polyps or severe allergic rhinitis cause loss of the senses of taste and smell?

The organs of smell – the olfactory lobes – are hidden away in the nasal sinuses almost under the brain. Thus, it is quite easy for access of air to these organs to be blocked off. Taste and smell are closely associated and the tongue and palate cannot do much on their own.

19 Managing eczema

There is a close relationship between asthma and eczema because they often co-exist, and when one complaint gets better the other may get worse. Many victims of the asthma/eczema syndrome, as it is called, recover spontaneously, but the unlucky ones can draw a true life sentence.

Steroid creams and ointments have revolutionized the treatment of eczema, but often at the cost of removing the incentive to look for causative factors. Oral steroids are usually reserved for short-term use in acute flare-ups, when they are dramatically effective because the drug is absorbed into the bloodstream, and then passes into the extra-cellular fluids to reach the cells of the skin, where both immediate and delayed allergic reactions are suppressed. Food or inhalant allergens can use the same route to reach the skin from behind, and by contact or by entry through tiny cracks in the skin, the allergens can also reach living skin cells from outside. The steroid compounds included in creams or ointments also gain access to the deeper layers of the skin, as do the emollients which help to keep the skin flexible, and may prevent the horny layer becoming too thick and cracking, as is so common in eczema.

The usual purely suppressive approach to treatment may not satisfy sufferers who may wish for a more investigative approach. Unfortunately, there are at present few dermatologists who view eczema from an allergic viewpoint and are prepared to investigate in depth.

What is eczema and what can cause it?

Eczema is commonest in infancy, most often in children of allergic parents but often disappears quite soon. Otherwise it may persist along with asthma, rhinitis and other allergic syndromes throughout life. Although the parents are often assured that the child will get better with time, this is by no means certain.

Eczema is caused by the formation of tiny beads of fluid in the depths of the skin, which cause great irritation, itching and scratching. The face, eyebrows, trunk and especially the backs of the knees and the folds of the elbows are the usual sites involved. When the condition is chronic the skin becomes thickened, with painful cracking round the joints, scaling, weeping, crusting and infection.

The blood in eczema contains very large amounts of IgE, so there can be no doubt that the disease is allergic. Well-organized trials in infants have produced good evidence that milk or egg can cause eczema, but attempts to oversimplify the situation by concentrating on one food, or even several foods, seem doomed to failure. My experience has been that several factors are usually present, and that results will not be obtained unless they are *all* avoided.

The case which first taught me that there could be *several* avoidable factors was a boy of 2 with very severe eczema, who had considerable relief after excluding milk products and beef, but on holiday became completely free from the disease. Returning from holiday by car they stopped to pick up the dog from the kennels, and by the time they reached home the child was frantically scratching himself. After the dog had been found a good home and the house had been thoroughly cleaned his eczema disappeared completely, but his parents found that as little as 2 hours' exposure to a dog was enough to cause eczema for a week. This means that an encounter with an animal once a week can keep the disease going indefinitely.

A similar case was a girl of 6 with very severe eczema which cleared completely in a week off milk. Three days later she was brought in with a severe flare-up, because she had been to see her grandmother who had a cat and a dog. Finally she was completely desensitized as an experimental procedure, can now tolerate cats and dogs, and no longer reacts to milk.

Most British skin specialists do not believe that eczema, one of the commonest skin complaints, can be caused by foods or environmental allergens, or that prick skin testing can be helpful in diagnosis and management. American and European allergists and dermatologists published many scientific papers on this subject between the wars, but they seem to have been long forgotten. Today, however, many sufferers have realized that steroid ointments only suppress, never cure, and eventually damage the skin, so a revival of interest in allergic aspects may gradually occur in future.

My personal interest in eczema began when some cases cleared as a fringe benefit from diets introduced in an attempt to improve their asthmatic problems. Other clinical experiences also focused attention on dietary factors, such as the patient with generalized eczema which was worst on the right hand. It was obvious that the right hand must be in contact with something that the left was not, and a month later the patient produced the answer. This was that she always made her own yeast bread, holding the bowl in the left and kneading it with the right. There was no effect from making soda bread (which contains no yeast), and by avoiding yeast her generalized eczema and asthma disappeared.

Eczema is certainly one of the allergic diseases, and a search for causative factors in the foods and/or in the environment or both may be very rewarding. In the present state of knowledge investigation may often prove disappointing, but to accept the dictum to learn to live with it is cold comfort for the sufferer. The role of house dust and mites as well as pets in the causation of eczema has been seriously underestimated, and several causes may be operative. Some clinical trials of the dietary approach alone may have failed to take this into account.

If patients with eczema get married to each other, will the children have eczema?

Children have a good chance of escape if only one parent has eczema or asthma, but if both parents are affected, and if both families are involved, then the chances are much greater of the children developing not only eczema, but all the other allergic problems as well. It is best to try as hard as possible to minimize the risk by breast-feeding and avoidance of early weaning, and avoiding contact with animals as far as possible.

How can eczema be prevented?

Mothers should breast-feed for as long as possible, and should not take much milk themselves, preferably very little, and avoid eggs as well, for as long as possible. Weaning should be delayed as long as possible, epecially if there is a bad family history, as the immature gut may admit food allergens and cause all manner of allergic problems. Tinned baby foods may contain additives so are better avoided.

Does eczema get better spontaneously?

It is true that eczema in babies is usually transient, but in the more severe cases the disease may persist, or change into asthma and/or rhinitis as infancy passes into childhood and exposure to environmental allergens such as dust and pets begins.

Medical reassurance that the condition will improve at the age of 7 or in the early teens is often quite incorrect. As a rule the earlier the eczema begins and the more severe the disease, the less likely is a favourable outcome. Long-term follow-up studies have shown eczema to persist into adult life in 30 per cent in some of the studies, and as much as 80 per cent in others, depending on criteria of 'cure'. The reasons for improvement or worsening are unknown.

In a few cases the eczema will clear completely after a few days on holiday in a certain place, or moving residence may cause a clearance. One case of very severe eczema always cleared completely on holiday in Guernsey, and relapsed within hours of return home. Holidays elsewhere were not effective. Cases which behave this way suggest that something in the environment or a change in diet must be the cause. These cases, and those cured by avoiding a known cause which has been positively identified, should encourage a more intensive search for causative factors in food and in the environment, but there is very little interest in this more tedious approach to eczema.

Is skin testing worth doing in eczema cases?

Many dermatologists believe that so many positive reactions will be obtained from prick skin testing that interpretation is impossible, and the tests meaningless. This is a mistaken belief, because simple prick tests can quite often point to an important causative factor, such as foods, pets or dust mite. Indeed, if some relationship to food or environment can be demonstrated only good can result from avoiding the suspected cause. Also, as eczema can be a lifelong problem, there is nothing to lose but a little weight by trying a restricted diet. However, disorganized dieting can only cause confusion and disappointment, informed dietetic advice is hard to find, and inhalant factors such as mites and pets are also important in many cases.

Skin testing can show whether removable causes, such as animals are important, and also if the dust mite is playing a prominent role in causing the eczema. An effective mite killing agent has been developed in Germany, which may soon be available here. Some cases have cleared dramatically after the house was cleared of mites, and relapse promptly if they are exposed, even for a night, to a normal house. Therefore mites are obviously a very important cause of eczema.

How should steroid and other creams be used in the treatment of eczema?

Steroid creams are the main effective suppressive treatment for eczema, and can be used quite intensively on hands and feet for periods of up to a week or two.

Various non-steroid preparations are also used on the skin to allay the itch and scratch, and to soothe the skin. Infection is common, and can be a serious problem. Application of antibiotics to the skin, especially neomycin, can cause sensitization of the skin to the drug, an ever-present danger with all medication.

What are the side-effects of steroid creams and ointments in eczema?

Steroid creams or ointments applied to the skin every day will eventually cause local side-effects, as a result of the destruction of the collagen in the skin, which loses its elasticity and becomes thin and fragile. The small blood vessels begin to show through the skin, particularly in the face, and wound healing is very slow. It may take many years for these side-effects to become obvious, but a state of alarm about these well-recognized side-effects has only recently passed into everyday practice. Both skin specialists and general practitioners have begun to restrict severely the usage of steroid creams on the skin, particularly on the face, with the result that many patients who have been well controlled for years have an acute flare-up, and weaker creams or non-steroid preparations are found inadequate to control the eczema. This creates a dilemma for both patient and doctor, because life without steroid creams may be very uncomfortable. The doctor may be reluctant to continue with steroid creams, especially if the dermatologist has advised against them, or has discharged the patient from the clinic. Thus, medical advice may alternate between 'carry on regardless' and forbidding steroid creams altogether.

A more serious side-effect may result from *excessively* lavish use of steroid creams in children with severe eczema. Enough steroid can be absorbed through the skin to produce an 'ointment dwarf', so-called because growth is stopped. This is unusual, but can occur if the parents are unaware that excess steroids on the skin can cause the same side-effects as tablets.

What is the place of Nalcrom or Becotide in treating eczema?

Nalcrom (Intal in capsule form) has been shown to have the ability to block the entry into the circulation of a food to which a patient is allergic. It is given dissolved in warm water some time before meals, beginning with two or three capsules, and increasing to as many as ten a day. The initial doses may make eczema worse, but this is actually an encouraging sign. Only a minority of patients respond to this treatment, which is also one way to find out if food is involved in causing the eczema.

It is not sensible to use an expensive drug on a long-term basis when the problem could be solved by avoidance of a specific food, but the food or foods must first be identified – a task which may be very difficult. When a great many foods are involved Nalcrom can be very helpful, as a blocking agent, but it should not be a long-term treatment unless this is unavoidable.

A good result from Nalcrom suggests that a food is causing the eczema, so the next step should be a diet excluding foods liable to cause allergy, while continuing on Nalcrom for about a week. If the offending food has been excluded the eczema should not relapse when Nalcrom is stopped. Foods are then reintroduced one by one to identify the causative foods, which are then avoided completely.

Thus, Nalcrom can be used to pick out eczemas with a definite food factor, can help in controlling a difficult dietary problem, and can be used as an investigative tool. Unfortunately simple straightforward food problems are rare, and the disease is often due to many factors.

Recently capsules of Becotide (Rotacaps) have also been found to help some cases of severe eczema, but given orally instead of by inhalation. As explained elsewhere, this drug does not cause general side-effects, and may have a surface effect on the lining of the gut similar to Intal's.

What is a commonsense approach to the management of atopic (allergic) eczema?

The appropriate treatment depends on the severity of the problem, but some general observations are in order.

Steroid creams can be used in moderation. It may be better to use them intensively for short periods, then stop to allow the skin to recover, rather than to use them daily for years. Oral steroids in a comparatively low dose (15 or 20mg prednisolone a day) will usually clear the skin dramatically, and can be stopped abruptly after 7–10 days. This treatment should be reserved for when the problem is severe, to clear the skin before changing the therapy or making dietary experiments, or in conjunction with antibiotics when there is gross infection.

A cream or ointment may eventually cause an allergic reaction in the skin after being used for some time. The ingredient to which sensitivity has developed may be found in several different skin applications.

Constant review of possible allergic factors in the environment is essential. For example, if the eczema clears on holiday, absence of an allergen from the environment or the food should be suspected, and should stimulate an intensive search. Sea bathing and sunshine may be helpful on holiday, not at home. Even if this search is fruitless do not give up, but try again later. Elimination diets, especially avoiding milk, eggs or yeast, can be very helpful, but without assessment of the whole environment may prove disappointing.

Tight clothes will soon be found to chafe, and look out for nickel sensitivity from jean buttons and earrings. Wool irritates the skin – cotton is best. Keep the nails short to avoid scratching.

Avoid using strong detergents, especially 'biological' types, for clothes or dishes. Try to avoid emotional crises which might promote itching and scratching. If infection becomes evident do not wait until you are in a mess before seeking medical advice. Pets are always a possible causative factor, and should be avoided in allergic families.

The skin can be kept supple and moist by a variety of preparations which are available. These emulsifying oils or ointments, and oatmeal baths, are of many types, some prescribable, some obtainable at any chemist, and are not harmful, unless the skin becomes sensitized to them also. The best cosmetic is none at all, but if you must use them it is really a matter of trial and error. 'Hypo-allergenic' preparations are not necessarily the best, and always cost more. Worry causes stress, which may promote itching, which leads to scratching, which makes the eczema worse and leads to more stress, itch, scratch, infection, worry and stress. Worry is not a true cause, but an aggravating factor. The good effects of a holiday in the sun can seldom be accounted for by 'absence of stress' and so on.

What is allergic contact dermatitis, and how does it differ from atopic eczema?

There is really little difference between the two forms of eczema except that the pattern and distribution of the skin eruption and a history of exposure to a known contact allergen may suggest the diagnosis. The two forms may co-exist.

This type of eczema is referred to as 'contact' eczema because it is acquired by contact of the affected parts with the allergen. This results in sensitization of the cells of the skin in that area only. The number of potential contact allergens is enormous and they may be encountered anywhere. Fortunately a relatively small number of allergens accounts for the great majority.

At work protective clothing, better ventilation and substitution of less allergenic chemicals may be possible. Barrier creams and gloves may help but complete avoidance is the ideal. If the cause can be identified and avoided there should be no further trouble, but a change of job may be necessary because further exposure will usually cause relapse of the dermatitis.

Nickel is one of the commonest sensitivities, and there are a great many people who cannot wear nickel-plated earrings or have contact with anything nickel-plated. The modern site for a patch of nickel dermatitis is under the plated buttons on jeans, but it used to be on the front of the thigh under the metal suspender clip. One patient was truly allergic to money when she developed eczema on the left hand only – the one which handled the change!

Money in a trouser pocket can also do this, and in severe nickel sensitivity with a widespread rash a nickel-free diet may be necessary, because traces of nickel are found in some foods. Modern jewellery made of white gold or 9 carat gold alloy may contain nickel and other metals. Allergy to nickel is illustrated by the case of the young woman who played in a band and suffered from reactions on the lips when a 9 carat mouthpiece was used, but not from one plated with pure gold.

What are the common causes of contact eczema?

Anyone can have skin irritation and damage from, for example, strong antiseptics, but someone who becomes sensitized will react to very small amounts of the substance, and the condition may be permanent.

There are so many possible causes that it is best to divide them into broad categories, as follows, to give an idea of the range of possibilities. The jungle of chemicals with which we surround ourselves today can all sensitize, but some are more potent sensitizers than others. The unfortunate part of the story is that once an area, such as the hands, has become sensitized, complete avoidance is the only solution, and exposure years later will bring out the rash at once.

Botanical

This group includes plants, some exotic woods, some fruits, vegetables, and spices. Examples are primula, chrysanthemum and poison ivy (USA).

Cosmetics

This very large group includes even toothpaste, creams, ointments, and so on.

Dyes

In cosmetics, clothing, leather, paints, inks.

Hairdressing

Lotions, bleaches, hair dyes, and so on.

Soaps

This group includes soaps, detergents with synthetic scents, and so on.

Metals

For example nickel and chromium (cement).

Oils and resins

In oils, paints, and polishes of all sorts.

Rubber compounds

Found in wellington boots, sneakers, sticking plaster, and so on. Synthetic rubber contains antioxidants, accelerators, and so on which are potent sensitizers.

Plastics

For example, plastic seat and badly cured dental plates.

A complete list would be impossible, and useless. If the reader understands the concept of sensitization and the possibilities in the environment, the way is open to finding a cause in any particular case.

What is photo-dermatitis?

This is a type of dermatitis caused by exposure to sunshine while taking a drug, or using an external application or certain soaps which contain a chemical which acts as a photo-sensitizer.

Treatment depends mainly on avoiding the sun and the cause, if identified, and also anything containing related chemicals. In some unfortunates the photo-sensitivity is long-lasting, and can be a serious handicap.

Photo-dermatitis is mentioned here because if the association with drugs taken internally or soaps or creams externally is more widely known the diagnosis may be achieved more quickly.

Is allergy the cause of urticaria and angio-oedema?

Urticaria is the medical name for nettle-rash or hives. Angio-oedema is a specially severe type of urticaria which tends to affect only one part of the body, such as the face and lips. This form of urticaria used to be called angio-neurotic-oedema, because until relatively recently it was thought to be all in the mind.

These curious conditions may be regarded as huge uncontrollable skin reactions which are very distressing, unsightly and itchy, and usually respond to anti-histamine drugs. The swellings and weals are caused by the leakage of fluid from the capillary blood vessels in the skin, brought about by the liberation of mediators from the mast cells. Gross swelling of the face, eyes and lips may occur. The condition is not dangerous unless swelling of the tongue or throat causes dangerous obstruction of the airway, when an emergency opening in the windpipe may have to be made (tracheostomy) but this is rare.

My experience has been that very often it proves impossible to track down a definite cause, even with the most intense investigation. Sulphites, yeast, beer, citrus fruits, cheese, additives in white bread and sundry chemicals have occasionally been found to be definite causes, but this is uncommon. Paradoxically, this condition, which resembles an enormous skin test reaction, usually proves to be negative to all skin tests, and blood tests are usually unhelpful.

Chronic urticaria is a most difficult problem because it is so often impossible to find the cause. In some cases it has been found that the dye in anti-histamine tablets is perpetuating the condition, the original cause for which the tablets were prescribed having long disappeared. Newer anti-histamines such as Zirtek and Hismanal can be very helpful.

Table 19.1 Principles for the management of eczema in relation to household tasks

Excessive exposure to soaps, detergents and other common household irritants is often made *worse* by wearing rubber gloves. Half of cases are sensitive to metals, rubber and chemicals. Commonsense measures are often the best treatment.

1. Use long-handled brushes for dishes and pots.
2. Soak dishes for half an hour in hot soapy water and let it cool so the hands will not be overheated.
3. If you must use rubber gloves wear cotton gloves inside them and use talcum powder.
4. Bath the baby with bare hands as baby soaps are so mild.
5. Use disposable nappies.
6. Wear cotton gloves for housework to keep hands clean and thus avoid excessive hand washing.
7. Avoid contact with fruit juices, onions, garlic, vegetables and raw meat.
8. Avoid contact with wool if it is known to irritate.
9. Avoid contact with hair lotions, and so on.
10. To cleanse the hands do not use household cleansers; avoid frequent washing. Pat skin dry, do not rub.
11. Use superfatted soaps which are mild and free from strong chemicals. Take great care to rinse off soap thoroughly.

Has fringe medicine anything to offer the eczema sufferer?

In my experience acupuncture, naturopathy, homeopathy, hypnosis, yoga, and sublingual therapy have not been able to produce any lasting improvement. Evening primrose oil may be helpful and is now prescribable on the NHS as 'Epogram'.

PART 7

Allergy and Intolerance to Foods and Environmental Pollutants

PART V

20 The importance of food allergy, food intolerance, and environmental pollution

Asthma and eczema were accurately described by the ancient Greeks and Middle Eastern physicians long before the birth of Christ. They also noted that occasional patients could become very ill from eating even a morsel of cheese, a few strawberries, honey, nuts, oysters, fish, eggs and milk – a list which includes foods which still cause allergic problems today. The proverb 'One man's meat is another man's poison' is accredited to Lucretius in the first century AD, in the second century Galen recorded allergy to goat's milk, and the Talmud of Babylon gave precise instructions on how to treat gut sensitivity to egg. In the eighteenth century William Cullen, Professor of Medicine at Edinburgh University, noted adverse reactions to drugs, and in 1873 a case in Germany was reported in which eating freshly cooked pork repeatedly caused a rash, but smoked pork did not.

With the dawn of the twentieth century allergic reactions to foods became increasingly recognized. As a result, publications in the medical journals of Europe and America reporting various foods as a cause of allergic symptoms became more and more frequent, especially in the 1920s and 1930s. The medical journals of the time make fascinating reading because the clinical aspects of allergy to foods were being established, but scientific explanations were unobtainable. The pioneers of the study of food allergy were often ridiculed by their colleagues, especially in America. The subject has only become acceptable at scientific meetings in recent years, now that some of their findings have been confirmed in the laboratory.

In spite of opposition the principles of dietary treatment were laid down by American pioneers before the Second World War, at a time when there were no antibiotics, no anti-histamines, no steroids, and only weak bronchodilators such as ephedrine and aminophylline. In fact, there were so few powerful drugs available at that time that there must have been much greater incentive than there is today to find the cause of the disease, so that it could be avoided and the patient thus relieved.

Daily foods may cause daily symptoms, so it is very difficult to know when to suspect allergy to or intolerance of food. In fact, the only way to exclude food as a cause is to try out a limited diet for a *short* time, but to do this without guidance may be unproductive, and to continue on a limited diet may lead to severe malnutrition. This situation has arisen when parents have refused to accept that the behaviour problems of their children are not caused by foods, and have continued on a foolish diet regardless of the consequences, to the extent that vitamin deficiencies have been observed. Also, to reject or refuse conventional modern treatments can have serious consequences, and it is ideal to have the advice, help and co-operation of a consultant, general practitioner, or qualified dietitian.

Sometimes sufferers from chronic and disabling diseases have discovered for themselves that foods or chemicals are the cause, and can be avoided with great benefit. These lucky people may wish to share their personal miracle by writing books describing their experiences, whilst others form pressure groups to obtain treatment and advice on the National Health Service. Their motivation is wholly admirable, but may give false hope to some who are afflicted with crippling diseases.

Food allergy or intolerance is probably quite common but seldom diagnosed because it is not considered a serious possibility. A skin rash will often be attributed to a drug, but very seldom to food. Dietary restriction is widely advised to counteract the evils cf obesity but often unacceptable for the treatment of allergic disease. It is not surprising that many patients find these inconsistencies difficult to understand.

The continual stream of medical information from newspapers, magazines, radio and television, must make people think deeply about their chronic ailments. Many must wonder if their drug treatment is causing some sinister side-effect, or if their illness is all due to an allergy to foods, preservatives, dyes, and so on. Much of their information may be as new to the doctor as to the patient. Doctors may feel disadvantaged when badgered about the latest television programme they did not have time to see, so be reasonable.

How does the alimentary tract work?

A few facts about the alimentary tract or 'gut' may help the reader to understand allergy to and intolerance of foods more readily. The gut begins at the lips and ends at the anus. It is lined throughout by living cells, which are constantly being cast off and replaced, backed up by muscles and glands. The structure of each part is ideally adapted to its function. Beginning at the mouth, the food is chewed and mixed with saliva, which contains enzymes to begin the breakdown of starches and sugars. It is then swallowed, and in the stomach is exposed to acid and more enzymes. When it is ready it is passed on through a narrow muscular part, the duodenum, into the small intestine. On the way the food is mixed with bile from the gall-bladder under the liver and with more enzymes from the pancreas, so that proteins and fats can be further digested.

The effect of all these digestive processes is to break down large molecules into smaller molecules which are easier to absorb into the bloodstream, and can be utilized as energy and serve other metabolic processes. All other essential nutrients, vitamins and minerals are absorbed as well. The surface of the small intestine is very special, as it is lined with enormous numbers of tiny projections, like the hairs of a short-haired brush, which contain blood vessels and glands, thus expanding enormously the surface available for absorption. Once the broken-down food molecules enter the bloodstream, all it takes is a few beats of the heart to expose every cell in every organ of the body to these substances. This also applies to all chemicals, preservatives, dyes and insecticides which get into our food.

The gut is also inhabited by countless myriads of harmless bacteria, some of which help digestion, while others manufacture vitamins. When the food reaches the colon (the large intestine) everything slows up and the excess water and salts are reabsorbed. Finally what is left over is stored in the rectum and evacuated through the anus.

What is the difference between food 'allergy', and food intolerance?

This distinction is important, especially as many doctors are not aware of the difference, and the word 'allergy' is often used carelessly.

In true food *allergy*, which is quite uncommon, tiny amounts can trigger off a reaction. Sometimes even touching or smelling the food is enough, and swelling of lips or tongue may prevent swallowing it. Reactions are fast, and can even cause anaphylactic shock, but this is very rare.

Most food allergic people are fully aware of their allergy, and do not need medical help except when accidentally exposed. On the other hand slightly sensitive cases may not realize that traces of a food, such as egg, are causing chronic problems like eczema.

Because specific IgE against the food is present in the blood and on the mast cells, skin tests and blood tests (RAST) are positive, so a laboratory diagnosis is possible. Food allergy lasts for many years, may be lifelong, and hence are called 'fixed' food allergies.

Food *intolerance* is quite different from food allergy, is much commoner, and is frequently undiagnosed because the relationship between the causative food or foods, and the effect is not obvious. Skin and blood tests (RAST) are negative, and at present the diagnosis can only be achieved by dietary manipulation. Large amounts of the food tend to be required to set off a reaction. Many cases react in 3–6 hours, others take longer. It may take daily feeds with the suspect food for a week before a reaction takes place, and it is not uncommon for several foods to be involved. This is the type of reaction to food with which this section is mainly concerned. Intolerance often passes off after a varying period of time, so is not fixed.

Many enzymes designed specifically to digest certain foods are produced by the gut wall, and if any of them are deficient or missing severe diarrhoea may result. The best example is absence of lactase, so that lactose from milk cannot be digested, but this is neither allergy nor intolerance. In other states, such as the so-called irritable bowel syndrome, specific foods will provoke the production by the bowel of powerful mediator chemicals such as prostaglandins, which will stimulate the production of diarrhoea.

The human digestive processes function efficiently in most of us, and usually tolerate a great deal of abuse without complaint. These processes are very complicated and are not yet fully understood, and it is too easy to attribute all manner of complaints to allergy or emotion. It is unwise and unsafe to assume that a digestive or bowel problem is due to food allergy or intolerance without excluding other causes of similar symptoms.

Would a specialist in digestive diseases (gastroenterologist) or in children's diseases (paediatrician) be able to advise on food allergy and intolerance?

Various problems involving the gut can be caused by foods at any age. These include severe diarrhoea, failure to thrive and malabsorption in infants, coeliac disease, chronic diarrhoea and – rarely – severe constipation. Other examples are the irritable bowel syndrome and spastic colitis (both rather vague entities), Crohn's disease, ulcerative colitis, and proctitis (itchy anus).

All these problems have been reported as being caused by foods many times in the last 50 years, but scepticism and prejudice may be found amongst those who specialize in diseases of the alimentary tract, and many paediatricians. As a result, the proportion of cases which might respond to dietary management is unknown because the idea is so often rejected without trial. Few dietitians are aware of the essential principles of elimination diets or have the know-how necessary for success.

Many patients who have tried diets on their own have been dismissed as faddists. As they do not return for a further consultation if they have solved their problem, the consultants and dietitians miss the opportunity to learn from the patients' experiences. It is important to report that improvement has occurred, as if the doctors become convinced of the importance of dietary control many others may also be helped. Patients with chronic recurrent abdominal symptoms are often extensively investigated in hospital, and when the results are all negative they are often labelled psychosomatic; yet it should be no surprise that a person with chronic symptoms which defy diagnosis should become anxious about themselves. As in asthma, cause and effect may easily become confused.

How can dietary advice be obtained regarding possible food allergy or intolerance?

Many books are available today which give all sorts of advice to those who suspect that they may have food allergy or intolerance. Unfortunately the information may be inaccurate, cranky or conflicting, and the diets too complicated or unsuitable for long-term use.

At this time, there are few hospital dietitians who are expert in manipulating diets for food allergy or intolerance. This aspect of diet is a modern challenge to experts in dietetics which will not be properly met until physicians collaborate fully with dietitians. The dietitian should be an essential member of the team, but without medical support results will be unsatisfactory. The hospital cook should also be part of the team, as unfortunate mistakes are easily made unless everybody involved understands precisely what the patient can and cannot eat. It is a hopeful sign that more and more dietitians are becoming interested in food allergy, but there are still considerable difficulties in obtaining informed advice for a suspected food allergy or intolerance problem.

Why do doctors often reject the idea that foods can cause allergic illness?

The patient must understand that doctors get very little training in dietetics or nutrition as medical students. In consequence, your doctor may find it difficult to advise you on other than basic dietary matters, especially if time is limited. Food-allergic patients are often emotionally upset, and can very easily be labelled as 'psychosomatic'. If you encounter resistance to your suggestion that you may have a food-allergy problem, do not become upset and aggressive, because it is very important not to alienate your medical adviser. You might need help at any time, and perhaps your problem is not a food allergy at all. It is good sense to exclude other serious causes of your symptoms before concluding that allergy is the cause of them. Try to enlist the help and co-operation of your doctor, who might eventually become interested in the result of your dietary experiments, if approached correctly.

Is food allergy all in the mind?

A publication in a leading medical journal alleged recently that this is indeed true, and has been widely quoted and accepted by those who prefer this view. This conclusion was reached following tests in which patients who suspected that they had food allergy were placed on elimination diets. The foods which produced symptoms were thus identified, and shown to produce symptoms repeatedly as long as the patients knew what they were eating. However, when the foods were put up in double-blind coded capsules and swallowed, very few patients reacted, suggesting that their reactions were psychosomatic. Those few who reacted did so quickly, and were found to be the immediate-type reactors with positive skin and laboratory tests (RAST), so they had true food *allergy*.

A diametrically opposite result was obtained by recent research in children with migraine, where the responsible foods were first of all pinpointed by dieting. Specially coded tins of food were then made up, some of which contained the offending food, but others did not. Ninety per cent had headaches *only* after eating the tins which contained the foods they were sensitive to, proving that foods really do cause migraine. In some cases epileptic fits and behaviour disturbances also disappeared.

These contradictory results would seem to be accounted for by the fact that only small amounts of food can be given in capsules, while the tins contained large amounts and were given for up to a week. The lesson is that if the methodology of a double-blind test does not mimic natural exposure closely, a fallacious result can be obtained.

This recent research only confirms the observations of many allergists over the last 50 years. The difference is that this new study was carried out under conditions where neither patient nor doctor knew what foods were in the tins so that criticism is difficult. This new research may at last place dietary treatment of migraine, epilepsy and behaviour disorders in children on a sound footing.

What is environmental medicine and what is clinical ecology?

The term 'ecology' refers to the relationships of living organisms to their environment and to each other. Human ecology concerns the adaptation of the individual to the conditions of existence – the environment. It is evident that we must remain perfectly adjusted (adapted) to every circumstance in our environment from the cradle to the grave. In this context partial failure of adaptation is disease, and complete failure is death.

Maintenance of the constancy of the internal environment in spite of all adverse environmental influences is essential for continued health, which can be defined as a state of perfect adaptation to the environment. The many bodily mechanisms which operate unseen to ensure our continued adaptation and survival must have been programmed by the environmental experience of our species over the millenia.

Obviously there is a continual interplay between the individual, with innate advantages and disadvantages as determined by genetic inheritance, and the many influences of the environment. The resultant of all these influences will normally be a state of health, but any major external or internal change can upset this delicate balance, and produce either malfunction or overreaction.

The study of disease in man resulting from failure to adapt completely and constantly to the ecological environment has been referred to as 'clinical ecology' for some years. However, interest in the adverse effects of civilization and industrialization on the ecology has increased so much in recent years that 'ecology' has acquired a confusing political connotation. The expression 'environmental medicine' seems a better alternative, which is easier to understand.

It seems obvious that there is little difference between environmental medicine and clinical ecology, and that the study of both in depth and in detail should not be a neglected aspect of medicine. Unfortunately the development of the major medical specialities according to the anatomical divisions of the body and the major organs has brought about almost complete neglect of the concept of a 'holistic' response of body and mind to continuous environmental challenge. During the last hundred years scientific developments have made it possible for man to man ipulate the environment as never before, often without consideration of any possible consequences. As a result our air, water and food become more and more polluted with new chemicals.

Insecticides, additives, preservatives, dyes, antibiotics and a host of other chemicals enter our bodies. It would be more surprising if nobody became intolerant and reacted against these new environmental pollutants than that a minority of us should do so. Table 20.1 lists possible causes of allergic reactions in the environment.

The effect depends on the capacity of the chemical to sensitize, which can vary a great deal, and the potential of the immune system of the exposed individual to overreact. Obviously the greater the amount and variety of environmental chemicals, the more likely they are to cause diseases due to failure of perfect environmental adaptation. The rapidity of these changes in the chemical environment, in contrast to more gradual natural evolutionary change, must overload the capacity of some individuals to adapt, with the production of exaggerated and self-destructive reactions which may effect many systems of the body.

To keep pace with the rate of change in our ecosystem presents a greater challenge than ever before to our ability to adapt, and to stay adapted, to our environment.

At the present time, therefore, more stress is being applied to the immune system by environmental pollution with chemicals than ever before, but the effects of adverse reactions to chemicals are so diverse that the connection may not be recognized, or may be mistaken for psychosomatic illness. A reliable laboratory test to detect these reactions and point to the cause would be a great leap forward.

Allergic reactions where cause and effect are obviously related went through a phase of clinical observation when there was much scepticism and prejudice in the medical profession as a whole. Scientific investigation has now provided explanations which have led to acceptance of the immediate type of allergy, but the simultaneous development of really effective drugs has led, at least in this country, to excessive reliance on suppressive treatment.

'Environmental' medicine should be allied with 'occupational' medicine, which deals with disease caused by bad working environments, and is increasingly concerned with chemical ex-

Table 20.1 Possible causes of allergic reactions in the environment

Causes	Comment
Indoor Air Nitrous oxides due to gas or oil heating and cooking.	Respiratory complaints have been commoner among children with gas cooking (several surveys).
Gases liberated from plastics, glues and fabrics; bleach; paint fumes; disinfectants; insecticides; air 'fresheners'; tobacco smoke; scent, aftershave, deodorants, cosmetics; shampoo, hair dyes; cavity wall insulation; lack of ventilation from double glazing.	Allergic reactions difficult to prove, and no tests available. Formaldehyde from cavity wall insulation may cause problems but subject very controversial and far from clear. Laboratory tests are slowly developing which provide objective data for chemical sensitivities.
Outdoor air Car exhausts, diesel fumes, carbon monoxide, nitrous oxides, insecticides, sulphur dioxide from power stations, industrial fumes.	Nobody likes fumes, but control is difficult and clear proof of effects is difficult to obtain. Recent work suggests that air pollution is causing the remarkable increase in allergy in Japan.
Water Nitrates and nitrites, bacteria, detergents, insecticides, industrial pollutants, local pollution in house storage tanks, lead pipes, aluminium etc.	Water authorities do have quality control, and effects of some pollutants are difficult to prove. (More publicity has been given to pollution of water recently.)
Food and drugs Preservatives, antioxidants, dyes, insecticides, plastic containers, waxed cartons, antibiotics, exotic foods; reactions to specific foods and drugs, anaesthetics and muscle relaxants.	Effects difficult to prove. Increased public awareness has forced food manufacturers to remove as much as possible. Blood tests now available for anaesthetics and muscle relaxant allergy.

posures. Hence, the allergist and the environmentalist should have common interests, particularly because both types of problem are so often present in the same individual, but this seldom happens.

Where are the main environmental pollutants to be found?

Our homes are increasingly polluted with insecticides, aerosol sprays, so-called air-fresheners, furniture polish, detergents, enzymes, synthetic scents in soaps and other toilet articles, cosmetics, aftershave and so on, *ad infinitum*. Our food, water and especially the air, are increasingly contaminated with numberless potentially allergenic chemical compounds. Even medicine can cause sensitization directly, or may contain unnecessary chemical additives such as colouring and synthetic flavouring. Table 20.1 lists possible environmental causes of allergic reactions.

To condemn outright all insecticides, preservatives, additives and other chemicals because they are relatively new to our environment would be just as foolish as to accept them blindly. It is necessary to emphasize that only a minority will react adversely to many chemicals. Total condemnation should be reserved for substances such as lead which are toxic to everyone.

Environmental pollution is not always the result of irresponsible management of chemical factories, but probably began with modern fertilizers and insecticides, which have had very serious secondary effects on the ecology of birds, animals, plants and insects. Farmers contend that they could not raise enough crops by the old-fashioned methods to feed the present population, and many arguments are brought forward in favour of modern methods of agriculture, harvesting, pest control and preserving. Food technology has mushroomed as a branch of applied science, and huge quantities of dyes and preservative chemicals are added to our food.

Recently, public awareness of these matters has increased remarkably, resulting in the removal of additives and dyes from many foods – but not yet from medicines!

A few case histories will serve to illustrate the problems which can be caused by environmental chemical exposure, and how they can be solved by avoidance as long as the cause can be identified.

A middle-aged man was admitted to hospital with severe asthma of several years duration, but recovered by the next morning without treatment, suggesting a cause in the home. On enquiry it was found that at home there were air-fresheners in almost every room and exposure to one of these in hospital caused another attack. The separate ingredients of the product were obtained from the maker and exposure to each in turn demonstrated that only one affected him severely. With total avoidance of air-fresheners and similar products he has had no recurrence but if the cause of his problem had not been identified he could have become an irreversible case of apparent chronic bronchitis (Figure 20.2).

A lady who had recently purchased a new caravan found that when in the caravan she developed huge swellings on one side of her face. She suspected the large amounts of plastic used in the construction of the caravan, but eventually the real cause was found to be a block of insecticide which was hung under an awning outside above the cooking stove. The clues were that she had no trouble except in summer, and no trouble when she forgot the insecticide, but if it was hung so that it was to the left of her face, the left side reacted, and vice versa, demonstrating that even a few molecules of this substance in the open air could cause an obvious reaction.

Another patient with a poor sense of smell had severe chronic asthma of totally unknown cause, and the only clue was that she felt wheezy whenever she was near the washing powders in the supermarket. Even in a strange supermarket she would react before she knew where the washing powders were. Washing powders with enzymes are well known as causing asthma, but she never used the enzyme type of powder. She recovered in hospital where she did not have to do the washing twice a week, but controlled exposure carried out by tipping scented and un-scented powder from one cup to another caused severe asthma which lasted 5 days after one of the tests. She had an immediate reaction to the scent, followed by a delayed reaction, but for the unscented washing powder she had a delayed reaction only, as shown in the graphs (Figure 20.3a & b). As one exposure to washing powder could cause asthma which lasted for 5 days, and she washed clothes twice a week, she had chronic asthma until a powder which did not have this effect was found.

Another woman became convinced that her chronic asthma

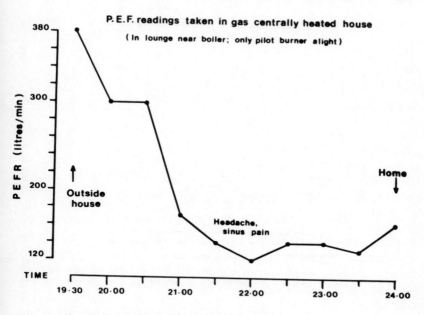

Figure 20.1   The effects of fumes from a gas pilot light.

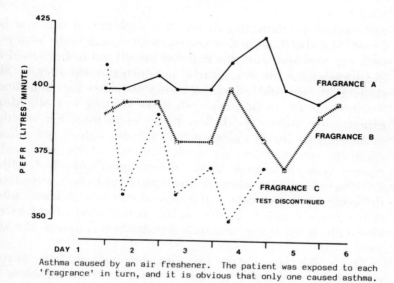

Asthma caused by an air freshener. The patient was exposed to each 'fragrance' in turn, and it is obvious that only one caused asthma.

Figure 20.2   The effects of exposure to fragrances in an air freshener.

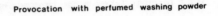

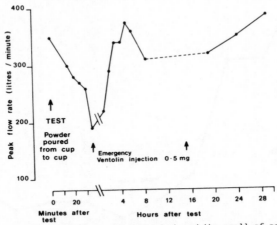

This chart shows that the dust and the smell of perfumed washing powder caused a sudden attack of asthma, so this patient was very sensitive to 'perfume'.

Figure 20.3(a)   The effects of washing powder on an asthmatic patient.

was caused by natural gas, but this explanation was not believed. She also thought that she reacted to going to the local pub with her husband, and this reaction turned out to be caused by the orange juice she drank there, to which she was allergic. She stated that she could tell within minutes whether a strange house had natural gas or not, even when the heating was off. Many experiments using a peak flow meter to monitor her reaction produced convincing evidence that she did indeed get asthma when she was near any gas appliance with a pilot light, and typical example is given in the illustrative Figure 20.1. Other cases have been seen where natural gas seems to be involved, but the evidence in this case is the most conclusive. It seems likely that nitrous fumes from incomplete combustion of gas at the pilot light is the cause, and with avoidance this patient remains well.

These illustrative case histories demonstrate how anyone could help themselves to find a cause for their problem by observing a reproducible pattern of reaction to specific circumstances.

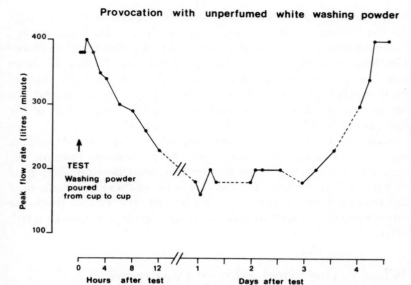

Figure 20.3(b)   The effects of washing powder on an asthmatic patient.

What illnesses may be caused by environmental pollution?

Doctors interested in illnesses caused by maladjustment to environmental factors may consider that a remarkably wide range of ailments can be caused by 'allergy'. They may also use tests which depend entirely on subjective symptoms reported by the patient as a result of provocation tests given under the tongue or by intradermal injection – conditions which make the patient susceptible to suggestion or bias.

There does not seem to be any really satisfactory confirmation of any of these tests at this time. Hence, it is no surprise that these claims are not accepted by the majority of the medical profession. The lack of any laboratory tests which can confirm objectively that environmental factors really *do* cause disease is a serious obstacle. In these circumstances it is obligatory for those who use these controversial techniques to prove them by double-blind methods. Unfortunately it may be very difficult to arrange for double-blind tests to be carried out, just as for food allergy.

An adverse reaction to an environmental pollutant can involve any body system, often producing symptoms identical to those which are truly psychosomatic in origin. For example, to feel very much better on holiday might suggest an environmental cause, but could also be accounted for by the tonic effect of the holiday itself. The distinction may be difficult.

How common is adaptation disorder of the self-damaging immune-response type? What are these aberrant immune responses? How can they be firmly diagnosed beyond all doubt? What are they caused by? One day some of these questions may be answered and steps taken to remove the causes from the environment, but until reliable tests are developed confusion will reign.

What is the 'total allergy syndrome'?

Sufferers of this 'syndrome' are alleged to be 'allergic to the twentieth century', hence unable to live normally in our modern polluted environment. The condition cannot be accurately defined, as the name was invented by a journalist. These cases have attracted excessive attention from the media, who produce experts who pronounce that the problem is either anorexia nervosa, over-breathing, psychosomatic or hysteria. No doubt it is impossible to define the cause once a patient has got into such a state, but it is evident that these people are very ill, and that it is uncharitable to dismiss them as psychiatric cases. Excessive publicity for these bizarre cases, which seem to be exclusively female has probably increased the common medical opinion that allergy is part of the lunatic fringe of medicine.

How can a diagnosis of allergy to chemicals be made?

At present the only way of making such a diagnosis is by removing the patient into an environment with pollution-free food, air and water. If improvement ensues, deliberate exposure to suspect chemicals, preferably without the knowledge of the patient, should reproduce the symptoms. Unfortunaely no reliable test has been developed, although progress has been made in demonstrating specific IgE against chemicals and drugs. Examples are antibodies to TDI, used in making plastic foam, to muscle relaxants for surgery, and to ethylene oxide used to sterilize plastic tubing.

The only method of diagnosis may be to demonstrate a clear and repeatable cause/effect relationship. This can be done negatively by removing the patient from the suspect environment to show improvement, and then positively by re-exposure to show relapse on *at least* two occasions. Reliance on the subjective sensations of the patient may be unreliable.

Isolation in a pollution-free environment is only possible in two centres in England at present, but several units exist in the USA and one in Australia. Costs tend to be very high, and in the event of improvement it can be very difficult or impossible to arrange for a suitable environment for the patient on discharge.

Can water cause allergic problems?

It is sometimes suggested that patients suspected of food or environmental allergy should drink only bottled spring water, in case pollution of ordinary tap water is relevant to the case. This is a harmless suggestion, but it is probably not important, unless the need for it has been clearly established. Nevertheless, ordinary water is becoming more polluted, and it may help readers to discuss this matter in more detail.

Drinking water must be free from infection, so chlorination is usually essential. Very rare cases of allergy to chlorine have been reported with convincing evidence, and the author has often seen patients who cannot tolerate swimming in chlorinated swimming baths because of asthma, but can swim in sea or lake without problems. Whether this is true allergy or just irritation is difficult to establish. Heavily chlorinated water smells and tastes unpleasant, but boiling will drive it off. Fluoridation does not seem to have been associated with allergy, and in any case the greatest source of flourine is tea. Bromine is becoming popular instead of chlorine for swimming baths, but has caused skin reactions in some people, and may soon be replaced by ozone, which can be irritating in excess. Iodine may be present in water in tiny amounts, but is usually added to the cooking salt, because this element is essential for the thyroid gland to function properly. Nevertheless, sensitivity to iodine and bromine can occur, and was not uncommon 50 years ago when only bromides were available as sedatives.

Water may be derived from lakes, or may be recycled from a river. All sorts of chemicals may drain into these sources from the land and pollute the water with residues of chemical fertilizers, insecticides, detergents, traces of industrial wastes, and so on. Water from deep wells or springs will have been filtered through a great thickness of rock, and hence be relatively free from such contamination. During a water shortage nitrates from fertilizers may reach high concentrations. The haemoglobin in the red blood cells of babies who receive this water to drink in their feeds may be converted into an inactive form which cannot carry oxygen, and the baby may turn blue. This is not an allergic reaction, but a chemical change which indicates the extent of pollution which can occur from fertilizers, and is now well recognized.

Excessive amounts of nitrates may also be found in some vegetables, and nitrates, such as saltpetre, are used as preserving and pickling agents. It has now been found that compounds called nitrosamines may be formed which have been shown to cause stomach cancer. Many foods and drinks are now screened for the presence of these substances.

Bottled spring water has been used for drinking in continental Europe for many years, and is now becoming much more popular in Britain. There is a shortage of good data on possible reactions to tap water, but it must be remembered that storage tanks in the attic can be grossly contaminated (often by dead birds) so if a little of the hot supply gets into the drinking water, or if the kettle is filled from the hot tap to save time, almost anything is possible. A paediatric colleague had a case where the bath water seemed to be the cause of severe eczema, as shown by the fact that a rash on the skin was seen below the level of the bath water if the child was persuaded to sit still in the bath.

Many water mains are very old, and may be colonized by tiny aquatic animals which may have to be removed by the occasional use of insecticides such as pyrethrum and old lead pipes may still pose a hazard in soft water areas. Traces of copper, aluminium, and now plastic residues may also be present. Thus the purity of our drinking water cannot be taken for granted. Some people may react to pollutants, and to drink bottled spring water may be necessary for some individuals, but too little research has been carried out for positive recommendations to be made.

These matters have become more widely recognized by the public in the last five years with a tremendous increase of sales of bottled water.

21 The effects of food allergy and food intolerance on the alimentary tract

From the lips to anus the alimentary tract, or gut, is exposed to everything we eat or drink. Sensitization of a part of the gut may be quite local, or affect larger parts, and reactions can be swift or slow. We are what we have eaten, controlled by our likes, dislikes, appetite, greed, tolerance and intolerance, and so on.

The amounts of food and drink consumed in a year, or in a lifetime, are astonishing, so it is remarkable what the gut can cope with, usually without complaint. It may be helpful to pass down the gut from top to bottom, indicating what sort of problems may be associated with allergy or intolerance to foods. We can then proceed to consider the problems which can be caused by food after it is absorbed into the circulation.

Can foods cause problems in the mouth or lips?

The lips may be very sensitive, as in the young man who suffered dramatic swelling of the lips and tongue after he kissed his girlfriend who had been eating fish and chips. Even lipstick can cause a reaction in someone the wearer kisses, or the wearer. Reddening and cracking at the corners of the mouth can be caused by foods or lipstick and, rarely, by vitamin B deficiency.

The mouth is the first part of the alimentary canal to be contacted by food, where it is chewed, mixed with saliva, and prepared for swallowing down to be digested further in the stomach. Thus, there is much close contact with foods and drinks, some of which may be absorbed direct into the blood

from the area under the tongue, to cause symptoms in a sensitized part of the body. This is why Nalcrom (Intal capsules)
should be dissolved in warm water and swilled round the mouth
before swallowing, to block entry of a food from the lining of the
mouth.

It is not widely known or accepted that chronic painful mouth
ulcers, which afflict some patients for many years, can be caused
by foods. Convincing evidence can only be obtained by dietary
restriction and reintroduction, especially as the reaction to the
causative food is quite slow. Mouth ulcers can be seen by
anyone, including the victim, and are easily visible evidence of
the kind of problems that can be caused by food anywhere in the
gut where the ulcers cannot be seen without special instruments.

Toothpaste, dental fixatives, chewing gum, and so on, must
not be forgotten as possible causes of trouble. Everything that
passes the lips is suspect until proved otherwise.

Can allergy in the mouth be dangerous?

Swelling of tongue or throat, such as may occur in persons
intensely sensitive to foods, can obviously be dangerous and
require emergency treatment using adrenaline. It may help to
spray the mouth and tongue with 20 puffs of an adrenaline
aerosol (Medi-haler Epi) which can be carried constantly.

If the cause, such as nuts, fish, chocolate, and so on, can be
identified it can be avoided, but sometimes this is difficult or
impossible. Where this is the case, patients may have to carry a
syringe and adrenaline.

Can false teeth and fillings cause allergic problems?

Acrylic plastic dental plates can cause inflammation and swelling if they are not properly 'cured', because of the presence of
free plastic molecules. Alternative material such as stainless steel
or even gold may be necessary.

An amalgam of mercury with gold and silver is used for
fillings. Sometimes patients become sensitized to mercury, but
the dangers of poisoning from fillings have been exaggerated.

What abdominal symptoms suggest food allergy?

All manner of symptoms can be caused by food allergy and different parts of the body may be affected simultaneously. Nausea, vomiting, excessive burping and wind, pain, an 'irritable bowel', chronic indigestion, constipation, diarrhoea, colitis, itchy anus (proctitis), colic, suspect gall-bladder trouble and many other complaints can be caused by food. The difficulty is in associating food with a variety of symptoms which may have many other causes. Some patients may have had operations which revealed no cause for their symptoms, others have had many investigations and x-rays which reveal nothing. The diagnosis of food allergy depends mainly on awareness of the possibility, because there are no special symptoms to point to food as a cause of the illness.

Can a duodenal ulcer be caused by allergy or intolerance to foods?

The author has seen one case due to egg, and another due to milk. Both had been put on a special diet for ulcers which contained large amounts of milk and eggs. The milk allergic was referred because of worsening asthma since the ulcer was diagnosed, and avoidance cleared both duodenal ulcer and asthma. In the other case avoidance of egg cured the ulcer. Occasional cases of allergic reactions in the stomach have been reported, but this may be more common than is usually realized.

It seems more likely that the majority of duodenal ulcers are not so much due to allergy to food, but to the eating of refined flour from which all the protein and fibre has been removed. This is because protein and fibre in wholemeal products soak up and 'buffer' the acid in the stomach, but purified sugars or sweets have very little ability to do so.

There is impressive evidence in support of this concept derived from the sufferings of prisoners in the last war. For example, ulcers were very rare among German prisoners in Russian hands eating only very coarse cereals and vegetables. In fact, those with chronic ulcers actually got better, but relapsed when they returned to Germany, and began to eat refined flour products and sweets again. These observations have not attracted sufficient attention from the medical profession.

A middle-aged man recently referred for advice regarding his nasal allergy, also gave a long history of stomach ulcers with persisting severe pain. He had an unexpected positive skin test for fish, which he ate at least three times a week on medical advice. Avoidance of fish resulted in complete freedom from pain for the first time in many years, and the allergic reaction could repeatably be provoked by eating fish again. Professor Romanski has repeatedly observed allergic reactions to foods as they happen, through the gastroscope, and has photographed them.

Can food allergy or intolerance affect digestion?

The effects on digestion are mostly in the small intestine in cases of intolerance to milk proteins or to gluten from wheat and other cereals. The delicate brush-like projections which absorb the nutrients are partly destroyed and inflamed by the local reaction, so the patient is starving in the midst of plenty because of malabsorption of foods. Fats are not absorbed, causing vile-smelling stools which float in the water closet, and/or chronic diarrhoea. The production of enzymes, such as lactase which digests lactose (milk sugar), may be stopped as a secondary effect, producing severe watery diarrhoea. Thus, a chronic reaction in the gut wall can cause general havoc to nutrition, especially in children.

Does food cause the 'irritable bowel syndrome'?

'IBS' is one of the commonest conditions seen by specialists in alimentary diseases. The patient has diarrhoea or constipation pain and wind, with negative x-rays, and so on. The usual opinion is that it is a 'psychosomatic' illness, but perhaps cause and effect have become confused or reversed.

Recent careful research showed that specific foods could produce the symptoms even when the patients were unaware that they had had these foods. Also, the symptoms were associated with the release of mediator prostaglandins. The symptoms were brought on by specific food only, particularly cereals, milk, coffee, tea and citrus fruits. Hence, there was a clear-cut specific reaction which is characteristic of allergic reactions, and avoidance has meant complete freedom from symptoms in two-thirds of the patients involved in the research. In spite of these results, some critics still consider it is 'all in the mind', and hypnotism has recently been alleged to be very beneficial treatment.

What is coeliac disease and how is it caused?

After our food has been partly digested in the stomach, it passes into the small intestine, which produces enzymes to complete the digestion of the food, and also absorb nourishment into the bloodstream.

Gluten is a very important protein found in wheat, and all cereals except rice. If the delicate lining of the small intestine becomes intolerant to gluten this lining is partly destroyed by the reaction and as a result the food can no longer be properly digested. This is called coeliac disease (also called gluten entero-pathy), which is characterized by fatty, stinking diarrhoea, malnourishment, failure to thrive, stunting of growth, and many other problems which occasionally include a skin disease called dermatitis herpetiformis. Coeliac disease can occur at any age, sometimes when weaning on to cereals, is seriously debilitating, and causes chronic ill-health for years unless positively diag-nosed by obtaining a tiny sample (biopsy) of the lining of the intestine for microscopical examination. Strict avoidance of all cereals containing gluten will bring about gradual and complete cure, but even a tiny amount of food containing gluten will cause a relapse which can be confirmed by biopsy. Gluten-free diets are so well established now that it is possible to obtain gluten-free foods in any large town and remain in good health. Constant vigilance is essential – for example, the communion wafers dis-tributed at Roman Catholic masses caused problems until a recent dispensation from the Pope permitted gluten-free wafers to be used.

Coeliac disease is sufficiently common for the sufferers to have formed the Coeliac Society, which gives their members up-to-date lists of gluten-free manufactured food, recipes and advice.

Meetings may give much-needed moral support and guidance, and joining a support group can be very helpful. Milk allergy, particularly in children, may also be present, so that complete relief will not be obtained unless milk products are also avoided. This possibility should be considered if the result of a gluten-free diet is disappointing.

It is important for the sufferer from this disease to realize that the diet is for life, and that even minor transgressions will eventually cause trouble. This is very difficult for children, especially because there is no reaction the same day, and it may be several weeks before symptoms begin to return. This is a disease which is fully accepted as being caused by gluten but is not usually classified as allergic.

Does food allergy cause Crohn's disease?

This very serious disease affects the small intestine, causing thickening of the wall and narrowing of the passage. The result is serious abdominal symptoms which often result in a surgical operation, when the diagnosis is confirmed. Unfortunately cutting out the affected part does not always result in cure as the disease can spread and occur again. There is some similarity to ulcerative colitis in the large bowel. Crohn's disease is becoming much more common, increasing fivefold in Nottingham and threefold in the whole UK and in Sweden from 1958 to 1971. The onset may be insidious and the diagnosis delayed for years, perhaps because it is not realized that any part of the alimentary tract may be affected, from the mouth to the anus.

For at least 50 years foods have been reported by allergists in America as causing this serious disease, but adequate proof has never been produced. At the present time the role of foods in this disease is being intensively investigated at British centres and these old reports are often being confirmed, giving new hope to sufferers.

One of the author's small patients provides an interesting example. She was referred with asthma and eczema aged 5. Egg was found to be the major cause and avoidance was very effective. Six years later she began to take egg again, apparently without any effect, but a year later she had acute abdominal pain and at operation was found to have Crohn's disease. When seen afterwards she was having occasional attacks of pain and diarrhoea, which could be reliably reproduced by eating egg. It appeared that the sensitized part of the body had changed from the bronchus to the gut.

Can ulcerative or mucous colitis be caused by allergy or intolerance to food?

Ulcerative colitis is a serious and very distressing disease of the large bowel, or colon, causing severe chronic diarrhoea with passage of blood and mucus. Mucous (or spastic) colitis is not so severe and there is seldom blood in the motions, but the conditions are closely related.

It is now over 50 years since it was first shown that food, especially milk, could cause colitis. According to American experts over half the victims can be completely relieved by elimination diets, but this approach has been rejected by most physicians. In England the exclusion of milk products, but not butter or beef, has been tried, with a good result in only one case in five. However, it is essential to exclude butter and beef from a proper milk-free diet, and many other foods can also cause colitis. Dietary treatment, if it has been heard of at all, is generally arbitrarily dismissed. In the last few years, however, there has been some revival of interest in diet treatment in certain centres, with encouraging results.

Removal of the whole colon is the popular treatment in severe cases today. This is because if the organ where the reaction is taking place is removed, a 'cure' is effected, but the patient will be left with the consequences of the operation. Major surgery can be life-saving, but it is common sense to try a special diet before taking such an irrevocable step, and at an *early* stage in the illness. Perhaps if all cases were put on strict dietary treatment as soon as the diagnosis was made the true importance of food in causation would be shown. Placing a very ill patient on a special diet is difficult to do, so an elimination diet should be the first step, not the last. Steroids by mouth and by enema and sulpha drugs are effective treatment, but are purely suppressive.

A 45 year old man had severe ulcerative colitis to the extent that removal of the colon was being considered. By chance his son heard that milk could cause colitis, and with avoidance there was considerable improvement. When he came for consultation it was found that he was still eating beef, and on avoiding beef completely he became completely symptom-free. One small steak would cause a week's illness, and with avoidance he has remained well, with his colon intact but his surgeon did not seem convinced or interested. It is not usually realized that even a few drops of milk may be enough to upset some of these cases, so dietary control has to be strict. Many other foods can be involved so the initial diet should be free from fruit, cereals, milk and beef, as discussed elsewhere.

Can constipation or diarrhoea be caused by milk?

Milk can cause both – a curious paradox – but constipation is rare. Three cases have been seen by the author, one in an infant who also had coeliac disease, and two children of 10 and 13, who both emptied their bowels only once in 2 or 3 weeks. The product in each case was described as being the diameter and length of a milk bottle which had to be broken up to prevent blocking the drains! The adolescent girl also had behaviour problems and asthma, which had been confidently attributed by a paediatrician to parental discord and divorce. Every problem vanished with avoidance of milk.

Chronic diarrhoea is more common, but seldom recognized. All manner of investigations are negative, but no diagnosis is made unless there is awareness of the possibility.

A woman with recurrent abdominal pain and diarrhoea for 5 years was fully investigated at great expense by a university medical department but no evidence of serious disease was found. She was classed as 'psychosomatic' and told she would have to learn to live with it, but refused to do so. Her doctor agreed and referred her for food allergy investigation.

Several members of the family could not tolerate milk, and a careful history showed that her pain and diarrhoea occurred only on Saturdays. Further questioning revealed that when she left the office at noon on Saturdays it was her weekly treat to buy a cream bun and eat it as she walked home. Shortly after she reached there she would have a colicky pain followed by explosive diarrhoea. She also had frequent vague abdominal problems but since avoiding milk products she has been in better health than she can ever remember.

Can food allergy cause problems with the anus?

All the food residues must pass out of the anus, which is, therefore, exposed to everything we eat. An itchy anus, or genitals, is a most embarrassing complaint. Apart from local irritations, it can be caused by allergy to foods, preservatives, drugs or dyes, so it could be well worth finding out what to avoid.

There may be local eczema, partly caused by scratching, and seasonal pollen allergy is a rare cause.

22 The effects of food allergy and intolerance on other parts of the body

Readers should now refer once more to Figure 3.1 which illustrates the holistic approach to allergic disease, because this concept is particularly relevant to this chapter.

Some foods can be inhaled as dusts, such as flour, but do not necessarily cause rhinitis or asthma, passing instead, in the bloodstream, to a distant sensitized organ. More usually, food proteins are absorbed from the gut without causing any digestive problem, and pass in the body fluids to reach the sensitized cells of any organ of the body. The absence of problems referable to the gut makes diagnosis very difficult. Improvement in emotional problems often comes as an unexpected bonus from a trial of an elimination diet given for an apparently unrelated problem.

These comments apply not only to foods, but also to drinks, additives, dyes, drugs – anything that passes the lips.

Can foods act as inhalants?

Any food which becomes airborne, either as a smell or as a fine powder such as flour, can cause asthma, hay fever, eczema or even emotional disturbance. For example, a lady of 32 had emotional instability and panic attacks within a few minutes of exposure to flour dust, while blindfolded, but not to rice flour. Eating wheat caused diarrhoea and violent behaviour. She once smashed up a coffee table after a small amount of wheat was eaten by mistake. As a secretary in a flour mill, she was always unwell both physically and emotionally, but recovered completely when she got a job in an office a few miles away. She was then sent to a branch office next door to the flour mill. The extractor fans blew flour into this office, and she again became emotionally unstable, only to recover on a wheat avoidance diet and in another job away from any trace of flour dust. Her wheat sensitivity was confined to her gut and her brain, but she got no asthma at all. Other patients, especially bakers, react to the inhalation of flour dust with asthma.

What is masked food allergy or addictive allergy?

Physicians with an interest in food allergy have been aware for a long time that some food allergic patients have a craving for the very food which is the cause of their problems. It appears that if the food is taken frequently enough to satisfy the craving, symptoms will be prevented from occurring. These patients feel much better soon after having another dose of the food to which they are addicted, but a few hours later the multiple symptoms, both mental and physical, will recur and can only be assuaged by another dose of the food. These sufferers may also have symptoms in the night, relieved by a snack, or they may feel more tired in the morning, with depression and sometimes confusion, than they felt at bedtime. These food-addictive allergics may become very fat. This type of patient often feels much worse during the first few days on a strict diet or a fast, but if they persevere the symptoms will subside and disappear. If a test dose of the suspect food is given just after this first period on a strict diet the reaction to it is often much more severe than previously, so the first test dose should not be too large.

Although the author has no personal experience, it seems probable that some alcoholics or even drug addicts may also fall into this category.

Is allergy to food or chemicals recognized as a cause of mental disturbance?

No! Yet if only one psychiatric patient in a hundred could be cured by dietary manipulation the benefits in terms of human misery, and the saving in National Health Service money, would be incalculable. Instead psychiatric treatment today relies to a large extent on drugs which are suppressive rather than curative, which many patients dislike taking for the rest of their days.

I have sometimes received letters from patients or their close relatives seeking guidance and help in finding out if the mental illness of one of the family could be caused by food. Usually nothing can be done without the co-operation of a psychiatrist, because after introducing a restricted diet it is necessary to withdraw the drugs to see what happens. In a severe relapse injury to self or to others could occur, so that specialized supervision is essential at this crucial time. Perhaps a few psychiatrists will eventually accept that foods can cause emotional illness, and actively search for it amongst their patients.

A hundred years ago a mystery disease, called pellagra, used to be found amongst the very poor in the deep south of the USA. Pellagra was characterized by diarrhoea and dermatitis, and especially by insanity. This disease, which filled the asylums and often caused death, was found to be caused by a deficiency of nicotinic acid in the diet, and to be completely curable by giving this B group vitamin before it was too late. This story proves that mental disorder can be caused by vitamin deficiency, but the role of allergy can be more complex.

The publication of *Not All in the Mind* and *Chemical Victims* by Dr Richard Mackarness, a psychiatrist, suggested that foods, drugs, and additives and preservatives can cause all sorts of problems in psychiatry.

One example out of many is of interest. A man of 42 had been unemployable for years because he would hardly ever get out of bed. Psychiatrists and drugs had been of no avail, and he requested an allergy investigation as he had heard of this possibility. When interviewed he certainly seemed mentally disturbed, and explained that he stayed in bed because he had such intense feelings of suppressed violence that he was afraid to get up in case he did someone serious injury. A basic diet produced a dramatic reversion to normal feelings and behaviour within a few days, and it was then shown that his mental state was provoked by a certain make of margarine, which contained large quantities of red and yellow dyes. He avoided foods containing them, remained well, and started work again.

Reluctance to experiment with dietary restrictions by psychiatrists seems inexplicable. What do they have to lose?

Where is the risk? What is the objection? Why not try to find a cause, if that is possible, and substitute avoidance for drugs.

Is there a behaviour pattern which suggests a food allergy affecting the brain?

I have repeatedly observed that a child patient who cannot sit still, or stop talking, grimacing and showing off, and who reacts excessively to examination or to skin testing, often has a hidden allergy to foods or dyes. These children may have clinical histories which suggest straightforward inhalant allergy, but this behaviour pattern, especially if accompanied by heavy dark shadows under the eyes, should suggest a food allergy as well.

On enquiry it will often be revealed that their unfortunate parents have been driven to the brink of child battering by their behaviour. The children cannot sit still, need little sleep, are totally undisciplined, and tend to hurt themselves deliberately. They may also have a history of screaming, vomiting, colic, diarrhoea or extreme constipation, and sometimes infantile eczema, which is suggestive of milk allergy. A child may be sent to a special school, but this can achieve little if the underlying cause has been neither recognized nor resolved. In my experience milk is the most common cause of this sort of behaviour pattern.

Can hyperactivity in children be caused by allergy to foods and dyes?

When we turn to possible effects of allergens on the emotions, as opposed to serious mental disorders, the situation is much better defined, but still not generally accepted. In 1975 Dr Ben Feingold first demonstrated that hyperactivity and misbehaviour in children could be controlled by a diet which excluded all synthetic dyes, flavours and preservatives. His researches attracted great public interest and, following the publication of his cookbook for hyperactive children, became a matter of public debate and medical controversy. Medical opinion in this country has been cool and lacking in enthusiasm, in spite of very good evidence that some children can react adversely to food dyes.

The result has been the formation of support groups composed of parents who have these exasperating problems with their offspring. My personal experience is that although avoidance of dyes can be helpful in some children, foods, especially milk, can be much more important. Even if the problems of only a few children with behaviour problems are caused by avoidable factors in the diet, there can be no excuse for reluctance to try out a restricted diet for a few weeks. What is there to lose by co-operating with concerned parents in the introduction of a trial diet for a limited period? If misbehaviour can be reproduced repeatedly by feeding the causative substance, perhaps confirmed later by double-blind methods, the connection must be accepted.

What sort of reactions can be caused by azo dyes in foods and medicines?

The answer to this question will be illustrative of the holistic nature of allergic reactions, and draws on both personal experience and that of colleagues.

Tartrazine (E102) added to cider to intensify the colour was noted to produce asthma or rhinitis both in consumers and employees. Symptoms did not occur when another cider was consumed which did not contain this dye. Rhinitis would also be produced when a yellow tablet was given for rheumatism, but not when the dye was washed off before taking it. One woman felt depressed when she started taking the contraceptive pill, so she was given vitamin tablets, which gave her a rash. Neither depression nor rash occurred when she was given white tablets instead of coloured, or they were washed before swallowing.

Antibiotics for children or infants are often dispensed as coloured and flavoured syrups or suspensions. Those who develop a rash are usually presumed to be sensitive to the antibiotic (often penicillin), while the undeclared additives are seldom blamed or considered at all.

It is common for children (and some adults) to complain of frequent sore throats, with enlarged glands in the neck and sometimes a temperature. Many are due to infections, but in some cases antibiotic syrups or suspensions do not help, or actually make things worse. The problem recurs frequently, yet throat swabs and other investigations are usually negative. Sucking coloured throat pastilles may even aggravate the sore throat. Avoidance of suspected dyes brings relief, and then provocation tests with one dye after another will repeatably reproduce the sore throat, enlarged glands, fever and an increase in blood eosinophils. Coloured toothpaste may also aggravate this problem, which is usually caused by red dyes.

Benzoates added to syrups as a preservative may cause any sort of allergic problem. As dyes are also present as a rule it may be difficult to sort out which is responsible. Clear syrups also contain benzoates.

Coloured milk shakes may cause symptoms which are blamed on the milk, but stopping milk does not help because the same food colours may also be put in soya milks to persuade the child to take them.

Perhaps the most subtle example of dye allergy began when dyes were avoided by some children who had recurrent fluid in their ears. Not only did their ear problems disappear, but some of them also stopped wetting the bed. This recurred when they had a provocation test or accidental exposure to dyes, along with irritation in the genital area in girls. One little boy whose rhinitis and headaches ceased when dyes were avoided was found to have a return of symptoms when given a certain dye. Also, every time he had a test with the dye he also complained of a sore penis.

Other cases who had bladder irritation and pain on passing water were observed to have mild inflammation of the inside of the bladder but no evidence of infection. Some of these patients improved on avoiding dyes, and commented that pink toilet paper irritated them. Hence, this observation can be a clue to the presence of dye allergy which may have many effects.

Finally, both dyes and preservatives may cause misbehaviour and delinquency. An adolescent at a boarding school began to misbehave, lose his place in the class, and became a persistent thief. This was traced to dyes in fizzy drinks, and so on, but improvement was not complete. A diet diary revealed that he frequently had corned beef, which contains a lot of nitrites. With avoidance of nitrites as well as dyes his behaviour became normal and he soon regained his place at the top of his class.

How many problems are caused by these unnecessary and noxious chemicals? How many careers are permanently blighted – even turning to criminality – by junk food? How many readers will identify similar problems in their own families? Obviously the psychiatric or custodial approach usually adopted will never help, and the holistic approach by an allergist must be tried out more often in an attempt to answer these questions.

Can child or adult violence be attributed to foods?

Until the true role of foods and chemicals in causing emotional instability has been established it is impossible to assess the importance of this avoidable cause of discord. Some investigators in the USA have put forward evidence that foods or chemicals can cause delinquency or even criminal behaviour, but their results are generally disbelieved – yet if even a few people with violent-behaviour problems could be found to be curable by diet control, it would be well worthwhile. Society has no solution to violence and mindless vandalism yet there is little interest in this possible answer to some of these problems. Altering the diet in a detention centre would be worth trying.

Can there be a connection between a battered child and reactions to food or chemicals?

It is possible for a child's abnormal behaviour, caused by food or chemicals, to drive a parent beyond endurance, resulting in violence towards the child. An avoidance diet for the child has saved several marriages in the author's practice, by transforming a little demon into a normal happy child.

Injuries can be self-inflicted in these children, so battering cannot be assumed to have taken place. Clumsiness, lack of co-ordination, head banging and uncontrollable tantrums can all cause accidental injury. Obviously one should be wary of providing an excuse for battering, but it should be possible to elicit a history to support this explanation. If adjustment of diet can bring an improvement in behaviour, and a dietary indiscretion cause a relapse, food may be the cause. Unfortunately scepticism and disbelief rather than interest is the usual reaction amongst other health professionals to this proposal.

A remarkable case history is worth relating here. John was a very large baby, so the midwife said he was 'too big to breast-feed'! Cow's milk formulae caused vomiting, but he tolerated evaporated milk. He seldom slept and screamed constantly, so the family doctor, thinking this was the result of hunger, intro-duced cereals to the diet on the sixth day! The hyperactivity and screaming subsided, but when he was a year old incessant screaming and head banging began again with uncontrollable temper tantrums, coughing and sniffling. By age 2 the tantrums lasted for hours at any time of day or night, and he was observed to be very clumsy and uncoordinated. He began to wander off and get lost, became destructive, and would inflict pain on him-self by punching his arms and legs, producing large bruises. Family life became a nightmare, and his mother felt that he had become 'a manipulative destructive monster'. The mother could take no more, and so she placed him with a registered child-minder and went back to teaching as headmistress of a local school. A cut head required attention at the local hospital, where he was found to be covered in bruises. The parents were sent for and accused of battering him, and it was with difficulty that they convinced the paediatrician that the injuries were self-inflicted.

At nursery and infant school he was unsocial, aggressive and had frequent episodes of respiratory infection, finally diagnosed as asthma when he was aged 7. His behaviour and asthma deteriorated, with rudeness, aggressiveness and often violence. He would run or jump on the spot and make silly noises for long periods, and would repeatedly throw himself down the stairs to hurt himself deliberately. His behaviour was destructive and vindictive, and he continued to pinch and even cut himself, his clothes and the furniture. He kicked holes in his bedroom wall.

The family then got a new doctor who referred him to a child psychiatrist. He blamed the boy's behaviour on parental mis-management, and their inability to communicate, and it was suggested that he was being provoked by his sister. His asthma got worse, finally causing an admission to hospital which was followed by referral for allergy investigation.

It was found that the cats were the cause of the asthma, and they were removed, but also his behaviour became normal within a week of removing milk products from his diet. Deliber-ate or accidental ingestion of milk or milk products resulted in dramatic relapses of behaviour. His teachers began to recognize when he had been cheating by taking milk chocolate or ice-cream because of his behaviour. His clumsiness also disappeared and his academic progress was excellent. The psychiatrist, who had been fully informed of these events, saw him once more and then discharged him. The paediatrician, on hearing he had been sent to an allergist, refused to see him again. The diagnosis of allergy as the cause of his behaviour problems was also supported by the family history. The mother knew that milk caused her eczema, and her daughter was sick if she took dairy products, but neither had behaviour problems. The maternal grandfather had had behaviour patterns very similar to those of his grandson, but he had been diagnosed as a paranoid schizophrenic and died in an asylum. Was milk the cause of his problems too?

This boy is representative of a growing collection of similar cases, which suggest that allergy should be seriously considered as a possible cause of delinquent or disruptive behaviour.

Can dyslexia be associated with food allergy?

Rapid improvement in reading abilities has been seen by the author in three cases after withdrawal of milk products. There is no reason why this disability should not be caused by food allergy. In the USA some investigators have reported dramatic improvements in learning ability amongst 'mentally retarded' children on controlled diets.

Can milk intolerance and coeliac disease run in families?

The story of a milk-allergic mother, a father with probable coeliac disease, and two very allergic sons is of interest.

The son of an allergic mother, who reacted to cow's milk, was first seen aged 2 with rhinitis, wheezing, eczema and aggressiveness, which had begun when breast-feeding ceased at 8 months. Carrots always caused acute diarrhoea and vomiting. He thrived on soya milk, but wheezed and became aggressive if he had milk or milk chocolate, which also provoked headaches.

On her own initiative his mother removed milk from the diet of his elder brother aged 5, and this child's diarrhoea of 3 months duration ceased, but after some months he could tolerate milk again. Both boys had been born in the Pacific Islands of the New Hebrides, and the elder had always had evaporated milk, which is heat treated, until returning to Britain. Both boys continued without milk, but the occasional licking of a finger dipped in cream, or inadvertent butter on sandwiches, would cause asthma in the younger boy. He also ate carrots by mistake and had projectile vomiting and diarrhoea for a week, and began to react to dogs and horses. Milk always caused asthma and tantrums, and by age 7 he had begun to have fairly frequent loose stools. A disguised milk drink produced acute diarrhoea repeatedly, but rigid exclusion was ineffective, and he also began to have chronic abdominal pains, as did his elder brother.

By the time he was 8 he had occasional severe asthma and both he and his brother continued to have frequent and very malodorous stools. The father, in Africa at that time, had similar stools and the mother said that she had naively concluded that males always produced very smelly motions. At this point both boys were put on a gluten-free diet, with the result that all their symptoms disappeared in a few days, they both grew over an inch in a month, and put on weight rapidly. (Being in Africa, the father has been unable to arrange a gluten-free diet as yet.) The average peak flow rate in the asthmatic boy also increased from 250 to 350 litres/minute in a month.

To make this case even more unusual, this child had been having reading difficulties for 3 years. Recently he was diagnosed as having dyslexia, but is improving rapidly on his present milk-free, gluten-free diet.

Can seasonal allergens cause emotional problems?

In recent years I have encountered some remarkable cases of 'midsummer madness'. The following is a typical case history.

Jonathan was a 12 year old who for 5 years from April to September had become consistently aggressive, physically attacking anyone who crossed him, doing badly in class work, refusing to sit still, and unable to concentrate. In contrast his behaviour was quite normal in the winter, he was fairly intelligent, could concentrate, and made such rapid progress that he usually caught up with his classmates in the winter. The long summer season and positive skin tests clearly indicated that seasonal mould-spore allergens might be responsible, a possibility supported by his mother's statement that he became much more aggressive after playing in woods, where there are many mould spores.

The boy was exposed to these allergens in the winter by a nasal challenge test with mould extracts. It was found repeatedly that temper tantrums would be produced in the winter by extracts of some of the moulds which were prevalent in summer, but not by control tests. Thus, there was good evidence that inhaled allergens, which did not produce any symptoms in the respiratory system, were passing to the brain to produce emotional disturbance. Immunization against these moulds might have been the best treatment, but another important allergy was suggested by a history of violent vomiting of his cow's milk formula as an infant, and a positive skin test for milk, suggesting a background allergy to milk. Milk products were rigidly excluded from his diet the following summer, when his behaviour problem did not appear unless he had a deliberate or an accidental provocation with milk or milk chocolate. It would appear that he had a masked allergy to milk which was constantly present, but this was insufficient to trigger off any symptoms on its own. In the summer the extra load of the summer allergens tipped him over into his characteristic reaction, but the summer allergens on their own were insufficient to trigger him off as long as he had no milk.

The school teacher who was having emotional symptoms from moulds has already been described.

What part does food allergy play in the causation of migraine?

Obviously very severe headaches should be fully investigated to exclude serious causes before considering food allergy. Some investigators are convinced that food allergy is a common cause of migraine and that most patients are sensitive to more than one food, while others contend that food is a rare cause of migraine. The truth probably lies somewhere between the two.

RAST testing for the detection of specific IgE to foods has been found helpful by some investigators, but not by others. However, this test will only detect antibodies associated with the immediate type of allergy and not with the delayed types. Other tests, such as the cytotoxic test, have not been validated scientifically or clinically and it is doubtful whether they are worth the money.

When migraine attacks are extremely frequent, the use of very restrictive basic diets for a short time is certainly worth trying, but if an attack occurs only once every 3 months, or more, it is obviously nonsense to stay on an inadequate diet for such a long time. Furthermore, if someone was misguided enough to stay on a very restricted diet for 3 months and no attack occurred, it would be impossible to find out whether the attack had not occurred because of the diet or whether it was postponed for any other reason.

The dietary manoeuvres may become exceedingly complicated and demand a high degree of co-operation from the patient. Challenge tests must show that certain foods will provoke an attack repeatedly before it is possible to say that the cause has been clearly identified. How often food is the answer to migraine will never be known until the dietary approach is used more widely. Recent trials in children have produced very encouraging results, proved by double-blind techniques, so there is no good reason for continued scepticism.

The clearest example of food-induced migraine I have encountered was an Irish lady who complained that migraine occurred every Saturday without fail. I asked if she was a Catholic, and then if she ate fish every Friday. By abstaining from fish she never had another attack except when she took fish to prove that it was the cause, and when she was too polite to refuse it! In her case the delay period was nearly 24 hours.

Another case was a man who had had daily migraine for 5 years, which cleared on a basic diet. He then found that a piece of cheese the size of a pea would put him in bed for a week with migraine. Another lady established that tomato and cheese had been the cause of her migraine of 20 years duration but obvious cases like this one are rare.

Which foods often cause migraine?

Over-use of monosodium glutamate as a flavouring agent in Chinese restaurants can produce a headache and a sensation of tightness and pressure on the face and chest. Repeated association of suspected cause and symptoms gives the diagnosis. Sometimes headaches are caused by eating hotdogs and similar foods, due to nitrites used as preservative which relax the blood vessels and bring on a severe headache. Another cause can be cold icecream in the mouth triggering off pain in the head, and relaxation of the blood vessels as a result of too much alcohol. Hangover headaches are probably due to chemical mediators produced when the alcohol is broken down in the body.

Certain foods can also trigger off an attack, because they contain certain chemicals, such as tyramine, which is found in cheese, red wine, Marmite, Oxo, Bovril and similar yeast extracts. Similar chemicals are present in chocolate, broad beans, tomatoes, pineapples and bananas. Thus, some attacks can be explained by an excess of these chemicals in certain foods and is not an allergy.

Are food additives necessary?

Many chemicals are added to foods to assist manufacture and to improve keeping qualities, palatability and eye appeal. The main categories of additives are emulsifiers, thickeners, colours, preservatives, spices, enzymes, smoking and curing agents and various inhibitors of bacterial and fungal growth. Food may also be contaminated by insecticides, fertilizers and fungicides.

The colour of foods makes them more attractive and appetizing to the consumer, and is the only valid reason for food dyes being used at all.

How can people find out which food dyes and additives are in their food?

Food dyes and additives are harmless, or apparently harmless, to the majority, but undoubtedly cause allergic reactions in some people. The true incidence of allergic reactions of all types to these substances is unknown, because the effects can be so varied that they are probably seldom recognized for what they are. There is no reliable blood test which could be used to establish how large a minority are sensitive to these chemicals. This subject has recently received belated official recognition by the compilation and issue of a free booklet entitled *Look at the Label*. This includes the list of code numbers which are used in the EEC to denote dyes and additives. It is obtainable from: Food Sense, London SE99 7TT.

When buying food look at the label, where you will probably see a list of numbers, all beginning with 'E', which are the EEC codes for chemical additives. The length of the chemical names explain why a code is used.

Many people will find the list of dyes and additives in *Look at the Label* daunting and confusing, perhaps even frightening, as it is a shock to find what curious chemicals we are eating unawares. The answer to the next question is an attempt to classify and simplify this information. The simplest plan is to avoid food with the suspect numbers on the labels, and not worry about the long names.

Antioxidants such as butylated hydroxyanisole (E320) are widely used to stop fats from going rancid. A list of foods in which they can be found would be very long indeed, including most of the supermarket beverages, potato flakes, breakfast cereals, dry yeast, lard, ice-cream, and so on. These chemicals have been reported in the USA to cause angio-oedema symptoms, with mild anaphylactic shock, a condition in which the cause is often difficult or impossible to find. Again, as there are no tests, it is only by demonstrating a cause/effect relationship that cases can be identified. Hence, we have no idea how frequently illness is caused by these chemicals.

The beautiful fruit from all over the world in the shops today would not be so cheap, plentiful or attractive to look at were it not for many insecticides. Most of us do not react to these chemicals, and to identify those whose physical problems may be caused by reactions to insecticides is very difficult. However, a few cases have been pinpointed by finding that they can tolerate only unsprayed worm-eaten inferior fruit from decaying orchards.

Thus, thousands of chemicals may be added to food, so that to identify the one which is causing symptoms is a daunting task. In fact, the only way to establish whether any of these chemicals is causing problems is to avoid *all of them* as far as possible and see whether improvement takes place. More information can be obtained from *E for Additives* (M. E. Hanssen, 1984).

What common preservatives in food, drink and drugs can cause allergic reactions?

Sulphur dioxide, and various sulphites and metabisulphites, and sodium benzoate, are commonly used as a sterilizing and preserving agent in foods, fruit drinks and other beverages ('Camden tablets'). Sulphites may be used in solutions of drugs as a stabilizer, and as an antioxidant spray to keep salads and potatoes and fruit looking fresh, especially in salad bars. Metabisulphites are often found in wine and beer, especially home made.

Serious reactions, ranging from anaphylaxis to severe urticaria and asthma are being reported more and more frequently from metabisulphites. Asthma has been found to result from the sulphur dioxide (and sometimes from the tartrazine) in soft drinks.

Sodium benzoate is widely used in foods as a preservative, and people sensitive to aspirin may also react to sodium benzoate or benzoic acid.

Patients on slimming or exclusion diets may eat more salads and fruit, hence exposing themselves to the hidden menace of the sulphites. If they have some alcohol, more sulphite will be taken, producing urticaria, angio-oedema, asthma or even anaphylaxis on rare occasions.

Astonishingly, several bronchodilator solutions in the USA contain sulphites, and severe life-threatening situations have been caused in this way. Dangerous reactions to injected drugs may be caused by sulphites in the solution as a preservative, rather than the drug, but they are not declared on the label. It has been estimated that there may be half a million people in USA who are sensitive to these preservatives – but many will not be diagnosed unless the physician is aware of this possibility.

How important is monosodium glutamate (MSG) in causing symptoms?

It is well known that this additive is used extensively in Chinese cookery, and that it upsets some people. In fact MSG is now used very widely in other products as well, and can cause a variety of problems.

MSG is a flavour-enhancer made from wheat gluten. It is to be found in soya sauce, spices, processed foods, and in stock cubes for soups. If there is an excessive amount in a Chinese meal some people react shortly after with sweating, fainting, flushing, headache, numbness in the back of the neck, and pains in the chest which may suggest a heart attack.

These effects are most unpleasant but not dangerous. Recently, however, MSG has been reported as being an occasional cause of very severe asthma, proved by a controlled challenge test after recovery. These attacks occurred as long as 12 hours after the meals, so that the connection between the meal and the asthma attack may well not be realized by patients or doctors who are unaware that this is possible. The reason for this effect of MSG is completely unknown.

MSG has been reported as causing eczema to flare up in some patients, and can cause angio-oedema or severe urticaria in others. How much trouble it actually causes is difficult to assess.

MSG's code number is E621 (also 622 and 623), and though not used in infant foods, it is common in snacks which children often eat – so look at the label. MSG may be found in bacon, crisps, hamburgers, tinned pasta, salami, savoury snacks, tinned and packet soups, and so on.

Can dyes and fillers in medicines cause allergic reactions?

Medicines are made up in solutions, capsules, tablets, and so on. They contain not only the drug which has been prescribed but also dyes, and often bulk fillers such as corn starch or lactose, to make up the size of the tablet. Gelatine capsules contain colour, tablets have coloured coatings, and syrups and solutions contain preservatives and colours. Syrups and suspensions for children frequently contain dyes to make them look attractive.

All these additives, none of which is essential for the effectiveness of the drug, can cause allergic symptoms in susceptible patients. For example, when a group of patients who had had chronic urticaria for a long time were re-investigated it was found that the skin eruption was actually being *caused* by the yellow dye in the anti-histamine tablets, and the original cause was no longer present. When the tablets were stopped so did the itchy rash which the tablets were supposed to be treating.

Eye drops, contact-lens solutions and nasal drops require preservatives and anti-bacterial substances which can irritate and sometimes cause an allergic reaction. Preparations ready to be given into a vein may contain undeclared preservatives which can cause a serious reaction.

Particularly disturbing, especially to doctors interested in allergy, is the fact that patients can now avoid food containing E102 (tartrazine) or other dyes, but can be innocently prescribed drugs containing it by their doctor. The drug-makers are aware of these facts, but have paid scant attention to them. Only a few drug companies are introducing dye-free drugs.

Unfortunately there is no EEC law to compel the drug manufacturers to disclose *all* the ingredients of these preparations, and to put the code on the label in case one of these hidden ingredients makes a patient *worse*.

The formulations of drugs are not disclosed to the public even if a request for specific information is made, but will be disclosed in confidence to a qualified medical practitioner. Generally, though, both doctor and chemist are completely ignorant of the extra ingredients being consumed by the patients. This applies not only to prescription drugs, but to all the usual over-the-counter remedies, and the myriad of pills and potions in health-food shops, as well as sweets, lozenges, toothpaste, and so on.

Adverse reactions to fillers such as starch and lactose are fairly rare, but colouring of drugs is another matter. Different colours help to distinguish one product from another; hence there is less chance of taking the wrong pill, and so on, but this is only one aspect of the problem. Although colouring and other additives are excluded from infant foods, coloured syrups containing antibiotics and other medicines are very commonly prescribed. Some curious reactions have been seen. For example, one infant got tantrums every time he was given penicillin with red colouring. His father persuaded the chemist to exchange it for the same product without colour, and there was no such effect.

Another child became so lethargic and stupid that a full investigation was required. Eventually the cause was found to be a green aminophylline syrup. It was recently reported that one child in twenty receiving theophylline (aminophylline) as a bronchodilator had behaviour or learning problems. When the drug was stopped the children were less restless and distractable, slept better and were more manageable, and IQ scores improved, as did memory, concentration, and flexibility of thinking. This study was carried out double-blind, and is important because this drug is so commonly used.

Will the prescription of drugs according to their chemical (generic) names cause extra problems in connection with allergy to drugs or additives?

The active drug should be the same, and the patient is either allergic to that drug or not. Colours, other additives, and fillers will vary from maker to maker, are quite unknown to the prescribing doctor, and will inevitably cause problems with the allergic minority. Obviously, the only solution is for *all* the ingredients to be declared.

Can sugars cause food allergy?

Sugar is made from sugar cane, beet and 'corn' (maize). Digestive and gut symptoms from sugars can be caused by absence of the enzymes necessary for the digestion of sugars, but this is not allergy. American investigators have reported specific allergy to each type of sugar, presumably to impurities left from the refining process, but the author has only seen sugar allergy once or twice. Obviously, traces of the plants from which the sugar is made could cause symptoms in sensitized people.

Honey is promoted as a health food, but contains many pollen residues. The origin of the honey can be ascertained from identification of the pollen grains contained in it. Patients allergic to the plants from which the bees gathered the honey can get severe symptoms.

Some American allergists consider that sugars derived from maize ('corn') cause many problems. These sugars are found in the syrup of canned fruits, sweets and soft drinks, and when people are sensitive to maize products these sugars can set them off. Other maize products are corn starch, corn oil, corn flakes and other breakfast cereals, corn whisky, and so on. Those who react to wheat and other cereals may also react to corn products, but in the author's experience corn is not a very common cause of allergic problems in this country, and some studies in the USA have also failed to confirm that corn causes allergic problems.

Can liquid medicines rot sick children's teeth?

Chronically sick children who frequently take liquid medicines, nearly always sweetened with sucrose, have been shown to suffer nearly three times as much dental decay as children taking tablets. Doctors should, therefore, prescribe tablets rather than liquid medicines. If a sucrose or glucose syrup is used the concentration should be stated on the bottle. Some medicines contain more than 60 per cent sucrose! This could also complicate the management of diabetes, and some food allergies.

Can bread cause allergic problems?

Apart from coeliac disease, for which gluten-free bread is essential, the ordinary loaf can also cause problems either in wheat-sensitive patients, or because of contaminants and additives. Wholemeal bread does not contain these additives, so may be more suitable for those who react to them.

It is curious that, with the objective of ease in mass production, wheat is processed to produce high-extraction flour, then chemicals and vitamins are added to 'improve' the baking qualities and nutritional content. Some patients will react to these additives, such as potassium bromate, chlorine dioxide, iron and vitamin B, fungal amylase, soya flour, azodicarbonamide, and so on. Chlorine dioxide was introduced to take the place of nitrogen trichloride, similarly used in the 'agene' process as a bleaching agent, because flour with this in, was shown to cause hysteria in dogs when fed with flour meal and biscuits.

Can potatoes cause allergic reactions?

The potato and tomato, and tobacco, all belong to the nightshade family. Although a daily food, potato can cause allergic problems. Unusual examples of potato allergy may be of interest. In the last three years the author has found many problems caused by potato, diagnosed by pricking through some fresh potato juice.

For 6 months a man of 40 suffered from intense itching and nettle-rash which kept him from sleeping and did not respond to treatment. A 'basic-basic' diet of rice, potato and mutton made him much worse within a few days, suggesting that one of these foods was responsible. Complete relief followed removal of potato, and itch and rash recurred every time he ate a potato, confirming the cause beyond doubt.

Scraping new potatoes creates an aerosol, and it is quite common for asthma to be caused by this chore. (Baking potatoes in their jackets is an obvious answer.) Eating potato as a cause of asthma is rare.

Eczema can be caused by potato, as in a toddler whose eczema flared up when he got his hands in the potato water, thus carrying out a skin test on himself. Fortunately, his mother connected cause and effect, and made the diagnosis.

Rarely, potato can cause psychiatric symptoms. One young woman always seemed introverted, depressed and tired, as well as suffering from hay fever, which was the initial reason for the consultation. One summer there was a shortage of potato, with a prohibitive rise in price. She stopped buying potato, and within a few days she became a bright, cheerful extrovert, quite unlike her usual self, to which she reverted promptly whenever she ate potato. One schoolboy's poor academic performance was due to potato, as when it was avoided he became top of the class again.

People who cannot tolerate potato sometimes react also to tomato, because of the botanical relationship.

Can you be allergic to alcoholic drinks?

Allergic reactions, usually slow in onset, are very common in association with various drinks, and can be caused by either the yeast or by other substances derived from the grain or fruit.

Yeast ferments starches and sugars (carbohydrates) and converts them to alcohol and carbon dioxide, but traces of the original material persist, along with traces of yeast. The distinctive taste and smell of various drinks depends on this complex

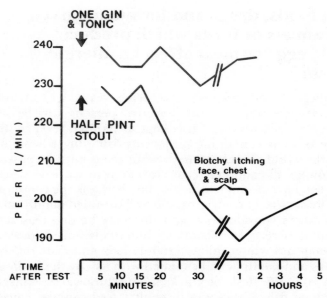

This lady had no adverse effects from gin or vodka, but reacted as above to stout, and also to red wine.

Figure 22.1   Reaction to alcoholic drinks monitored by a peak flow meter.

mixture of chemicals, rather than the alcohol. Allergic reactions to yeast or other ingredients are common – particularly to yeast – and can be very specific (Figure 22.1). For example, a man began to have severe asthma every Sunday, which was pinned down as being caused by the yeast in the beer he drank on Saturday nights only. This had been his habit for many years, with no such effects. Further inquiry revealed that the asthma had only occurred since he had started drinking a different make of beer. Some patients cannot tolerate vintage wines, but can drink cheap 'plonk', while others are the reverse. Several patients react violently to champagne, and one had such severe asthma that she ended up in hospital dressed in all her finery when she went to a wedding. Another patient reacted with asthma to some wines, but not others. We found that the wine which upset him gave a positive test when pricked into his skin. He loves wine, so when he goes to a wine tasting he takes disposable needles with him to test the wine as well as taste it!

Can foods, drugs and hormones given to animals or birds which produce milk, eggs or meat affect an allergic person?

It is illegal to sell milk from cows being treated with an antibiotic such as penicillin because sensitive persons can be affected. However, milk production is kept at its high level by the provision of diets containing many surprising ingredients from all over the world. Traces of these exotic foods must be passed on in the cow's milk, and may cause reactions in sensitive people, but very few have been identified so far. Perhaps the composition of milk from cows entirely grass-fed and those fed mainly on special diets differs considerably, and this may be one reason for the apparent increase in milk allergy and intolerance in recent years. Summer and winter milks certainly look and taste different.

Eggs and poultry can be tainted with fish by the feeding of fish meal, and the flesh of chickens and turkeys can affect those allergic to fish. Antibiotics in poultry feed can also cause problems in the consumers of eggs and poultry.

When we turn to meat the situation becomes even more complicated. Apart from possible problems caused by antibiotics, and other unusual items of diet, we now have to consider tenderizing enzymes injected intravenously just before killing the animal, and hormones used to promote rapid growth. Thus, the possibilities for sensitization or for reaction by those already sensitized become ever greater. Pigs are intensively reared on special feeds which may contain authorized antibiotics to promote rapid growth, and again hormones may be used. Surplus milk is often used to feed pigs as is swill and anything else available, hence pork may affect milk allergic patients. Once the pig has been converted into pork all sorts of chemicals are used for preserving and curing, some of which may cause trouble also.

Hormones are extensively used to boost meat production. A pellet of the drug is implanted in the base of the ear to release the hormone slowly. Anabolic steroids (similar to those misused by athletes) and oestrogens have been abused extensively in the past. The European veal market almost collapsed when early sex changes were seen in little boys being fed on Italian veal-based baby foods. Excessive amounts of diethylstilboestrol were found in the tins. This is the hormone which is known to have caused vaginal cancer in the adolescent daughters of mothers who were given high doses during their pregnancy in the 1940s or '50s to prevent a miscarriage. It has been banned in many countries, and new steroids and new methods have been developed to take its place.

The World Health Organisation and the EEC have been involved in the control of these methods of boosting meat production, and in ensuring that residues of these drugs are not present in the meat. There will always be unscrupulous farmers, but methods have now been developed to detect residues in the meat.

Orville Schells 'Modern Meat' is a frightening report on the American meat industry, which exposes the excessive use of hormones and antibiotics, and the possible development of 'superbugs' such as resistant salmonella.

Can food allergy or intolerance cause asthma and/or rhinitis?

Reference to the holistic diagram (Figure 3.1) will remind the reader of the importance of knowing which part of the body has become sensitized, and that how the allergen gets into the circulaton is immaterial.

Hence, any food absorbed from the gut can strike any sensitive area, including the bronchi, but all tests are usually negative, and the only clues may be in the history – often in the infant feeding history.

For example, one 28 year old woman had had chronic asthma since childhood, was given a few steroid tablets, and had an acute emotional reaction. She was admitted to a psychiatric hospital, and steroids were blamed for this reaction. (Such reactions to steroids are *extremely* rare.) On admission the psychiatrists, apparently not understanding the problems of the asthmatic, took away her Ventolin aerosol, hence her asthma got worse. The facts that she had recently had her first baby, that her husband had been made redundant, and that he had broken his leg and was in plaster, were apparently considered unimportant. She discharged herself against advice, but when she got home the asthma got so bad that she was admitted to hospital. It was found that she had a history of projectile vomiting in

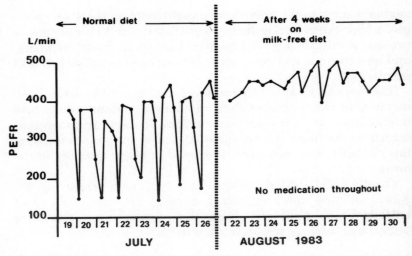

This patient aged 43 made a complete recovery without drugs, and can be called a real 'cure' of lifelong asthma.

Figure 22.2   Severe asthma caused by milk.

infancy, which slowly resolved as the chronic asthma began in early childhood.

She responded to steroid treatment, milk products were excluded, all drugs stopped and tests with milk were carried out. The results when she took a glass of milk were dramatic. By avoiding milk this patient has hardly ever had a day's illness since, but skin tests for milk are negative.

This case illustrates the importance of the infant feeding history, and how a sensitive gut can finally change to a sensitive bronchus. Any food can sensitize the respiratory system.

How important is food allergy as a cause of eczema?

This matter has been discussed in the appropriate section, but it is mentioned again here to emphasize the part foods may play in the causation of eczema.

Elimination diets can be helpful in eczema, but have to be carried out meticulously, especially when avoiding egg, which may have to be banished from the house. One attempt to establish the importance of dietary factors in eczema by a double-blind trial of milk- and egg-free infant formulae was moderately successful, but the role of foods in eczema will continue to be inconclusive until it is acknowledged that each case has an individual pattern of reaction.

Eczema cases cannot be put together in a group, and inhalants can be as important as foods in causation. By this it is meant that eczema may be caused by environmental factors, such as dust mites and pets, and food as well. To concentrate on foods alone as a cause is an over-simplification which has resulted in inconclusive results.

Can food allergy be seasonal and can seasonal allergies affect the gut?

Seasonal foods, such as fruits and vegetables, can be a rare cause of seasonal allergic problems. Eating nuts on Christmas Eve caused one patient to spend Christmas in hospital year after year until the cause/effect relationship was realized. (He never ate nuts except at Christmas.)

Less obvious seasonal influences on the gut are inhalant allergens. For example, grass pollen can cause ulcerative colitis, with severe bloody diarrhoea every June and July only. A colleague who found one such case decided to prove it beyond all doubt by a provocation in the winter because the skin test was negative. He did this by inserting an instrument into the rectum and puffing in a little grass pollen, and watching the intense reaction which occurred. The patient was successfully desensitized to pollen and has had no further trouble. The fact that pollen can cause colitis indicates that it must be possible for other allergens to play a similar role.

Can the smell of food cause symptoms?

Immediate-type allergic reactions to smells can be extreme, as in a patient who got severe asthma whenever she passed a fish shop, and a farmer who got asthma when the west wind carried the smell of horses from the stable a hundred yards away from his home. Some patients get symptoms just by being in the kitchen when an egg is opened, and failure of elimination diets in infantile eczema can be due to exposure to the smells of food in the kitchen, where a child may spend much time.

Extreme examples can be almost beyond belief, as in the child who began to itch whenever he got near a dressed fowl, or whenever eggs, fish, pork or bacon were cooked. Perhaps the best story of all is regarding the man sensitive to salmon who got asthma from eating a salmon croquette. The cook put the remainder in the fridge near the butter, and the next day the patient got another attack of asthma from bread and butter. These examples show just how sensitive people can be and just how careful they have to be if they know what to avoid.

Can 'premenstrual' symptoms such as swelling of ankles, joints and abdomen and emotional disturbance be caused by food allergy?

Women often find that they hold extra fluid just before their menstrual periods. Their weight increases, rings get tight, and there is some bloating of the lower stomach. This is a very common problem, but if it is much worse than usual, food allergy may be the answer. Swelling round the eyes, or dark shadows under the eyes, is often associated. Difficulty in thinking, confusion, headaches and anxiety are often associated, frequently attributed to emotional factors. The presence of multiple symptoms affecting many different body systems is characteristic of both food allergy and psychosomatic problems, which may become confused unless the possibility of allergy is considered.

For example a woman aged 35 suffered from all the above symptoms for about 15 years. In the last few years she had also experienced episodes of high emotional tension, irritability, and such vile temper as to threaten the stability of her marriage of 13 years duration. These episodes would alternate with periods of deep black depression, uncontrollable purposeless weeping, and even suicidal thoughts. The usual tranquillizers had no effect whatever, so she was referred to a psychiatrist who tried very hard to help her, devoted much time to delving into intimate problems, and also interviewed the husband. He recommended more powerful drugs which she refused to take, and concluded that the root of the problem was marital discord. He asked if she had ever considered divorce and suggested that an affair with another man might help her cope with her problems more effectively!

All her problems vanished in a few days on a strict diet, and it was repeatedly shown that the episodes of high emotional tension were caused by fish, and all the other symptoms were caused by milk products. She has now been discharged by the psychiatrist, who refused to believe that allergy was the cause of her problems, and she feels in better health than for the last 15 years. This case emphasizes once again how allergy to foods can produce widespread symptomatology the causes of which can only be defined by dietary experiment.

Can food cause arthritis?

Food was first reported as a cause of arthritis and swelling of the joints 67 years ago, but little or no attention has been paid to the occasional reports which have appeared in the medical journals and in books on food allergy. Rheumatoid arthritis was first treated with steroids over 30 years ago, when this treatment was hailed as a miracle cure until the side-effects of long-term treatment became evident. For this reason steroids tend to be withheld, and anti-inflammatory drugs are generally used. However, some of the newer drugs have had serious and fatal side-effects and have been withdrawn from use.

Rheumatic diseases have become a specialized area of medicine, so food as a possible cause is not usually considered, just as in alimentary disease such as colitis. A trial of an elimination diet in a large number of cases in the early stages of rheumatoid arthritis might be worthwhile. If carried out properly the true importance of food in joint problems might become evident with less chance of side-effects. One successful trial has already been published.

A middle-aged woman had suffered from arthritis affecting all her joints for 4 years, and as she derived little benefit from specialized treatment and the condition became so severe as to prevent her driving, she requested investigation to make sure that there was no avoidable food allergy present. When placed on a very restricted diet her joint swelling and stiffness improved very rapidly within about 10 days. The cause was shown to be milk and milk products because the reintroduction of a small amount of milk produced a relapse of her arthritis lasting for over 2 days on three separate occasions. The patient was delighted with this improvement, but she still had some days when her joints were slightly affected. Her husband observed that she always complained of her joints on the morning after they had had intercourse. It was suggested that a condom be used to see if this would prevent the effect on the joints, and when this proved to be effective the husband was also placed on a milk-free diet. It could then be shown that the effect of intercourse on her joints occurred only when her husband was taking milk, so that the infinitesimal amount of milk protein in his semen was enough to trigger off a reaction. As an unexpected bonus, the chronic eczema of the ears from which the husband had suffered for 30 years also cleared up, so it appeared that he was also intolerant of milk.

A 28 year old mother of 2½ year old twins developed rheumatoid arthritis severe enough to require many powerful drugs, some of which produced quite troublesome side-effects. The pain in her wrists was such that she had difficulty in bathing the children, and she found great difficulty in getting out of bed in the morning. She had noticed that some drinks and foods seemed to make her joints worse, and insisted on exploring the possibility that foods were the cause. A 'basic-basic' diet produced dramatic relief, and test feeds caused repeatable reappearance of swelling and pain in the joints. She has a more difficult dietary regime because she cannot tolerate milk products, beef and pork, any food containing yeast, any alcohol, some cooking oils, and soya products. She is still adding foods one by one to her diet, but her arthritis has completely disappeared.

What are the permitted food colours, preservatives and other food additives and what problems can they cause?

Azo Dyes

Additive	Comments	Reactions
Yellow: E102 Tartrazine E104 Quinoline Yellow E107 Yellow 2G E110 Sunset Yellow		Allergic and hyperactive reactions of all kinds are possible with any of the azo dyes – even coloured paper hankies and toilet paper.
Red: E122 Azorubine E123 Amaranth E124 Ponceau 4R E127 Erythrosine	All used very widely in food, drink, and drugs such as tablets and antibiotic syrups, etc.	E127 contains a tiny amount of iodine which could upset iodine-sensitive people, or those with thyroid disorders.
128 Red 2G	Used only in UK for meats and sausages.	
Blue/brown/black: E131 Patent Blue E132 Indigo Carmine	Few foods are blue so usually used only in small amounts to adjust colour.	

Vegetable and Animal Dyes

Additive	Comments	Reactions
E100 Circumin	A wide variety of coloured plant extracts – but few are widely used because the colour is less intense, and some are very expensive. Chemical dyes are soluble, strong, reliable and cheap.	Reactions have rarely been identified but are always possible to any vegetable products.
E120 Cochineal	Made from squashed South American beetles. Expensive, usually used in kitchen, not in processed foods.	
E140 Chlorophyll E141 Copper complexes of chlorophyll	The natural green colour of plants.	None known.
E160 (a to f) E161 (a to g) E162 (Beetroot Red) E163 Anthocyan-ins	Plant and fruit extracts.	None known.
E150 Caramel	In the kitchen made from burnt sugar but also several varieties such as ammonium sulphite caramel used in beer, gravy browning, soft drinks and vinegar. Is a commonly added food colour.	No evidence but sulphite-sensitive persons might react to it.

General Preservatives

Additive	Comments	Reactions
E200–203 Sorbates	Used in cheese to restrict growth of yeast but does not affect lactobacilli. Also wide variety of foods and drinks.	Reaction to cheese or moulds much more likely.
E210–219 Benzoates	Used extensively in all sorts of foods and drinks, sweets, etc, as a preservative.	All sorts of allergic reactions in sensitive persons.
E220–227 Sulphur dioxide and sulphites	Used extensively in all sorts of foods and drinks, and may be sprayed on salads to keep them looking fresh, and oven-ready chips, crisps, etc.	Definite asthma reaction to SO_2 in drinks which may irritate but main problem is severe angio-oedema-type reactions to sulphites, even anaphylaxis.
E230–233 Biphenyls	Used to treat the skin of citrus fruits to stop mould growth, along with many pesticides – all of which may get in the marmalade.	Reactions reported but difficult to implicate any one of them because of multiple spraying.
E234 Nisin	A type of antibiotic used in cheese and other milk products as a preservative.	Harmless.
E249–251 Nitrites and nitrates	Used as preservatives and for curing meats. Nitrosamines may be carcinogenic. Excess can cause problems with haemoglobin, as in babies due to excess in drinking water during drought.	Can cause reactions similar to sulphites.

General Preservatives

Additive	Comments	Reactions
E260–263, 270, 280–283, 290, 296, 297	This group of miscellaneous preservatives are harmless as far as is known.	Harmless.

Antioxidants

Additive	Comments	Reactions
E300–304 Ascorbic	In various forms, stops foods going off.	Harmless.
E306–309	Vitamin E in various forms which also acts as an antioxidant.	Harmless.
E320 Butylated hydroxy-anisole (BHA) E321 Butylated hydroxy-toluene (BHT)	Found in a vast range of edible products.	Skin rashes, symptoms resembling those caused by MSG, angio-oedema, and urticaria.

Emulsifiers and Stabilizers

Additive	Comments	Reactions
E322–620	None of these agents are known to cause problems except rarely to vegetable gums.	
E621–623	The glutamates are used as flavour enhancers. The effects of these are described separately (MSG, etc).	

Emulsifiers and Stabilizers

Additive	Comments	Reactions
E627, 631, 635 Granylates	A flavour enhancer often found in precooked rice, crisps and gravy granules.	Nothing reported but unsuitable for patients with gout.
E636–904	Miscellaneous waxes, etc.	Not known.

Mineral Oils

Additive	Comments	Reactions
E905–907	Oils and waxes to improve the appearance of the product.	Harmless.
E920–923	Additives for bleaching and 'improving' white flour. Colour, soya flour and milk may also be added for loaves.	See comments in text.

23 Food allergy and intolerance in infancy

Public interest in possible allergic problems in infancy has increased greatly in recent years, but both medical and other professionals involved with infant care have been very slow to accept allergy as a significant problem in infancy. Parents must therefore be prepared to meet resistance, scepticism or even open hostility to the concept of allergy to milk and other foods.

Babies are often weaned rather early to tinned convenience foods. Nevertheless the range of foods and the types of reactions which may occur at this age are really quite limited. Reactions to a particular food are, therefore, more likely to be found at this time of life, and may be correspondingly simpler to sort out as long as there is an awareness of the possibility of allergy.

This is the reason why this book deals with infantile problems before the more difficult and complicated problems of allergy and intolerance in children and adults – the patterns found in infants may also be helpful in the understanding of the more complex problems.

It is hoped that some of the suggestions in this chapter may enable parents to produce convincing evidence and, more importantly, significant relief of symptoms. It is also important to convince their advisors that the allergic nature of the child's symptoms is not a figment of a disordered parental imagination. Unfortunately those whose suggestions are summarily rejected seldom return to their doctors to discuss the outcome of successful dietary manipulation, but in the absence of such practical demonstrations of results medical opinion is unlikely to alter.

The key to the diagnosis of allergy of milk, eggs or other common infant foods is a high index of suspicion, but the tendency to jump to conclusions, blame everything on allergy, and make haphazard alterations in the feed must be resisted. Furthermore, parents must be warned against giving infants dietary formulae which are nutritionally inadequate.

Who supervises infant feeding in Britain today?

The pregnant mother can attend her doctor or the hospital for antenatal care, and also classes for exercises and information which today lay commendable stress on the importance of breast-feeding. When the time comes the baby is delivered in a local hospital maternity unit, attended by the hospital midwife and medical staff, and the baby will be checked over by the paediatric unit for congenital defects. In the absence of any complications mother and baby will be at home in 48 hours or so, having commenced breast- or bottle-feeding.

At home the community midwife will supervise mother and child closely for the first 10–20 days, then hand over to the health visitor who will continue supervision. Sometimes there is a community dietician as well, and the child also attends a 'well baby' clinic for monitoring. The health visitor may chase up mothers who do not attend clinics, and so on. The family doctor may be consulted regarding feeding problems if the midwife or health visitor ask for help.

Thus a large team of health professionals, particularly nurses, are involved, who may hold many divergent views, which might even be contradictory. Thus the mother of a baby with feeding problems may become confused and anxious, but may be unable to get helpful advice from any member of the team. Even if the paediatrician is consulted it is quite likely that the possibility of milk allergy or intolerance will not be seriously considered. If the baby is still on the breast the possibility that allergy to milk, eggs or other items of the maternal diet is the cause of the problem will be even less likely to be considered possible.

It may be helpful to join a local branch of the National Childbirth Trust. The aims of this organization are to support and educate young mothers and encourage breast-feeding.

Can the development of allergy be predicted in new-born babies?

In Sweden testing blood obtained from the umbilical cord at birth has shown that when detectable IgE, the allergy antibody, is present these infants are very likely to develop allergy. Further blood tests at one year have confirmed that a high IgE at birth clearly predicts allergic problems by the age of 4. In France it has been found that severely allergic mothers are much more liable to have allergic children, but having an allergic father is less important. Specific IgE antibodies against milk and egg have also been found present at birth, as a result of these foods being eaten by the mother.

The predictive value of IgE estimation in the newborn and in infancy is now well established so that there are good reasons for doing this test when there is a positive family history, especially maternal. However, unless dietary control is introduced when the IgE result is positive the information provided by the test will have been wasted. Breast-feeding, modified diets and avoidance of exposure to pets would be sensible precautions which may prevent development of allergy in this group of infants.

It is unfortunate that there seems to be very little interest in prediction and prevention of allergy in the UK.

Can babies become sensitized to foods before birth?

Many years ago, when most babies were breast-fed, it was recognized that the foetus can be sensitized by the maternal diet. These observations were forgotten when bottle-feeding became the rule, but with the revival of breast-feeding sensitization before birth is becoming more common.

Mothers who are themselves allergic subjects would be well advised to avoid excessive quantities of milk, eggs, citrus fruits, wheat and nuts in pregnancy. They are often advised strongly to take large amounts of these very foods, but excess is surely unnecessary.

Rejection of the first feed of breast milk may indicate that the baby has been sensitized before birth. Avoidance of cow's milk by the nursing mother may relieve the symptoms.

Can allergy occur when they are still being totally breast-fed?

The effects of maternal diet have been noted since ancient times, yet tend to be overlooked today. Purely breast-fed infants can still react to foods, especially eggs and milk, from traces of these foods in the breast milk. Experiments where the suspect food was withdrawn and reintroduced to the maternal diet have produced clear evidence of a cause/effect relationship, especially in eczema. In 1978 an interesting report was published from Scandinavia regarding colic in breast-fed babies. Not only was the maternal milk intake related to the screaming, but cow's milk protein could be demonstrated unchanged in the breast milk. Drugs also pass through, and any chemical to which the mother is exposed, even insecticides from food.

There is a most important difference between infants who react to traces of foods in the breast milk, and those who react to the cow's milk formula in the bottle. Those who react to tiny amounts in the breast milk have been shown to have positive skin tests and also blood RAST tests, and can be dangerously sensitive, but maternal avoidance of the foods will avoid problems. They may have to avoid even traces of milk or egg for many years, sometimes for life; this is 'fixed food allergy'.

Milk-intolerant babies being fed on cow's milk formula are taking relatively large amounts of cow's milk protein (an adult would have to drink 10 *litres* a day to take in the same amount in proportion to body weight), and have no skin test reactions or RAST tests. If milk is avoided for a year or two they can usually tolerate it again.

This obvious difference, and the fact that the skin test can give the diagnosis in breast-fed infants, has only recently been realized, and can be very important. Those who give positive skin tests and react immediately should be recognized as soon as possible to avoid disasters – even cot death.

How do babies get sensitized to cow's milk after birth?

In the first section of this book I explained how exposure to an allergen can sensitize the individual prone to allergic reactions, so that an excessive reaction may follow subsequent contact with that allergen. This sequence often happens in milk-allergic babies because of the old-fashioned and ill-advised nursing practice of giving any baby in the nursery who cries at night a milk feed, instead of putting it to the mother's breast.

There is much to commend the baby being placed beside the mother from the start so that a feed can be given at any time, and breast-feeding can be established as soon as possible. The immune system of the new-born child then avoids being programmed wrongly. Quite recently a mother who was herself a state registered nurse told me that she had to threaten to throw the bottles of cow's milk formula at her colleagues before they would take her seriously in her attempts to feed her baby entirely on the breast. It is unfortunate that these nursing practices still persist today.

The first milk-formula feed is the sensitizing dose. The mother may not be aware that it is being given, or later forgets – until breast-feeding is discontinued months later or supplementary cow's milk formula feeds are introduced, when rejection of the cow's milk protein upwards by vomiting or downwards by diarrhoea may herald the development of milk allergy. The vomiting may be so violent as to be called the 'projectile' type, when the feed is no sooner swallowed than it is shot forcibly across the room.

When feeding problems commence as breast-feeding ceases, milk allergy should be considered as a possibility, especially when changes of formula bring no relief. Other causes of upset should be excluded first, before trying out formulae which do not contain milk.

What can babies become sensitized to?

Infants have very limited possibilities for becoming sensitized, and foods rather than environment are the most likely sources of allergens. These allergens may be supplied direct, as in the case of cow's milk formula, or indirectly from the food (or drugs) consumed by the breast-feeding mother, such as eggs, yeast, nuts and so on.

With such a limited range of possible allergens one might expect feeding problems in infancy to be more commonly recognized as being caused by food allergy or intolerance, and the identification of the few possible causes to be correspondingly simple and straightforward. Exactly the converse is true, and only a minority of paediatricians, general practitioners, health visitors, midwives and even dieticians believe that allergic reactions to cow's milk are a common cause of problems with infant feeding.

A century ago milk was not easily so freely available, and often carried dangerous infections such as tuberculosis and abortus fever before pasteurization became widely used. Breast-feeding was the rule and, if necessary, wet nurses were employed who were probably much safer than cows at that time. Today the amounts of milk and milk products produced are enormous. To maintain a high milk yield cows are fed on all sorts of exotic foods, and even spices, as well as their natural diet of grass and hay, so modern milk may contain many potential allergens.

What difficulties may be met by parents suspecting milk allergy or intolerance in their child?

Awareness that cow's milk proteins can cause serious allergic illnesses of many types, including colic, screaming, diarrhoea, vomiting, projectile vomiting, eczema, malabsorption, failure to thrive, asthma and even bedwetting, is being promulgated by radio and television and also by features in magazines popular with mothers. This information is being given out by pressure groups because the majority of paediatricians and dermatologists do not accept that milk and other foods can cause disease. Thus, it is not uncommon for this suggestion to be quite violently rejected and many parents, often more open-minded than their counsellors, have to be very persistent before they can obtain correct advice. Fortunately these facts are becoming very slowly more widely acknowledged, but problems can arise when an infant or child is admitted to a children's hospital unit for some other reason, such as simple surgery. I have known of cases where both nursing and medical staff have stated that they do not believe in all this nonsense, and insisted, against the protests of the mother, in giving cow's milk, with dramatic effects.

How can cow's milk allergy or intolerance be diagnosed?

Cow's milk allergy can affect any organ or system of the body, causing confusion and controversy, but in infancy the symptoms are usually confined to the gut.

Diarrhoea is the most common symptom, sometimes with mucus and blood. If diagnosis is unduly delayed damage to the gut wall will bring a whole range of other problems. The main effects are lactose deficiency, which makes the diarrhoea worse, malabsorption of food, causing failure to thrive, fatty smelly motions, anaemia, and rarely very severe constipation.

Rejection of milk by vomiting, and sometimes so-called cyclic vomiting causing severe upset and dehydration, is also common. Alterations in formula bring no relief, and abdominal pain is a frequent symptom. Colic and crying after a feed with relief after vomiting can be a suggestive symptom. An infant may sleep badly, cry a lot, and scream as soon as the bottle is finished, but the more the baby is fed the worse the screaming becomes.

These are the main features of a very trying situation, to which eczema or asthma may be added later. The diagnosis can only be achieved by avoiding cow's milk completely (and at first any trace of beef), substituting a soya-based formula and observing the results.

Deliberate test feeds, using small amounts for safety, should then reproduce the symptoms. It is necessary to give a test feed twice or three times to be quite sure, unless the result of the first test feed has been obvious and dramatic. What is observed clinically can be very obvious, but very difficult to confirm unless it is a true allergy with positive skin and blood tests.

Much more research must be done before it will be possible to develop a test which will give the diagnosis of milk intolerance. For the moment we have to be satisfied with the results of soya formulae and repeated challenge tests, and from the point of view of the desperate parents this is often more than enough.

What conditions can be confused with cow's milk allergy or intolerance?

The symptoms associated with cow's milk allergy can also be caused by many other conditions, so it is unwise to jump to conclusions and risk overlooking other problems. Allergy to other foods will cause the same symptoms, so other foods may also be involved. Exceptionally allergy may occur to items in the diet of the cow, such as wheat, nuts, linseed, antibiotics, and so on. Diarrhoea and vomiting can be caused by overfeeding, too concentrated a formula, or weaning too early, but these problems will almost certainly be excluded by advice from midwife or health visitor.

Milk sugar is called lactose, and a special enzyme, lactase, is normally present in the small intestine to digest lactose. Rarely, there is a congenital deficiency of lactase, but it is much more common for lactase deficiency to be a *result* of damage to the lining of the gut from gastroenteritis, milk allergy or intolerance, or other chronic forms of diarrhoea. The same comments apply to other sugars and the special enzymes required for their digestion, so several enzymes may be absent but usually reappear after a time.

Lactase is normally present in all infants, but is often deficient in adults because the presence or absence of this enzyme is greatly influenced by ethnic origins. For example, over 80 per cent of Scandinavians and North Europeans can digest milk, but 30–40 per cent of Mediterranean and Middle Eastern races cannot. Ninety per cent of Orientals cannot digest milk, as they do not produce lactase at all after infancy.

Coeliac disease is caused by intolerance of gluten from wheat and other cereals, causing damage to the lining of the gut similar to that found in severe milk allergy. Milk allergy or intolerance, can co-exist with coeliac disease, temporary lactase deficiency can be a side-effect of milk allergy or gastroenteritis, and avoidance of gluten as well as milk is necessary for recovery.

A 4 year old girl was referred for chronic asthma. Her mother was the first asthmatic in Derby whose asthma was found to be caused by the yeast in beer and stout, and her grandmother, now 80 and still steroid-dependent, was the first case of allergic aspergillosis diagnosed in Derby.

The child had been bottle-fed, and had been in hospital as a baby with gastroenteritis, suspected malabsorption, and failure to thrive. Vomiting and diarrhoea were associated with cow's milk, and beef was specifically refused. All tinned baby foods of a type with a common beef-broth base caused vomiting and diarrhoea, but she tolerated perfectly other baby foods made without a beef broth base.

When these problems subsided at age 2 the asthma began, and by 4 years of age, when first seen for investigation, she was a stunted, miserable, hyperactive girl with a pigeon-chest deformity, and negative skin tests. Milk products and beef were withdrawn, and the hyperactivity, tantrums, loose motions and asthma all improved dramatically in 3 days. Accidental provocations such as ice-cream caused a return of all symptoms in

4 hours, especially the tantrums. Her growth accelerated, but slowed up 2 years later, probably as a result of taking some milk products, because the stools became frequent and offensive again. Over the next few years she developed inhalant allergies with positive skin tests for grass pollen, dog and horse. She improved when the dog went, and horse-riding was avoided. By age 10 she still reacted to milk, but had become a very active, cheerful, delightful child with a normal peak flow rate, who was an excellent swimmer. At age 12 she won a 5 mile cross-country race against much bigger children, and further progress has been uneventful.

This case illustrates the wide range of manifestations of allergy and intolerance encountered in one family, and in one case over a period of 10 years.

Is goat's or ewe's milk a satisfactory substitute for cow's milk formula?

Goat's milk is frequently tried by parents, often on medical advice. There is such close similarity between the proteins in goat's milk and in cow's milk that a good result is, in my experience, uncommon. It is a mistake to assume that because the child is not better on goat's milk the cause cannot be milk.

The sensible approach is first of all to establish clearly that cow's milk is indeed the cause of the problem. Accredited pasteurized or sterilized goat's milk can then be tried as a substitute while the child has no symptoms. It will be found that goat's milk can be tolerated by some infants only. The same comments obviously apply to ewe's milk or any other animal milk.

Goat's milk is unsuitable for babies under the age of 6 months because it lacks sufficient vitamins A, C and D and because severe anaemia may arise because it lacks vitamin B12 and folic acid. Also, goat's milk is much more difficult to modify to resemble breast milk than is cow's milk.

The standards of hygiene for goat's milk may not be up to those mandatory for normal dairies, so to consume *raw* goat's milk is to risk milk-borne infections, especially abortus fever. It *must* be boiled for at least 2 minutes for safety.

What are the prospects for the milk-allergic or intolerant infant?

True allergy to cow's milk in infancy may be the prelude to a lifetime of misery. The feeding problems often gradually clear up, but are replaced by other allergic problems such as eczema and asthma. In some children milk will cause emotional and behavioural disturbances after the feeding problems have subsided.

Research on large groups of American children suggests that many of these problems could be prevented by more breast-feeding, persistence with breast-feeding up to at least 6 months, and the delayed introduction of allergenic foods such as egg, wheat and yeast. Once milk has been eliminated the outlook is good, but if other foods are involved complete relief may not be achieved. For example, sensitivity to orange, soya, egg, wheat, tomato, rice, pork and beef may be present, and these foods may also have to be avoided to get a good result.

Some infants or children lose their milk intolerance in a few months often by the age of 1 or 2 years. In patients of all ages milk intolerance may vanish if milk is avoided for up to 2 years, but this is only in those who have a delayed reaction to large amounts.

A few patients who have reacted to mother's milk containing traces of cow's milk from the maternal diet, and who have a positive skin test or RAST test, may have a fixed allergy to milk which may persist for life. In some cases in this category *dangerous* sensitivity to milk may be present.

When an infant predisposed to allergic problems is exposed to the home environment further sensitization may occur to inhalant allergens, such as dust mites and pets, causing asthma and/or allergic rhinitis.

Is cow's milk allergy or intolerance becoming more common?

My impression from very wide experience is that milk intolerance is increasing, but this is mainly the result of increased awareness of the possibility on my part. Enquiry regarding infant feeding problems in patients of all ages reveals that it is common for feeding problems in infancy to fade out, to be replaced by asthma, eczema, or some other allergic manifestation in childhood.

The most interesting and striking result of these enquiries was the finding that cow's milk tended to cause various allergic problems in several generations or in close relatives of the same family. For this reason it is worth suspecting milk as the cause of illness in other members of the family, and making very pointed enquiries about their tolerance of milk.

Cow's milk allergy was first recorded by Hippocrates in the fourth century BC, and goat's milk allergy by Galen in the second century AD, but it is probably mainly a twentieth-century disease. This is because abundant supplies of safe clean cow's milk are a development of the twentieth century, and the invention of ready-made cow's milk formulae provided a convenient outlet for surplus milk.

Allergy or intolerance resulting from feeding infant formulae was first reported from Germany in 1905, France in 1908, Sweden in 1910, the USA in 1916, but from Britain not until 1940.

Perhaps this partly explains the slow recognition of cow's milk intolerance or allergy in Britain. As a result paediatricians, family doctors, and especially community midwives and health visitors, who have the most direct contact with the nursing mother, may hold vastly divergent views regarding allergy or intolerance to cow's milk formulae. The range of opinion can vary from incredulity at the idea that such a valuable food can cause disease to suspecting that every minor tummy upset is caused by milk allergy. At present, rejection is the common attitude and it will take a long time for a balanced view to prevail.

Why is breast best?

Breast-fed babies have been repeatedly shown to develop less illness and to have a lower mortality rate than bottle-fed infants. Cow's milk was intended for baby cows, not humans. The composition of cow's milk and the proportions of fat, protein and carbohydrate are quite different from those of mother's milk. Milk formulae are usually adjusted as far as possible so that these differences are less evident, but the differences are still very important. Human milk contains antibacterial and anti-viral substances, antibodies, white cells which will engulf bacteria, and even lymphocytes, as well as protective IgA. Breast-fed babies have abundant harmless bacteria in their acid motions called lactobacilli, related to the bacteria used to make yoghurt. Bottle-fed infants have colon bacteria, some strains of which can cause severe diarrhoea. It is no surprise that infant mortality in the Third World has increased sharply since many of the babies existing in the poorest and most unsanitary circumstances have been put on the bottle and thus deprived of their natural and safe diet. The manufacturers have been rightly criticized for this.

It would seem obvious that breast is best, particularly in allergic families, but the clear-cut evidence from 30 or more years ago has not been as easily confirmed in recent years. In fact, the most recent survey suggested that breast-fed babies were *more* liable than bottle-fed babies to eczema, which is becoming more common in recent years. Chemicals such as insecticides in the cream of the breast milk have been suggested as a possible cause. So the eczema question is unresolved, but for the reasons above breast is still obviously best.

What drugs pass into breast milk and may affect the baby?

Alcohol or barbiturates passed by means of the mother's milk may sedate the baby. Some laxatives and ampicillin may cause looseness of bowels. Aminophylline drugs, often used in asthma, can cause irritability. Anti-thyroid drugs can affect the thyroid gland of the baby, and sulpha drugs can cause jaundice. Drugs are better avoided by the feeding mother if that is possible. If in doubt ask your doctor, who may, however, find difficulty in finding out if a drug for you is also safe for your baby. If breast-feeding never take any sort of medicine without medical advice.

It is not only ingested drugs that get into mother's milk, as even preparations for vaginal use are absorbed. A case has been reported of the use of povidone-iodine gel (Betadine) causing the infant to smell of iodine. Both breast milk and baby contained excessive amounts of iodine, and possible problems were only avoided by an alert intelligent mother. This preparation is widely used as a gargle and mouth wash, and allergy to iodine does occur.

A popular anti-histamine has been reported as causing

drowsiness, irritability, refusal to feed, and a high pitched cry in a 10 week old baby. Another report concerns transmission of undesirable amounts of vitamin D in the milk of a mother who was being treated with large amounts of the vitamin.

Is early weaning wise?

Early weaning has now become very popular, yet common sense alone suggests that the immature intestine cannot reasonably be expected to cope with cereal and egg and other allergens at the age of 6 weeks – yet a survey in Sheffield revealed that at this age all the babies surveyed were on solids! Another survey in London in 1978 revealed of 265 babies aged 12 weeks only 18 were breast-fed, with 197 on solids. Such figures may explain why the incidence of allergy in very young babies may be increasing.

Two surveys of patients with ulcerative colitis revealed that early introduction of artificial feeding increases the liability to develop colitis later in life.

What causes eczema in babies?

Eczema is common in babies, but in the majority it is slight and disappears in a few months. Under 1 year old milk and egg are probably the most usual causes but the early introduction of all manner of solid foods widens the range of possible allergens.

Some unfortunate parents have a screaming scratching demon of a child who does not sleep, produces an unbelievable amount of excreta and perhaps vomits as well. All sorts of advice may have been given, all to no avail, but there is nothing to lose by trying a soya-bean formula such as Prosobee. Indeed, there is no alternative to trying a milk-free, egg-free diet, because there is no other conclusive test available unless it is a true allergy with positive skin and RAST tests. Medical approval and help are useful here, as soya-milk formulae are (on the recommendation of a consultant) prescribable on the National Health Service in milk-allergy cases.

Eczema can have several causes, such as milk as a background plus animals and dust mites as well. Thus, a child may improve only slightly when milk is avoided, but when the dog or cat is also removed the eczema may disappear completely.

Can children get colitis?

Ulcerative colitis is rare in children but does occasionally occur, even in infants. It has been described as eczema of the bowel, and is more likely to be caused by food allergy, particularly to milk, in children than in adults. To remove the colon in a child as a life-saving operation is a very serious decision with long-term consequences. This operation has been said to resemble cutting off an eczematous hand instead of attempting to find a cause for the condition. Trial of dietary treatment should be an obvious first choice at an early stage of the disease. A recent investigation has shown beyond doubt that severe colitis with bloody motions in infants resolves completely on exclusion of the causative food, usually cow's milk.

Can foods cause bladder problems and bed-wetting?

All sorts of bladder symptoms can be caused by allergy. This was first reported in 1922. Foods and inhalant allergens can be the cause, but this is seldom considered. Failure of symptoms of infection to improve after repeated courses of antibiotics suggests allergy, easily confirmed by examination of the cells in the urine. Of course, such cases are very rarely seen by an allergist.

Bed-wetting is another urinary problem which can be caused by allergy to foods. One British author in the 1930s reported that 5 per cent of allergic children were bed-wetters, and the author has also noted several cases of food allergy where cessation of bed-wetting was a surprising spin-off from dieting. Another rare symptom can be vaginal itch and discharge, sometimes for years, caused by milk or other foods.

24 Dietary manipulation in the diagnosis and treatment of food allergy and intolerance

Can food be the cause of my illness?

This question is often asked by sufferers from illnesses ranging from asthma to arthritis, from colitis to Crohn's disease. Many people know from experience that they react violently to certain foods and avoid them. We are not so concerned with these obvious immediate reactions, but with those occurring after a delay of several hours or even an entire day, due to intolerance. Many foods may be involved, often those eaten frequently or daily, so the symptoms occur relentlessly day after day.

How can I find out if food is making me ill?

This is the next question most frequently asked. The only way to ascertain that food is or is not the cause of symptoms is by complete fasting or by a very limited diet, because there are no scientific tests available at present. The simplest way to get the answer is to eat nothing at all for five days or for a week, drinking only bottled water. Some people feel much worse during the first few days, but if they persevere they may improve definitely by the end of the week, showing that foods must be causing the symptoms. Everything that passes your lips, including toothpaste, chewing gum, sweets and all medicines are suspect.

Is there any alternative to fasting?

Fasting is not for everyone, so the compromise is to live on a very limited diet containing only foods rarely involved in food allergy or intolerance. This diet is called the 'Basic Diet', and consists simply of lamb and all lamb products, rice and/or potatoes, sometimes pears, and bottled water. This diet should be persisted with for 10–21 days, but unless the diet is strictly adhered to it is a waste of time and effort. Occasionally potato, sometimes lamb, and very rarely rice, causes trouble, but excluding each in turn should give the right answer.

During the trial period on the basic diet **nothing else**, repeat **nothing else**, can be eaten or you will defeat the whole object of the exercise. **Never** eat or drink anything not prescribed. The plan is that at first you will have the basic diet only.

The basic diet is safe, and gives adequate nutrition for short periods not exceeding 2 or 3 weeks. However, it is important to discuss dieting with your doctor, particularly if you are taking any medication and especially if you are already underweight. Dietary trials in infancy should be carried out only on medical advice, but as small children tend to have a more restricted diet anyway the problem should be easier to sort out.

Do not continue the diet longer than 3 weeks without medical advice.

Can dieting be dangerous?

Restrictive diets or fasting should never be undertaken lightly. It is dangerous to become obsessive regarding food allergy as a possible cause of your problems or those of your children. Very inadequate diets have been imposed on children by mothers who had become convinced that their children were food allergics, and severe malnutrition has been reported. An inadequate diet will eventually cause malnutrition, and also diseases caused by lack of vitamins and minerals, so basic type diets must not be persisted with for longer than 3 weeks.

If no improvement has occurred by 3 weeks the cause of the problem cannot be food, so further dieting is pointless. If the basic diet has given relief of symptoms then test feeds may show that many foods must be avoided to remain well. In this situation it is often difficult to be sure that the diet is adequate for

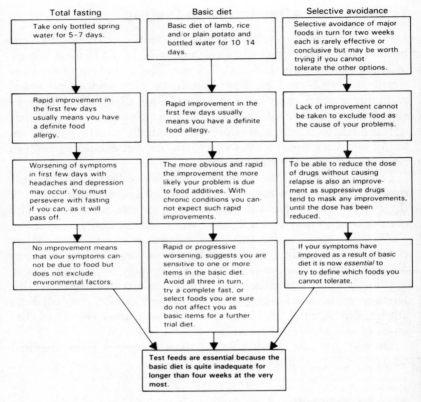

Figure 24.1 How to find out if your symptoms are due to food.

long-term use, and advice from a trained dietitian may be essential. Restrictive diets can also cause all manner of problems within the family, and compliance with diets may be difficult. In young women excessive zeal in dieting may be the prelude to anorexia nervosa.

What is meant by 'test feeds' and how should they be carried out?

The basic diet is for investigation only. After 10–21 days it should be evident whether food is causing problems or not. If no better the basic diet should be abandoned, but if symptoms have

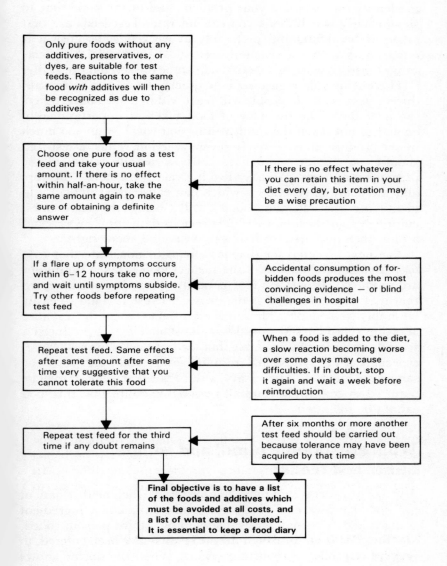

Figure 24.2   How to find out which food is causing your symptoms.

definitely improved, test feeding can begin. This is the only way to identify the causes of your problem, and at the same time to show clearly which foods you can tolerate. Test feeds are best taken at breakfast, and preferably at weekends, because it is often hours before a reaction occurs. At weekends the effects cannot disturb work or school, and can be observed more easily.

There is no rule regarding how quickly foods can be reintroduced, because some people will react within a few hours, others the next day. The quantity of food taken is important, as if enough is not taken the result will be equivocal, while too much might produce an excessively severe reaction. Thus, a test feed should contain just enough to cause a definite return of the previous symptoms. We have two big variable factors – the dose and the delay in reaction – which can cause great difficulty in identifying the offending food. Milk, being the commonest culprit, is a good example. If the previous daily intake was about a pint, then a quarter or half a pint may be about right.

The next essential for diagnosis is to demonstrate that *every time* an adequate amount of the suspect food is taken symptoms are produced. If one test feed is positive, it cannot be assumed that that particular food is the cause, because it could so easily be simply coincidence. Thus, it is essential to repeat the test after allowing symptoms to subside. If the same effect is produced a second time it is very probable that the test food is the real cause, especially if the symptoms are quite severe and occur after the same time interval. If necessary, a third positive test feed may be required to confirm beyond all reasonable doubt that this food cannot be tolerated.

What are 'double blind' and 'single blind' test feeds?

A test of any sort is said to be 'double blind' when neither patient nor doctor is aware of which test contains the active ingredient being tested. The material is made up by a third person, coded, and the code is not broken until the results have been entered, to prevent any bias in reporting results. When the doctor knows which mixture contains the active material but the patient does not, the test is called 'single blind'.

Double blind food tests are sometimes made up with the taste disguised in a soup, or given through a small tube into the stomach. Alternatively, coded capsules of food are given by mouth. Usually this elaborate type of test is carried out in hospital, but sometimes the suspect foods, or foods known not to cause symptoms, are made up in tins which are numbered but not labelled. In this way large amounts can be given for up to a week, as in the recent migraine trial, and the food can be taken at home. The latter type of test is the best, because it simulates natural exposure to normal amounts of food.

Can test feeds be dangerous?

Much depends on the nature of the reaction involved, and whether this could be dangerous, such as severe asthma, or an epileptic fit. Hence just touching the lips with the food, followed by building slowly up to normal amounts within two days may be the safest approach when there is any suspicion that the food being tested might produce acute reactions. This is particularly important in food allergy, but much less likely in food intolerance.

Shortly after a food which is causing problems is withdrawn, sensitivity to that food may actually increase, so a test feed can produce a nasty reaction. The more rapid the improvement the more likely it is that there will be a severe reaction, especially if there are withdrawal symptoms and a craving for the forbidden food. Of course, test feeds with foods such as egg, to which immediate or obvious reactions are already known to occur, are potentially dangerous, quite unnecessary, and should not be attempted under any circumstances without medical advice.

If a total fast or a very limited diet does not give relief is it still possible for food to be causing symptoms?

There are still several possibilities, such as inhaling odours of fish, eggs, coffee, spices and other foods, cooking fumes, or inhalation of flour from the air. Cheating, especially in children, must be considered a possibility.

As a rule, improvement should occur by the fifth or seventh day (time has to be allowed for the offending food taken before the diet started to get out of the body). In fact, symptoms may actually get worse in the first few days, so a great deal of resolve may be required to carry on. Severe headaches and lassitude are commonly experienced. If you are no better after two weeks, food is unlikely to be involved in your problem, but lack of improvement or actual worsening on the basic diet *may* point to one of the ingredients of the diet as a cause, making it necessary to avoid these items and substitute other foods. It must not be forgotten that everything that passes the lips is suspect, even toothpaste.

It is often difficult to know when to stop the diet and eliminate food as a possible factor in your problems, particularly when the condition for which dietary treatment is being tried is very chronic, with much inflammation which will take some time to subside. Examples are some cases of rheumatoid arthritis and ulcerative colitis. This is the type of case where the co-operation of the patient's medical advisers is most necessary.

Lack of improvement may also mean that the cause is in the environment or home or work. A good example is that of a woman who had generalized eczema for 3 years; she had little help from several skin specialists who assured her that it was all in the mind and she would have to learn to live with it. The eczema responded to a few days of oral steroids, during which time a basic diet was introduced, but as soon as the drug was stopped the eczema relapsed. Fasting was tried, and the eczema improved slightly but persisted in a variable manner, so foods were added one by one. Salmon, and then haddock, both caused an acute flare-up within 6 hours, and then the pieces of the puzzle fell into place. Her husband was a very keen salmon fisher, she was very fond of fish, and was frequently cutting up and cooking the salmon. Of course, face and hands were the worst areas.

The lesson is that we must not overlook cooking with inevitable exposures to foods by contact and inhalation rather than ingestion. Failure of dietary measures does not exclude environmental factors.

Can anyone try out a special diet without medical advice?

There is nothing to stop you as we have voluntary control over what we eat or do not eat, but there are certain conditions to be observed. For example, total fasting should never be carried out without medical advice, and if you fast, ten days is the absolute maximum.

With the full co-operation and participation of the family cook results *can* be obtained at home more readily than in most hospitals. Obviously it is essential to eat enough to maintain normal nutrition, but nobody will go short of essential vitamins or minerals over a period of weeks, so do not worry, as most allergy elimination diets are of short duration.

How quickly can foods be added to basic diet?

There are no firm rules, because the frequency with which foods can be added depends on the speed with which the patient will react to the food. It is easy to spot the cause if the reaction takes place within a few hours, but if nothing happens until next day or even longer a decision becomes increasingly difficult. To be absolutely sure that a food is harmless some authorities insist that it is given in normal amounts every day for a week, or until a reaction occurs, before deciding if it is tolerated. Unless adverse effects occur fairly soon, this process can be very tedious. On the other hand, some of the less conventional food allergists introduce several foods each day, but it is impossible to understand how delayed effects can be associated with the correct food.

Any symptoms which seem to be associated with a food must be allowed to subside before another food can be introduced, so impatience or hunger could easily ruin the whole experiment. Of course it must be shown as soon as possible by means of test feeds that symptoms are produced every time the suspect item is added to the diet, thus proving to yourself and to others that it is really necessary to follow a difficult special diet for some time.

Which foods are most liable to cause allergic problems?

Clinical experience has shown that some foods are more likely to cause allergy or intolerance than others, but to give precise figures would be misleading. This is partly because awareness of the many and devious ways in which allergic reactions to food can become manifest has been constantly increasing, and also because once an interest becomes known all sorts of cases suspected of being caused by food allergy are referred for investigation, greatly widening the experience. All I can give, therefore, are general impressions.

Allergy to only one food, most commonly milk, is found in about 35 per cent of my cases, but allergy to inhalants is also present in another 15 per cent. An overt allergy to, for example, house dust may conceal a major food allergy, so food and inhalant problems may co-exist. In about 30 per cent of cases allergy to several foods may be present, and another 15 per cent may have inhalant problems as well. Thus, the patterns are difficult to unravel, and the case may often be more complex than it appears to be to begin with. Enquiry may reveal several complaints which were not suspected of having an allergic origin, affecting various parts of the body, as detailed elsewhere. Each case has to be viewed as a whole, not in separate compartments.

Milk and other beef products

Milk and milk products are by far the commonest foods to cause allergy or intolerance, including beef in about one case in four. Very few sufferers can tolerate goat's, ewe's or other animal milks. Milk chocolate usually causes reactions to the milk, rarely the chocolate, except in migraine.

Egg and fish

Each of these allergies is quite common, skin tests and RAST usually being clearly positive. Patients often make the diagnosis themselves, by having an obvious incident, but small daily amounts can cause much trouble if unsuspected.

Yeast

Yeast is contained in so many foods and drinks that it is nearly as common a cause of allergic problems as milk. This can be diagnosed only by direct provocation test, and the results of such a survey are shown in Table 24.1.

This table, if it were updated, would emphasize even more the role of beer in the Midlands of England, where the figures

Table 24.1 Figures for proven allergy to drinks and yeast 1961–1971 (author's own survey)

Cause	Total	Cause	Total
Yeast	121	Yeast tablets (taken to get better!)	8
Beer	100	Vitamins (crude yeast type)	3
Sherry	22	Yeast-extract spread	3
Whisky	6	Beef extract	4
Wine	19	Hops	4
Home-made wine	5	Malt	7
Gin	1	Vinegar (malt or wine, not acetic acid)	3
Asthma worse eating yeast bread	93		
Asthma better eating soda bread	89		
Chronic indigestion relieved by soda bread	12		

come from. Sherry is also a common cause. I have watched polyps swell up and block the nose completely after a glass of sherry. The increase in home brewing is causing an increase in yeast allergy.

Cereals

In my experience wheat and corn (maize) have not been such common causes of allergic problems as reported by American allergists. Perhaps this is being confused with yeast allergy, which seems less well recognized in the USA.

Nuts

Allergy to peanuts, the oil from which is often used for cooking, and which are often popular with children in the form of peanut butter, is becoming an increasingly common cause of problems. Dangerous swelling of mouth or tongue may occur. Small children should not be given nuts anyway. The results of skin tests are very reliable and dramatic for allergy to peanuts. Hazelnut and brazil nuts are also sometimes important as the cause of allergy.

Citrus fruits

These can cause many problems, but skin tests seem valueless. Allergy is not very common, but can be important as many mothers feel their children are deprived if they do not get orange juice, yet it can be the cause of the problem.

Legumes

This group includes beans, peas and soya, and allergy is not common. The widespread use of soya milk as a cow's milk substitute has already caused an increase in soya allergy in the USA. Soya flour is often used in loaves and buns without being declared.

Potatoes and tomatoes

The nightshade family includes potato, tomato, tobacco, and several less common plants. Potato is a staple food, and the author has found that allergy or intolerance to potato is much commoner than is realized. The main problems caused are skin, particularly eczema, and emotional effects.

For example, a boy of five was seen whose behaviour was quite dreadful. The whole family went on lamb and rice to help him stick to a basic diet. Within a few days not only did he become an 'angel', but his father, who had definite aggressive tendencies, also became a much nicer person. Even a small amount of potato would trigger off an emotional reaction in both father and son. Another patient, a student, was stupid, sleepy, and introverted, having apparent psychological problems until, during a shortage, she ceased to eat potato. Suddenly she became a happy extrovert, but relapsed when she ate potato again.

For many years it has been recognized that scraping potatoes creates an aerosol which can cause sneezing and wheezing, but the effects described here were not known. Pricking through a drop of potato juice may produce a diagnostic skin reaction.

Potato can also cause severe eczema, either alone or in combination with other foods. A middle-aged lady had been using steroid creams for 30 years and was worried because the skin was so fragile and easily bruised. The clue was itching of the hands when peeling potatoes, confirmed by a skin reaction to potato juice. Her eczema did not recur after avoiding potato, and the skin slowly reverted to normal, and is still clear six years later.

Why should food allergics avoid ready-made foods?

We are quite ignorant of what we are eating if we buy ready-made or prepared foods. Food additives of all sorts are used to improve flavour, colour or keeping qualities, but may cause allergy in certain people. For example, sodium benzoate is used, quite legally, as a preservative in prepared meats, Lucozade and other soft drinks, and may sometimes upset those sensitive to aspirin. Soft drinks often contain synthetic colourings to which some persons are sensitive, especially the red and green dyes, also found in ice lollies.

Milk chocolate, ice-cream and sweets can contain egg, vanilla, coffee, honey, molasses, cereal extracts and spices, without their presence being declared on the label. One small boy got swelling of mouth and tongue after eating one kind of milk chocolate and not with another. Enquiry from the makers revealed that one sort of chocolate contained egg.

Not even frozen foods are entirely safe; tenderizing enzymes are often injected in to animals just before slaughtering, and hormones are also used to promote rapid growth. Sauces contain all sorts of gums, spices and especially yeast, which is also found in some tinned soups, stock cubes, beef extracts and gravy salts, and yeast-extract spreads.

For these reasons it is very difficult for the food allergic or intolerant patient to be sure of what they are eating. Fortunately public pressure resulting from the investigations of Geoffrey Cannon and Derek Cooper has made the food manufacturers label their products with all the ingredients. In fact 'no preservatives or additives' has become an effective sales pitch. However, this does not apply to medicines.

372 · ALLERGY AND INTOLERANCE TO FOODS

What is involved in total avoidance of milk products?

The first point to be made is that milk is *not* essential for adults. The second is that *in the initial diet phase beef and all beef products must be excluded because cows are the source of milk.*

Apart from avoiding all milk products in the home, you must get into the habit of checking *all* labels on manufactured foods before purchase. Also beware of changes in the composition of familiar products, as manufacturers can do this without notice.

For example, a young man's eczema was found to be caused by milk products, and his skin was clear for the first time in his life. His eczema suddenly relapsed and his father traced it to a certain brand of tinned soup. The makers confessed that they had changed the recipe, and were now including beef without declaration on the label. This case also had problems getting milk-free margarine.

The labels can be confusing, but the mention of any kind of milk, milk solids, whey or whey protein means you must not eat the product. When on a strict milk-free diet lactose, casein and non-dairy creamers for coffee, and so on, must be cut out but later it may be found that they are tolerated. Some ice-creams use vegetable fat, but non-fat milk simply means that the cream has been removed, leaving the milk protein which is the main cause of the allergy.

It is impractical to list all products containing milk but some guidelines are given below:

Bakery products

Milk or butter or soya is added to many breads, cakes, biscuits and ready-made puddings, but is not declared as there is no label.

Confectionery

Milk chocolate contains concentrated milk and cream. Milk or butter is added to fudge, toffee, caramels and many other sweets.

Beef

In the initial strict diet stage avoid all beef, and beef extracts. If you are very fond of beef then it could be reintroduced first. The best test is a rare grilled steak, as longer cooking may destroy the allergen. Gelatine may be a beef product (used to make capsules for drugs) and so is best avoided in the early strict diet stage unless vegetable gelatine from health shops is used.

Butter, cheese and milk

These must all obviously be avoided in their pure form, but remember that they may be less obvious ingredients in sauces, soups, souffles, pies and savoury and sweet dishes of all kinds. Many ready-made sauces will contain milk products, as will most of the many convenience foods involving batter. Convenience and processed foods are best avoided at first.

Margarine and milk substitutes

This is the obvious butter substitute, but margarine may contain a small amount of milk solids, or whey protein – so look before you eat!

Proprietary milk-free spreads include: Tomor (Van den Bergh); Vitaquell, Vitaseig (for cooking) and Telma (Fauses Vilquellwerk); Rakusen (Israel Products Ltd); and Weight Watchers low-fat spread (widely available). But do remember that recipes can change without notice.

Milk substitutes include Prosobee soya milk (Mead Johnson), S-Formula soya milk (Cow and Gate) for children and infants, and may be prescribed on the NHS for milk-allergic infants.

Products for adults include soya milk (Granose); soya milk (Plamil); S-Formula soya milk (Cow and Gate). Lists of milk-free manufactured foods and recipes may be obtained from most hospital dietitians.

How difficult is it to avoid beef and pork?

Tinned products, especially baby foods, often contain a beef-broth base, and must be avoided. Checking labels is essential. Do not eat sausages as many things (even eyes, spinal cord, brains and genitals) can be included at the whim of the butcher. Medicines in gelatine capsules have been recorded as causing acute reactions in people who are ultrasensitive to the animal from which they were made.

The most remarkable story of beef allergy involves an interminably screaming baby with constant stinking watery diarrhoea. The paediatrician diagnosed milk intolerance, but a 'milk-free' diet was ineffective. In spite of this the family went on a bus tour of France for two weeks, during which he was a normal child! Home again, he relapsed and a second medical opinion was requested. Investigation revealed that during the holiday he was fed on tinned baby foods which were beef and milk-free. On return his diet reverted to his former brand which had a common beef-broth base – so the diarrhoea began again!

Reactions may also be caused by medicines which are made from the glands of animals, such as ACTH from pig pituitaries. A lady was referred with a persistent rash of 2 years duration, which had baffled several skin specialists. Her own doctor had forgotten 2 years before he had prescribed tablets of thyroid extract, derived from sheep, and she was still taking them. A change to the synthetic thyroid hormone resulted in the disappearance of the rash. Problems can also be caused by preparations of pancreatic enzymes from various animals and, of course, preparations of horse serum, and so on.

How can egg be completely avoided?

Egg, particularly white of egg (the albumen), can cause all sorts of allergic symptoms. Some people are aware from early childhood that eggs make them ill, but they may not know all the foods that contain egg, which may be the unsuspected factor making their chronic asthma or eczema worse. Others may be completely unaware that egg is an important cause of their allergic symptoms, whatever they may be. Egg is the perfect convenience food in the perfect package, containing every essential nutrient, and it has become a very common ingredient of manufactured foods. Some patients can tolerate well-cooked egg, such as hard-boiled egg or well-fried egg, or egg in cakes or puddings, so they may tolerate egg in manufactured foods. The reason is that the heating distorts the protein molecules so that they no longer act as an allergen for that patient. For others, however, very strict avoidance may be essential for health. Occasionally it is necessary to exclude egg completely from the house, or to exclude the patient from the kitchen when egg is being handled or cooked.

The egg-sensitive patient must learn to *read the labels* on everything before purchase or before consumption. Lecithin (E322) is mainly derived from egg yolk, and is often used as an emulsifier. Albumen on its own is also a very common ingredient.

Avoid all manufactured foods containing eggs, egg white, meringue, ovomucin, ovalbumin, ovaglobulin and canalbumin. This means being wary of the following, all of which *may* contain egg: noodles, pasta, biscuits, cakes, puddings, pastries, breads, baby foods and cereals, desserts, creams, ice-cream and sorbets, dessert toppings, processed meat, anything in breadcrumbs or batter, sauces, salad dressings and mayonnaise, soups, stock cubes, vegetables and salads covered with a dressing or sauce, lemon curd, chocolate ready-prepared and marshmallows. Even some wines are cleared with egg white.

Some manufactured baby foods are egg-free, such as Boots Baby Rice Cereal, Robinsons' Baby Rice Cereal, Farley's Rusks and Farex and Milupa Plain Rice Cereal. Investing in a food blender and preparing the foods at home is the best, safest and most economical approach – then you *know* what is being given to your baby.

Allergy to egg may mean that only male birds can be eaten, as unlaid eggs may contaminate the flesh of the hen, or that chicken meat cannot be tolerated at all, though allergy to chicken flesh itself is very uncommon.

How safe is immunization in egg-allergic people?

Vaccines to give immunity against measles, German measles, influenza, yellow fever, and other virus diseases are grown on chick embryo. They may contain a trace of egg, which can cause serious reactions in egg-allergic people.

The doctor should always enquire about egg allergy before giving the injection, but a history of some sort of reaction to egg does not mean that protection by means of vaccination cannot be given. Prick skin tests, or intra-dermal skin tests with the diluted vaccine can be performed to reach an informed decision. In most cases the vaccine can be given safely after these tests.

How can wheat and other cereals be avoided?

Cereal grains are the seeds of wheat, rye, oats, barley, maize and rice, which are all domesticated crop grasses and form a large part of the Western diet. Rye and barley are used for bread-making in Europe, but make a very heavy loaf unless mixed with wheat. Oats are usually used for oatcakes, and porridge and muesli only. Rice is not such a common item of diet in the West and does not contain gluten.

Allergy can develop to one or more cereals, but wheat is the usual offender. If cereals are suspected of causing symptoms wheat must be avoided, but to begin with exclusion of all cereals is advisable, just to be sure, for not longer than 2 weeks. If there is no improvement by then cereals cannot be the cause of the symptoms.

If symptoms improve or disappear during this time then cereals are probably the cause. The more quickly the improvement occurs the more likely is wheat or another cereal to be the correct answer to your problems. At this point, no matter how well you feel, wheat must be reintroduced to the diet because it is essential to demonstrate a cause/effect relationship with wheat (or any other cereal in the same manner). Deliberate 'test feeds' are essential, so that you can prove to yourself and your medical advisers that cereals, especially wheat, are the repeatable answer to your problems and must continue to be avoided. Gluten allergy causing coeliac disease may co-exist, so a slow partial improvement from a cereal-free diet may imply that gluten allergy is also present.

On a wheat-free diet look for the *wheat-free symbol* **W** or the gluten-free symbol on manufactured foods. Check carefully that your food does *not* contain gluten, flour, wheat flour, wheat starch, wheat protein, wheat germ or edible starch. Examples of foods which may contain wheat or other cereals include: bread, crispbreads, popadoms and chapatis, breakfast cereals, chocolates and other sweets, flours (including gluten-free flours and cornflours), biscuits, cakes, pastries, puddings, desserts (including some flavoured yoghurts), meat or fish in bread-crumbs or sauce or batter, sausages, gravies, sauces, soups, stock cubes, soy sauce, pasta, semolina, processed cheeses, cheese and other spreads, and communion wafers!

Instead of wheat use flours made from arrowroot, millet, buckwheat, rice, soya, potato, peas, and chick-peas. Wheat-free cornflours are made by several well-known manufacturers. Your Health Shop will offer a variety of alternatives.

How can gluten be avoided in the diet?

Gluten is a protein found in wheat, rye and other cereals. Check carefully all the labels on manufactured foods. If the label uses the term 'starch' – perhaps food starch or edible starch – which may be obtained from any cereal, do not buy it because it may not be gluten free. Look out for the symbol – a wheatear in a circle with a line crossed through it – on manufactured foods.

Monosodium glutamate is a flavour enhancer used in many products, which sounds similar to gluten but is gluten free.

A booklet, *Gluten-Free Manufactured Food Lists* may be obtained from the Coeliac Society. For examples of foods which may contain gluten, see the list at the end of the previous question.

Gluten-free products which may be obtained from the chemist on National Health Service prescription include: bread (Juvela), biscuits, flour, baking powder and pasta (from G F Bakeries Ltd); bread mix and flour (from Welfare Foods Ltd); and Cantabread bread mix (Trufee) (from Cantasium). When baking with gluten-free flour, it is more successful to make a small loaf or rolls rather than a large loaf. Bread should be mixed to a batter rather than a dough. Your doctor will prescribe, but only if convinced that gluten-free products are essential.

How can yeast be avoided?

Yeasts are living micro-organisms which leaven our bread, ferment our wine and beer, produce B group vitamins, and are used as a flavouring agent. If you are allergic to yeast you must avoid everything containing yeast or yeast derivatives. This is a difficult task but worth it if it works! When shopping you *must* read every label. You have to know the various names given to yeast, and remember that ingredients may change. Names used for yeast are leaven, barm and hydrolysed protein. Many foods and drinks contain yeast without it appearing on the label, so be careful. Yeast is also contained in some tablets – Abidec, Multi-vite and tonic yeast tablets are examples.

Below are listed some of the foods which may contain yeast. When in doubt, do without!

Bread

The usual British loaves *all* contain yeast. So does pitta bread, but many ethnic breads are unleavened – i.e. without yeast (e.g. Jewish matzo, Indian chapatis and Mexican tortillas). Soda bread, which *can* be made palatable, contains no yeast, nor do scones or pancakes, and many crispbreads are yeast-free.

Cakes and buns, and so on

Cake mixes, cookies, cream crackers, slimmers' rolls, pretzels, doughnuts, muffins, pikelets, teacakes, pastries, and so on. Why not make your own with self-raising flour or baking powder?

Breakfast cereals

Many cereals and porridge-type breakfast foods have added yeast, even some especially formulated for infants.

Flavouring agents and sauces, and so on

Malt vinegar, wine vinegar, pickles and sauces with vinegar, gravy thickeners, horse-radish, mayonnaise, salad-/french-dressings, tomato sauce – all may contain yeast. Yeast-extract and beef-extract spreads are made with yeast and spices. Soup, soup powders, tinned soup, processed cheese, synthetic creams . . .

Meat and fish products

Hamburgers and beefburgers, black puddings and sausages may contain bread or rusk. Watch out for breadcrumbs on fish and meat. (Friendly butchers will often help if asked.) Some will even make special sausages for you!

Fermented liquors

Beer, wine and rum all contain yeast. Gin and vodka do not. 'Beer' includes herb beer and ginger beer. Wine and beer making at home must stop even if you do not drink it yourself! To avoid yeast is difficult, but often worth it. To begin with avoidance has to be meticulous, but after the level of tolerance is found it is not necessary to be so careful.

Why is some form of dietary rotation advisable for people with food allergy?

The discovery of a definite food allergy can give a new lease of life to a patient who may have been chronically ill for many years, but if several foods are involved the diet may become seriously limited. Thus, excessive amounts of the foods which are tolerated may have to be taken to satisfy requirements, but this may eventually sensitize the patient to them, thus restricting the choice of foods further. In cases where very few foods are tolerated any further restriction may cause a serious problem. This can be partly overcome by careful planning of daily menus so as to include foods to which reactions are relatively slight by eating them only once in a week or 10 days, in rotation. Avoidance of excessive daily intake of tolerated foods prevents the insidious development of further intolerances, and even less choice of food.

The following history illustrates how new intolerances to different foods can arise, which might have been avoided by constantly changing the items in the diet.

A 5 year old boy was referred with allergic rhinitis and cough. Tests were negative but his behaviour was appalling. Projectile vomiting in infancy and infrequent large pale and vile-smelling stools suggested food intolerance. Within a week milk-free diet resolved all problems, but symptoms recurred within a few hours after reintroduction of a little milk. Six months later a return of violent behaviour and diarrhoea followed consumption of one slice of bread (even gluten-free). His craving for bread was such that he gobbled stale bread off the bird-table. Except for rice, intolerance to other cereals followed. Egg caused diarrhoea and colic. As a teenager he is still very difficult and must remain on a severely restricted diet.

Is avoidance the only answer to food allergy or intolerance?

Avoidance of a food which can be clearly shown to cause the problem every time it is eaten is indeed the only sensible answer, but it need not be permanent. After 1 or 2 years of avoidance many foods can be introduced gradually without trouble. Patients apparently sensitive to many foods have a very difficult problem, and can be very difficult to manage. These are the cases where the clinical ecologists claim success for sub-lingual neutralization, or for neutralizing injections. This is a controversial area where great claims are made, but there seems to be little hard evidence in support of them. It would seem wise to wait and see how these methods develop and whether any confirmation of results using objective methods will be forthcoming in the future.

Sodium cromoglycate (Nalcrom) in large doses does help a few cases by blocking the entry of the food molecules into the circulation, but it is more useful as an investigative tool than a daily treatment. It is very expensive and has only limited application to the food-allergy problem.

Why were lamb, rice and potato chosen as the basic diet?

The reason for the choice of lamb as a major protein source in the basic diet is that sheep are relatively uncontaminated with chemicals, and very few people react to mutton. Unfortunately factory farmed lambs are now becoming available so that intolerance or allergy may become commoner. Possible alternatives are game birds and animals which have not been intensively reared, such as wild rabbit, hare, venison, wild duck, wild geese, wood pigeons, and pheasants, because they are relatively uncontaminated.

Carbohydrate sources are limited, as intolerance may be present to all cereals, but this is uncommon. Rice is the only cereal free from gluten, and most Westerners can tolerate it, so this is the ideal carbohydrate source, and gluten sensitive patients also improve. If there is any suspicion of intolerance towards all cereals, potato is to be preferred, but rice and potato are both tolerated as a rule. Tapioca or sago flour is an unusual source of carbohydrate to which few people are sensitive, but cooking may present problems. Bottled spring water is advised for the first week at least, to exclude those rare cases who are reacting to impurities in the water.

Some exclusion diets allow some vegetables, and without them constipation may be a problem. Intolerance is uncommon, but it is also true that the greater the number of items in the diet the more likely it includes something to which the patient will react. Pears are often advised, and apples which are in the same botanical family, but occasionally are not tolerated. The keynote is to keep it simple.

It might seem that such an irksome diet could be avoided if the major foods are excluded in turn for two or three weeks each, but the result is usually muddle, confusion, and discouragement. The reason is that many patients are reacting to several foods, so that it is necessary to avoid them all at the same time to get an obvious and convincing result. Nevertheless, selective exclusion of foods known to cause problems, such as milk, may be worth trying first of all.

What are the important trace elements which are essential for proper nutrition and health?

About 60 years ago the cause of a mysterious anaemia in cattle was found to be a deficiency of cobalt. Veterinary scientists soon found that other problems were caused by lack of different metals, but only traces of the missing elements were necessary to cure the condition – hence the term 'trace elements'. These workers led the way to the study of similar problems in man, but progress has been less rapid. It is very probable that millions of people have substandard health due to nutritional and mineral imbalances, which would have been sorted out and treated long ago if we had been farm animals, whose diets are supervised more carefully than our own.

The list of essential elements now includes iron, zinc, copper, manganese, nickel, cobalt, molybdenum, selenium, chromium, iodine, fluorine, tin, silicon and vanadium. They are essential for growth, pregnancy and lactation, so vitamins alone are not enough. Too much of one element may distort the balance and cause malabsorption of another, so the relationships are very complex, and also involve elements which are essential in larger quantities, such as sodium, potassium, magnesium, calcium, phosphorus and sulphur. Balance is maintained by selective absorption of what is needed and excretion of the surplus in the urine.

How important is zinc as a trace element?

It is only in the last 20 years that the importance of adequate zinc in the daily diet has been realized, because so many body enzymes depend on it. Deficiency can lead to skin problems, slow wound healing, slow growth and sexual development, and loss of taste and appetite, and impaired reactions of immunity. As meat is a major source, vegetarians may lack zinc, and as the British diet is reported to be lower in zinc than is thought desirable, marginal deficiency may be quite common. Measurement of zinc in the blood or cells is surprisingly difficult, but inability to taste a weak zinc sulphate solution is suggestive of deficiency.

Lack of zinc may reduce the desire for food to the extent that anorexia nervosa may result. In fact, cure of this distressing condition by giving zinc sulphate has been reported, so some cases may be due to zinc deficiency, especially as starvation increases zinc excretion in the urine.

A bizarre case of abnormal appetite (pica) in a child aged 18 months has been reported. She began to eat any metal object she could get hold of, such as keys, and gnawed the metal strips at the edge of the carpets. All this curious behaviour stopped in 3 days when zinc was given, her appetite recovered, and growth restarted.

Zinc has turned out to be one of the most important trace elements, and the widespread effects of deficiency are recognized more and more, often in allergic patients, and those with bowel disorders where absorption may be diminished.

The daily needs for zinc amount to about 15mg but greater amounts seem harmless. Calcium, iron and phytic acid from wheat flour in the diet may combine with zinc and prevent it being absorbed, so that only a proportion of the dietary zinc may be available. There is much more in human milk than in cow's milk. Zinc supplements have been suggested in pregnancy, as low zinc is associated with premature small babies. The effects of zinc deficiency have been reported frequently over the last 20 years, but have not yet filtered down to everyday practice. A total of 150mg of zinc sulphate a day can be given to supply 34mg of zinc, if deficiency is suspected, but only the taste test is readily available to access results. Much more research, especially into the significance of mineral analysis of the hair, is urgently required.

Can metals cause allergic problems?

Some metals, such as lead, cause toxic effects only. Other metals, such as nickel, chromium and mercury, are also potent sensitizers.

Nickel often causes local contact eczema of the skin, under plated earrings, plated clips on underclothing, jeans buttons, money, watch straps, and so on. There is some nickel in food, and generalized eczema occurs occasionally. Metal plates used to mend fractures may liberate enough nickel or chromium into the circulation to cause generalized allergic reactions. Enough nickel can be dissolved from a needle inserted in a vein to give an intravenous drip to cause generalized rashes, and exceptionally to cause an acute allergic reaction. Chromium is often alloyed with nickel, but the main problem it causes, is contact dermatitis from handling cement. Chrome-free cement is mandatory in Scandinavia, but not in this country, where it causes much industrial dermatitis.

Mercury is a very toxic metal, and also a potent sensitizer. It forms an amalgam with silver and gold for stopping teeth, but local or general reactions to fillings are very rare. In one case a mouthpiece plated with pure gold was necessary to stop swelling of the lips, which persisted even when a 9 carat gold alloy mouthpiece was used. Mercury used to be used as a drug, as a sterilizing solution (mercuric chloride), and as an antiseptic (mercurochrome). The red oxide is used as a colour for tattooing and if the victim is sensitive to it a nasty reaction may occur. Playing with mercury can cause severe poisoning and contaminate a whole house. Swallowing tiny deaf-aid batteries also causes poisoning, so they have to be removed surgically at once. Mercury allergy can cause many symptoms but it is not known how often it does so.

Removal of amalgam fillings and substitution with plastic is increasingly recommended but is very expensive. The National Health Service may pay for the fillings which show, but not for those which do not. Clear proof of toxic effects on the nervous system has not yet been published, but excessive amounts of mercury have been found in the brains of dentists in Sweden who had been exposed to amalgam for many years. The best advice would seem to be to insist that amalgam is not used in the first place, especially in children, as there are now many alternative materials for fillings.

Platinum causes extreme sensitization and severe asthma in refineries, but gold seems well tolerated unless alloyed with nickel.

How can we be sure that we are getting enough vitamins?

Public awareness that vitamins are essential for continued health, and may give increased vim, vigour and vitality, sells at least twenty million pounds worth of vitamin products a year in Britain alone. In the western nations disease due to vitamin deficiency is rare, as a good mixed diet provides all that is necessary. It seems paradoxical that we should take more vitamins than we need, while the Third World is so short of both vitamins and food. Impure products, such as yeast tablets or capsules containing yeast, can actually cause worsening of symptoms in yeast-sensitive individuals. A good mixed diet contains adequate amounts of vitamins and minerals essential for nutrition.

Very large doses of vitamins ('mega vitamin therapy') are sometimes advocated, especially in cases of mental disturbance, but the author has no personal experience of this. The published evidence is interesting, encouraging but difficult to evaluate. It has been claimed that there is great individual variation in requirements, so that if none overflows into the urine a relative deficiency may be present. Obviously, much further research is needed to find out if these claims can be confirmed, and if vitamins can be used as drugs.

The use of large doses of vitamin C (ascorbic acid) to prevent colds and for many other illnesses is still controversial. There is no doubt that there are increased needs for ascorbic acid after operations, injuries and illness. Vitamins cannot be discussed in isolation from the trace elements, and the mineral and nutritional requirements of the body, as is often done. A holistic view is necessary, to begin to understand how all these factors contribute to normal health.

Can one be allergic to vitamins?

This has been reported, but is uncommon. The various components of the vitamin B complex are easily obtained in yeast, but are contaminated with the other proteins from yeast. Hence, yeast-sensitive people cannot tolerate B vitamins from yeast, but can usually take synthetic B group vitamins.

Vitamins A and D are found in fish, liver and fish oils. Hence, fish allergics may not be able to tolerate these vitamins, unless they are synthetic. One patient found that her chronic eczema got better when she stopped margarine, which contains fish oils in varying and unstated proportions according to availability and price.

Intravenous injection of vitamin B has rarely been known to provoke dangerous reactions, but the preservatives in the solution may cause problems. Solutions of drugs ready for intravenous use may contain preservatives which are not declared on the label.

Are health foods always healthy or are they just a fad?

The concept of health foods, or organically grown foods, as being always safe and health giving is naive. Everybody is different from everybody else, no two food allergics are alike and one man's food can very definitely be another's poison.

Wholefoods such as wholemeal bread are definitely better for you because the product is not over-refined and the vitamin and fibre has not been thrown away. The present fashion for so-called health foods free from all preservatives and grown without fertilizers is rather unrealistic, as it is quite impossible to produce organic food in sufficient quantity without modern methods. There are probably very few people who really benefit from food which is as far as possible free from all contaminants, but the public are being encouraged to think that it is essential for all of us to eat these foods. Commercial interests will obviously promote a tendency to food faddism, perhaps based on incomplete or inadequate information, if it will promote sales at inflated prices. Exaggerated claims for tonic effects which would be very difficult to prove are made for some natural products. Careful research is obviously required to prove or disprove the claims made by manufacturers of health foods.

Bibliography

The books listed below were the sources of some of the information upon which this book is based. Other sources were innumerable scientific papers published in medical journals, and what I have learned through my practical experience of trying to help allergic patients.

Armstrong, D. and Cant, A., *The Allergy-free Cookbook* (Octopus, 1986)

Ed. The Asthma and Allergy Foundation of America and Craig T. Norback (consulting ed. R. G. Slavin), *The Allergy Encyclopedia* (New American Library, 1981)

Bahna, S. L. and Heiner, D. C., *Allergies to Milk* (Grune & Stratton, 1980)

Blackley, C. H., *Experimental Researches on the Causes and Nature of Hay Fever or Hay Asthma* (Dawson Pall Mall, 1959)

Brostoff, J. and Challacombe, S. J. (eds.), *Clinics in Immunology and Allergy* (W. B. Saunders, 1982)

Brostoff, J. and Gamlin, L., *Food Allergy and Intolerance* (Bloomsbury, 1989)

Clark, T. J. H. (ed.), *Asthma* (Chapman & Hall, 1977)

Clark, T. J. H. (ed.), *Steroids in Asthma* (ADIS Press, 1983)

Cleave, T. L. (ed.), *The Saccharine Disease* (Keats Publishing Inc., 1975)

Dickey, L. A. (ed.), *Clinical Ecology* (Charles C. Thomas, 1976)

Dong, C. H. and Banks, J., *The Arthritics Cookbook* (Granada Publishing, 1974)

Fisher, A. A., *Contact Dermatitis* (Lea & Febiger, 1975)

Frazier, C. A., *Parents' Guide to Allergy in Children* (Doubleday, 1973)

Freed, D. L. J., *Health Hazards of Milk* (Bailliere Tindall, 1984)

Freeman, J., *Hay Fever: A Key to the Allergic Disorders* (William Heinemann, 1950)

Gerrard, J., *Understanding Allergies* (Charles C. Thomas, 1973)

Gerrard, J. (ed.), *Food Allergy: New Perspectives* (Charles C. Thomas, 1980)

Goetzl, E. J. and Kay, A. B., *Current Perspectives in Allergy* (Churchill Livingstone, 1982)

Goldman, L., *When Doctors Disagree* (Hamish Hamilton, 1973)

Hanssen, M., *E for Additives* (Thorsons, 1984)

Hippchen, L. J., *Ecologic-Biochemical Approaches to the Treatment of Delinquents and Criminals* (Van Nostrand Reinhold, 1978)

Lessof, M. H., *Immunological and Clinical Aspects of Allergy* (MTP Press, 1981)

Lobstein, T., *Children's Food – The Good, the Bad and the Useless* (Unwin paperbacks, 1988)

Mackarness, R., *Not All in the Mind* (Pan, 1976)

Mackarness, R., *Chemical Victims* (Pan, 1980)

Miller, J. B., *Food Allergy: Provocative Testing and Injection Therapy* (Charles C. Thomas, 1972)

Moore, P., *No Milk No Eggs* (Foulsham, 1983)

Mygind, N., *Topical Steroid Treatment for Asthma and Rhinitis* (Bailliere Tindall, 1980)

Oseid, S. and Edwards, A. M., *The Asthmatic Child in Play and Sport* (Pitman Press, 1983)

Pepys, J., *Clinics in Immunology and Allergy* (W. B. Saunders, 1984)

Pepys, J. and Edwards, A. M., *The Mast Cell* (Pitman Medical, 1979)

Price, W. A., *Nutrition and Physical Degeneration* (The Price-Pottenger Nutrition Foundation, 1945)

Randolph, T. G., *Human Ecology and Susceptibility to the Chemical Environment* (Charles C. Thomas, 1962)

Rapp, D. J., *Allergies and the Hyperactive Child* (Cornerstone, 1980)

Rapp, D. J., *The Impossible Child* (Practical Allergy Research Foundation, 1986)

Rapp, D. J., *Allergies and Your Family* (Sterling, 1981)

Rich, A. R., *The Pathogenesis of Tuberculosis* (Charles C. Thomas, 1946)

Rowe, A. H., *Food Allergy: Its Manifestation and Control and the Elimination Diets* (Charles C. Thomas, 1972)

Sacks, O., *Migraine* (Pan, 1981)

Schell, O., *Modern Meat (Antibiotics, Hormones, and Pharmaceutical Farm)* (Random House, 1983)

Schroeder, H. A., *The Poisons Around Us* (Indiana University Press, 1974)

Seely, D., Freed, D. L. J., Silverstone, G. A. and Rippere, V., *Diet-related Diseases – The Modern Epidemic* (AVI Publishing Co Inc., 1985)

Speer, F., *Migraine* (Nelson-Hall, 1977)

Speer, F., *The Allergic Child* (Harper & Row, 1983)

Speer, F., *Food Allergy*, 2nd edition (PSG Publishing Company, 1983)

Urbach, E. and Gottlieb, P. M., *Allergy* (William Heinemann, 1946)

Workman, E., Alun Jones, V. and Hunter, J., *The Food Intolerance Diet Book* (McDonalds, 1986)

Index

abnormal appetite, 382
Achilles' tendon, 168, 169
ACTH, 162–6, 181–2, 374
acupuncture, 282
adaptation, diseases of, 19
addictive allergy, 313
additives, 73, 137, 293, 295 *see also* food additives
adrenal glands, 163–4, 164–5, 181–2
adrenaline, 160, 162, 193, 209
adrenocorticotrophic hormone, *see* ACTH
aerosols, 159–60
air conditioning, 60, 63–4, 69, 72
air filters, 205
air-fresheners, 295, 296, 297
albumen, 374
alcohol, 136, 325, 332–3, 340, 369, 379
alcoholics, 314
alimentary canal:
    food allergy and intolerance and, 112–13, 304–12
    working of, 287
    see also under components of
Allen & Hanbury, 184
allergens:
    antigens and, 12
    amounts needed for reaction, 34
    distribution of, 20, 34
    extracts, standardization of, 144–55
    see also following entries and chemicals
allergic salute, 123
allergy:
    body entry to, 33–4
    case history, 127–37
    causes, 15, 22–3, 25, 125
    changes in through life, 21
    childhood and, 21
    doctors' attitudes to, 25

fallacies about, 140–1, 217–19
family and, 15
family doctor and, 245–6, 246–7, 249
holistic approach, 20–25
identifying, 121–4
investigation, 126–7
scientific tests, 138–54
second opinion on, 247–8, 249–50
sensitization, 17–18, 19
specialized investigation, 217–19
specificity of reactions, 16
symptoms and treatment chart, 58
symptom suppression by drugs, 157–77
training in lacking, 217, 245, 246
unusual symptoms, 22
    see also under types of (eg, asthma, hay fever) *and* desensitization, drug treatment for allergy
Alternaria, 50, 52, 146
'alternative medicine', 250, 282
aluminium, 152, 302
alveolitis, 46, 70, 71–2, 108
aminophylline, 160, 172, 193, 286
amoeba, 3
'Ana-Kit', 86, 87, 164
anaphylactic shock, 16
    causes, 84–5
    definition, 84
    emergency treatment, 86–9
    prevention, 87
    symptoms, 86
angio-oedema, 75
    causes, 281, 327
animals, allergy and, 43–6
    hay fever, 96
    occupation and, 68–9
    see also pets
anorexia nervosa, 382
antibiotics, 67, 137, 238–9, 240–2,